PROFIT

FROM THE

SOURCE

PROFIT FROM THE SOURCE

TRANSFORMING YOUR BUSINESS BY PUTTING SUPPLIERS AT THE CORE

Christian Schuh   Wolfgang Schnellbächer   Alenka Triplat   Daniel Weise

HARVARD BUSINESS REVIEW PRESS
BOSTON, MASSACHUSETTS

Library of Congress Cataloging-in-Publication Data

Names: Schuh, Christian, author. | Schnellbacher, Wolfgang, author. | Triplat, Alenka, author. | Weise, Daniel (Writer on industrial procurement), author.
Title: Profit from the source : transforming your business by putting suppliers at the core / Christian Schuh, Wolfgang Schnellbacher, Alenka Triplat, Daniel Weise.
Description: Boston, Massachusetts : Harvard Business Review Press, [2022] | Includes index. |
Identifiers: LCCN 2022003884 (print) | LCCN 2022003885 (ebook) | ISBN 9781647821395 (hardcover) | ISBN 9781647821401 (epub)
Subjects: LCSH: Purchasing. | Business logistics. | Industrial procurement. | Shopping. | Success in business.
Classification: LCC HF5437 .S354 2022 (print) | LCC HF5437 (ebook) | DDC 658.7/2—dc23/eng/20220223
LC record available at https://lccn.loc.gov/2022003884
LC ebook record available at https://lccn.loc.gov/2022003885

ISBN: 978-1-64782-139-5
eISBN: 978-1-64782-140-1

Companies play a vital role in society. In the past, their role, and their success, was framed within a narrowly financial context, and the wealth they created was shared among a privileged few. They viewed their suppliers as a source of savings and their procurement function as the instrument for extracting those savings. In the future, they must contribute to the broader well-being of society—*the common wealth*. They must benefit the many, not just the few.

As we show in *Profit from the Source*, some CEOs have already begun to encourage their procurement teams to engage with suppliers in order to profit in the broadest sense of the word: yes, to save costs, but also to produce goods and services for the betterment of society, ones that are more innovative, better quality, faster to market, less risky, and above all, more sustainable. In all but the last of these, the metric of corporate success is to be better than the competition. But if they are to be truly sustainable, companies cannot measure themselves by how well they perform against their rivals or how well they meet minimum environmental, social, and governance regulations. Sustainability is an absolute: either a company is sustainable, or it's not.

We know the task of becoming truly sustainable isn't an easy one. Indeed, it is the most difficult, most important, and most urgent task facing business leaders today. We would therefore like to dedicate our book to the individuals and companies who can show all of us the way to a better, more sustainable future.

CONTENTS

Introduction   1
Suppliers and Procurement: The Keys to Your Company's Future

PART ONE

How *You* Need to Change

1 **Start at the Top**   25
   Make Your Suppliers and Your Procurement Function
   Leadership Imperatives

PART TWO

How *Your Company* Needs to Change

2 **Treat Your Suppliers as Friends**   43
   Forge New Dynamic Relationships with Your Most
   Important Suppliers

3 **Empower Your "Shoppers"**   69
   Put Your Procurement Team at the Very Heart of Your
   Product Life Cycle—from Ideation to Postproduction

4 **Go Bionic**   95
   Create a Procurement Function That Combines the Virtues
   of Human Creativity and Digital Technology

PART THREE

How *Your Company's Ecosystem* Needs to Change

5   **Cut Costs—Fast**   123
Demand *Up-Front Double Savings* from Your
Top Suppliers and Double Down on the Rest

6   **Dream Big Together**   135
Achieve *Breakthrough Innovations* by Pooling
R&D Resources with Your Suppliers

7   **Settle for Perfection**   155
Deliver *Unbeatable Quality* by Joining Forces with
Your Suppliers to Wage a War on Errors

8   **Share Your Tomorrows**   171
Become *Truly Sustainable* by Allying with Your Suppliers to
Meet Environmental, Social, and Governance Standards

9   **Get Quicker, Faster—as One**   191
Go *Twice as Fast* by Collaborating with—
Not Competing Against—Your Suppliers

10 **Anticipate the Inevitable**   205
Halve Your Risks by Working with Your Suppliers
to Predict the Unexpected

Afterword   225
Acknowledgments   229
Notes   233
Index   249
About the Authors   261

Suppliers and Procurement

The Keys to Your Company's Future

In August 2011, a little-known former chief procurement officer stepped into the shoes of the most celebrated chief executive on the planet. Up to that point, Tim Cook had spent his career in the backroom divisions of technology companies, far from the glare of publicity. He had been director of fulfillment at IBM and, briefly, CPO at Compaq Computers before joining Apple as senior vice president of worldwide operations and taking charge of procurement. Now he was going to replace the creative genius who had founded Apple Computer Inc. and who had, after a twelve-year hiatus when he left the company to pursue other interests, returned as a savior and made it into the epitome of cool: the irreplaceable Steve Jobs.

At the time, Cook's elevation to the top job was highly controversial. Many industry observers questioned whether he was the right man to run a company where style and "looks" were seemingly paramount. And the doubters appeared to be vindicated when, a couple of months later, Cook launched the iPhone 4S to a muted reception. As the *New Yorker* reported: "Apple seemed to stumble with its theatrics. The company held one of its fabled launches—led for the first time by the bespectacled Tim Cook, not the turtlenecked Steve Jobs—and bored people."[1]

But there were others who hailed Cook's appointment as being truly inspired. For them, it showed that the board—and Jobs, who had handpicked Cook as his successor—understood what made Apple tick: its supply chain. In a world of hyperconnectivity created by rampant globalization, Apple had shown itself to be a master of procurement, working with suppliers around the world to create the highest-quality and most-innovative products, all for the best price. The iPhone was (and remains) the classic example of a modern global product: designed at Apple's headquarters in Cupertino, California; assembled by workers at Foxconn's factory in the Chinese city of Zhengzhou, southwest of Beijing; and made of raw materials and components sourced from forty-three countries across six continents.[2] In 2018, Apple shipped more than 217 million iPhones.[3] Never before has such a complex product been manufactured in such numbers.

The next few years proved that the skeptics were wrong about Cook. He demonstrated that he knew how to deliver spectacular profit numbers that kept shareholders happy. Under his guidance, Apple has gone from strength to strength. In 2022, it reached an astonishing $3 trillion in market valuation, having become the first public company to reach $1 trillion just four years earlier.[4]

Cook has earned plaudits for his stewardship. But curiously, procurement as a business discipline has not enjoyed the same kind of adulation. At the time of Cook's appointment, it was widely thought that procurement would at last step out from the shadows and receive the recognition it deserved as the engine room of a modern globalized business. Now that a former CPO had reached the top of the corporate ladder, surely others would follow?

The answer to that question, however, has been "no." Few of the CEOs running today's major companies have served as CPOs. Apple may be among the world's most admired companies, yet one of the biggest things that sets it apart—how it puts suppliers at the core of its business—has been broadly disregarded by most major corporations.

• • •

In many companies, if not most, procurement is an unglamorous, un-loved part of the business. When the boss offers someone a job in procurement, they know they're on the fast track to nowhere. It's the corporate equivalent of being sent to Siberia—there's no way back. By our calculation, CEOs devote only a fraction of their mindshare (the amount of time they spend thinking about different tasks) to suppliers and, by extension, the procurement function. They rarely mention the work of the CPO in shareholder meetings or on earnings calls with analysts. Indeed, according to research by Harvard Business School's Michael Porter and Nitin Nohria, CEOs spend just one percent of their time with suppliers.[5] Given that spending on suppliers—the job of procurement—accounts for more than half of a typical company's total budget, this makes no sense. In effect, it means that CEOs spend next to no time either thinking about or being actively involved in how their companies spend more than half of their budgets. That's a mismatch with potentially existential consequences for companies.

The CPO and the procurement function are marginalized because procurement is a *deeply misunderstood* corporate capability. In most companies, the principal task of the CPO and their team is to purchase goods and services from suppliers for the lowest price. Over the years, CEOs trying to save money and drive both increased profits and total shareholder returns have instructed their CPOs to find less expensive vendors for raw materials, core components, and other production inputs as well as for services such as IT maintenance, accounting, and legal advice. As a result, procurement has become associated with a narrow, restricted interpretation that has left CEOs blind to its phenomenal potential.

In our view, however, the CPO and the procurement function, by virtue of the fact that they "own" the corporate relationship with suppliers, should be positioned at the heart of a company. They are the CEO's secret keys to success in troubled times—and long after, too. Even before the global crisis triggered by Covid and the conflict in Ukraine, the CEO's job of leading a company was challenging enough: globalization was stalling; new digital technologies were disrupting business practices; and seismic but slow-moving social and political changes, including aging populations, increasing inequality, the rise of China, and the development of Africa, were beginning to have a far-reaching impact.[6]

Now the job is tougher than ever. In early 2020, as governments imposed pandemic-related lockdowns and companies were forced to close factories, the *Economist* opined that "the epidemic will put the question of supply chain management squarely on the desks of . . . CEOs."[7] In subsequent months, however, the situation worsened. Companies had to deal with volatile swings in consumer demand. The global airline industry was all but grounded. Shipping was severely disrupted as labor shortages left container vessels unable to unload their cargo. And the automotive industry was halted by a semiconductor "famine" caused by factory shutdowns in Asia (manufacturers were obliged to cancel their plans to build ten million cars during the course of 2021).[8] Indeed, in its "Briefing Room" blog, the White House noted that the paucity of semiconductors was not only affecting the automotive industry but also "dragging down the US economy" and "could cut nearly a percentage point from GDP growth."[9] That a shortage of so ordinarily commonplace a piece of technology could have such a devastating effect alarmed politicians and policymakers. So great was the fear that supply issues could leave a permanent scar on America's future that President Joe Biden ordered a one-hundred-day review of the resilience of the country's supply chains for select critical products—not only semiconductors but also batteries for electric vehicles, active ingredients for pharmaceuticals, and critical minerals and specialty packaging.[10] Announcing the measure, Biden said: "The American people should never face shortages in the goods and services they rely on, whether that's their car or their prescription medicines or the food at the local grocery store."[11] Since then, the conflict in Ukraine has compounded the supply chain challenges.

Amid this turmoil, CEOs and their leadership teams have been expected to do the seemingly impossible: cut costs while improving the quality of their companies' goods and services and while making their businesses faster, more innovative, and more sustainable. They will come under increasing pressure not only to build back as things were before but to build back better. As the *New Yorker* noted, "Supply-chain trouble suggests that something is off with the way we're operating in the world," adding that short-term fixes will be neither satisfactory nor sufficient. "The real challenge, when it comes to thinking about supply chains, isn't making sure that a container ship is unloaded. It is deciding how we want to live."[12]

In the years ahead, companies, as motors of the global economy and major participants in global society, will necessarily have to play a big part in solving the manifold and complex issues arising from the Covid-19 pandemic. But where are CEOs and their leadership teams going to find solutions?

The answer, as we explain in *Profit from the Source*, is their suppliers and their procurement function.

Why do we say this? Typically, the procurement function not only controls more than half of a company's costs, it also determines the quality and sustainability of a company's products and services. It affects the speed of a company's operations. It has the potential to transform (or quash) a company's innovative spirit. And it can protect a company from as-yet-unknown risks in the supply chain. In other words, if CEOs use their procurement capability wisely, they can do much more than simply contain costs. They can tap five mission-critical sources of competitive advantage: innovation, quality, sustainability, speed, and risk reduction. More than this, they can realize their dreams for their company.

Even in the best of times, CEOs all too often fail to fulfill the lofty ambitions that they set for themselves when they took the top job. The urgent gets in the way of the important, short-term firefighting trumps long-term thinking, and quarterly financial pressures take priority. But since the start of the 2020s, business leaders have been experiencing the worst of times. Many of them have told us that if they could find a way to get back on track and beat market expectations, they could buy themselves some time and the room to maneuver that would allow them to pursue their dreams for their company. In our experience, time and the room to maneuver are exactly what a sophisticated approach to suppliers and procurement can offer.

One of the counterarguments we hear is that as soon as some kind of normality returns, all the anxiety over supply chains—and the associated need for an expanded role for procurement as the vital link with suppliers—will fade. In other words, with a little patience, CEOs and leadership teams will be able to ride out today's storms, and they won't have to reorient their companies for a different future. We argue that this is a forlorn hope. Right now, there is an ongoing, fast-evolving, once-in-a-generation transformation occurring in the way companies operate, and it will reward those CEOs who put suppliers at the heart of their organizations and empower those procurement executives responsible for working with the suppliers.

As we have said, procurement accounts for more than half of a company's revenue, on average. In some companies—notably some of the world's most successful technology companies—the percentage is significantly higher. We think this trend, which began long before the pandemic, will continue long after the pandemic has passed, as companies are forced to become ever more outward-facing and to re-organize themselves in new ways to capitalize on the rise of business ecosystems: loose networks of companies that come together with suppliers, distributors, government agencies, and other participants to deliver products and services in a frictionless way to customers.

This is why there is no time to lose. CEOs and their leadership teams need to take swift, radical action. Specifically, they need to put suppliers at the core of their businesses and empower their CPOs and procurement executives to extract the maximum value from those relationships.

How We Got Here: A Brief History of Buyers, Suppliers, and Procurement

Before we lay out precisely what actions CEOs need to take, it is important to understand how we got to where we are today. Why is it that so few CEOs really get the potential of suppliers and their procurement function? To answer this, it is necessary to delve into history.

Long before companies woke up to the importance of professional procurement managers, governments—and specifically defense departments and the military—were sophisticated buyers of goods and services from private contractors. As with so much of business thinking, procurement strategy can trace its origins back to the generals who needed to supply their armies with men, machines, and matériel.

But the modern story of how companies procure goods and services from suppliers begins a little over one hundred years ago, when Henry Ford, a farm boy turned self-made millionaire, was dealing with the consequences of World War I on his automotive company.

Henry Ford, the decline of trust, and
the dawn of vertical integration

In 1908, six years before the outbreak of World War I, Ford unveiled his spectacularly successful Model T. It clearly delivered on his promise to "build a car for the great multitude:" the Model T was affordable, simple to drive, and simple to fix for any moderately capable farmhand (if it ever broke down). Since limited customization was available—"Any customer can have a car painted any color that he wants so long as it is black," Ford famously said—it was relatively simple to make.[13]

For the first few years, Ford enjoyed remarkable success. He was heavily influenced by the distinguished mechanical engineer Frederick Winslow Taylor, the architect of scientific management, whom Ford hired as a consultant to observe his employees and develop ways for his company to become more efficient and productive. By 1914, Ford's newfangled assembly line at Highland Park in Detroit was churning out one Model T car every ninety-three minutes. But with the outbreak of war, Ford ran into difficulties. In particular, he struggled to obtain the raw materials needed to build the Model T. For instance, the rubber for the Model T's tires came from Ceylon (now Sri Lanka), and the supply was monopolized by the British, who were embroiled in the global conflict. These new problems compounded an existing one: what Ford considered the unscrupulous practices of his suppliers. This, after all, was a time when capitalism was red in tooth and claw. The heyday of the so-called robber barons was over, but trust—the invisible force that unites people in a productive partnership—was still a rare commodity.

In this febrile environment, Ford decided to take control of everything from sourcing raw materials to producing the finished goods. In other words, he decided to take ownership of the entire supply chain. It was a bold ambition. Until then, Ford had been an assembler, putting together handcrafted components produced by specialist suppliers. Now, he bought his own rubber plantation in the jungles of Brazil, where he founded a little town called Fordlandia. Also, he acquired coalfields, iron-ore mines, and timberlands, as well as a fleet of ships and a railroad to transport the raw materials to his factory. Eventually, in 1927, he built his own enormous steelworks, parts manufacturer, and assembly line at River Rouge, not far from Detroit.

This strategy, now known as vertical integration, transformed the fortunes of the company and turned Ford into the richest man in the world. Also, it meant that there was no need for procurement professionals, because there was nothing to procure—Ford had everything he needed to build the Model T. There were significant drawbacks to this strategy, however. For a start, it was costly. Second, it was bureaucratic, making the company less agile than some of its competitors. As a result, by the early 1930s, Ford had been overtaken by General Motors and Chrysler.

It took another war—and the influence of his great rival Alfred Sloan—for Henry Ford to think about a different approach.

Alfred Sloan, General Motors, and the rise of captive suppliers

Trust is essential in a functioning economy. When absent, as it was in the wake of World War I, business leaders take things into their own hands (as Ford did). By contrast, when trust is present, they are more willing to collaborate with others for their mutual benefit.

This is what happened during and after World War II.

In January 1942, just a few weeks after the Japanese attack on Pearl Harbor that triggered the United States' decision to enter the war, President Franklin D. Roosevelt established the War Production

Board. Its purpose was to take command of America's supply chain, controlling the distribution of essential materials and converting factories into manufacturing plants for planes, tanks, armored vehicles, and other military equipment. In a stroke, with the US government acting as a kind of guarantor, trust was restored in the economic system. Over the next three years, American factories became, in Roosevelt's words, "the arsenal of democracy."[14]

Ford's industrial might was put to good effect. The company produced B-24 Liberator bombers at the rate of one per hour at its converted plant at Willow Run, outside Detroit. But the biggest corporate winner was Ford's biggest rival, General Motors. GM was awarded government contracts worth $13.8 billion (compared with Ford's $5.26 billion).[15] As a result, its approach to business management, and the way it procured goods and services from suppliers, influenced other companies, including Ford. It was no coincidence that Peter Drucker chose GM as the subject for his pioneering study of corporate organization that led to the creation of schools of management across the United States.[16]

Under the guidance of president and CEO Alfred Sloan, GM developed a variation on the theme of vertical integration. Sloan created a series of what have since been called "captive suppliers": independent parts-making divisions such as AC Spark Plug, Harrison Radiator, and Saginaw Steering. The idea was to have all the benefits of a vertically integrated company plus the benefits of the free market on cost and efficiency.

Ford Motor Company sought to learn from its great rival. In 1946, the company, now run by Henry Ford's grandson, Henry Ford II, poached several GM executives. Also, Ford recruited military personnel who had been involved in fast-paced, high-pressure procurement work during World War II. Foremost among these were ten officers from the US Army Air Corps' elite Statistical Control unit, which had been established to help expand the country's ability to launch bombing raids in Europe, North Africa, and the Pacific. Hired en masse by Henry Ford II and let loose on Ford's vast River Rouge complex, the former officers subjected the company to a ruthlessly rational, forensic examination. How did the organization work? How were the cars built? Why were these components used?

The ten were nicknamed the Quiz Kids, a joking reference to the popular radio show featuring supersmart children, and before long, their work was having a dramatic effect. In 1946, when they arrived, Ford's profits had been a paltry $2,000. The following year, profits shot up to $64.8 million, and by 1949, that figure had tripled in size.[17] In tribute, the media renamed the young officers the Whiz Kids—a moniker that has stuck ever since. The standout Whiz Kid was Robert McNamara, a former Harvard professor who eventually became Ford's president. He might have remained at the firm for the rest of his career had President John F. Kennedy not appointed him US secretary of defense in 1961. By then, Ford, along with many other companies, was operating a well-staffed procurement function that worked with a wide network of suppliers.

Taiichi Ohno, Toyota, and the transformative power of keiretsu

In the first twenty-five years after World War II, Ford and GM, the world's two largest industrial manufacturers, enjoyed a period of commercial dominance. But then, out of the blue, they were knocked back by a new exogenous shock. Not war this time, but the energy crisis of the early 1970s.

In 1973, Arab members of the Organization of Petroleum Exporting Countries (OPEC) imposed an embargo on oil sales to the United States after the American government supported Israel in the Yom

Kippur War against Egypt. The price of crude oil rose dramatically, as did the price of gas. US auto companies, which were producing big cars (commonly referred to as gas guzzlers), were badly hit. In this moment of weakness for America's industrial giants, the great Japanese automakers saw an opportunity to capture the growing market for smaller, more fuel-efficient cars.

But what really separated the Japanese automakers from their American and European rivals was the quality and affordability of their products, and this had everything to do with their manufacturing process—specifically, the way they procured goods and services from suppliers. In this, the trailblazer was Toyota. Guided by its founder, Kiichiro Toyoda, and especially its chief engineer, Taiichi Ohno, a management genius in the tradition of Taylor, Ford, and Sloan, Toyota pioneered new forms of process innovation. Together, these forms made up the foundation of what became known as the Toyota Production System. One innovative process was *kanban*, or "just in time" manufacturing. Another was *kaizen*, or continuous improvement. Arguably, the real game changer was *keiretsu*, a collaborative corporate network wherein Toyota bought significant minority stakes in key suppliers. In a way, it was an evolution of GM's system of captive suppliers—but at arm's length. What held Toyota and its suppliers together was a sense of mutual obligation reinforced by the fact that they each held stakes in the other company.

The effect was remarkable. In 1970, on the eve of the global oil crisis, Toyota's workers were each, on average, producing thirty-eight vehicles per year—up from five in 1955. By contrast, Ford's workers were producing twelve per year and GM's workers just eight per year—the same number as fifteen years earlier.[18] It was a rate of efficiency that led John Krafcik—who later became CEO of Waymo, the autonomous-vehicle company owned by Google's holding corporation, Alphabet—to coin a new phrase: lean production.[19]

Jack Smith, Ignacio López, and the
start of global sourcing

By the early 1980s, American and European automakers, the world's biggest industrial companies, were facing the full force of their Japanese rivals. They had to react, but being unable to match the quality of the Japanese cars, they chose to focus instead on a radical cost-cutting program—and the reputation of procurement as a cost-cutting function was established. As we will show more fully in chapter 1, the leading innovator was GM CEO Jack Smith, who hired a brilliant but little-known Spanish engineer, José Ignacio López de Arriortúa, to the newly created post of vice president of worldwide purchasing and charged him with reducing the company's payments to suppliers. As well as squeezing suppliers to lower their prices, López launched GM's now celebrated global sourcing program, finding new suppliers in different countries around the world. In doing so, he capitalized on the growth of globalization and thereby took an approach quite different from that taken by the Japanese, who largely relied on Japanese suppliers.

For the next thirty years, companies enjoyed the benefits of globalization. The Berlin Wall came tumbling down, opening Eastern Europe and adding one billion people to the global economy as workers and as consumers. And China joined the World Trade Organization, making the world's largest low-cost labor market available to global companies. In recent years, however, the tide has been turning, and what once looked like smart procurement has started to look like an approach that was simply riding a favorable macroeconomic wave toward lower costs. Labor costs were rising in China even before the United States–China trade war further complicated matters. So too was competition. Together, these have triggered a margin squeeze in developed markets. Costs are being forced up, not down. What's even worse is that many CEOs appear powerless to counter the negative effects of the new macroeconomic trend. They have stuck with an out-of-date approach to procurement, practicing the not-so-fine art of coercing suppliers into yielding a portion of their profit margin in return for continued business.

This is a pointless, zero-sum game that is failing to deliver. Fortunately, procurement doesn't have to be like this. There is another way, one that is being pioneered by the Big Tech companies.

Apple, Dell, & Co—how Big Tech is reinventing the global corporation

Once upon a time, all the Big Tech companies were Little Tech companies—they started out as startups and, like Ford when it was founded more than one hundred years ago, relied on suppliers. Reflecting on his early years as an entrepreneur, Michael Dell observed:

> "When you start a company with as little as $1,000, as I did, you spend each dollar very carefully. You learn to be economical, efficient, and prudent. You also learn to only do those things that really add value for your customers and your shareholders. From almost the day Dell was founded, we asked: Should we build components ourselves or have someone else manufacture them to our design specifications?"

Dell's decision was to turn to suppliers, and they soon became allies "without whom you couldn't survive and thrive."[20] Whereas Ford was forced by circumstances to discard his suppliers and pursue vertical integration, technology companies were now operating in a fast-globalizing world that was becoming flat, as *New York Times* columnist Thomas Friedman put it. They were able to stay close to their suppliers in ways that could not have been imagined a century ago.[21]

Who would have thought that the world's most valuable company would be one that doesn't actually *make* anything? And yet that is precisely what Apple has managed to do. Its success, like the success of other technology giants, is usually attributed to beautiful design, remarkable technical innovation, and a deep understanding of the consumer. These are all important factors, certainly. But one capability trumps them all: an extraordinary capacity for managing a large network of suppliers.

We are living in a world that is being shaped by digital technology. At its heart is the internet, which by definition facilitates interactions among people. Over the past twenty years, people have learned to live their lives online—shopping, banking, even dating. Not for nothing has our time been dubbed the age of the "trust economy" or the "shared economy," and from a business perspective, what's now important is not simply what you *own* but who you *collaborate* with and how you collaborate with them. As a result, it is those companies that are part of or, better still, orchestrators of networks of companies that are really prospering. These corporate ecosystems are held together not by financial stakes—as with the Japanese *keiretsu*—but by bonds of trust and mutual interest. By collaborating with specialist suppliers that are the best in the world at what they do, the Big Tech companies are reaping the benefits of economies of scale and generating extraordinary value. In a sense, they are taking Adam Smith's concept of the division of labor to its logical conclusion.

How are they able to do this? Above all, it is because they have put their suppliers at the core of their businesses and have empowered the procurement executives who are responsible for managing the collaboration with other companies.

But, as we will show in *Profit from the Source*, if the Big Tech companies have shown the way for other companies, there is much further even they can go.

Why Now Is the Time to Put Suppliers at the Core of Your Business—and How You Can Do It

It is not easy to fathom just how valuable Apple is. In 1997, when Steve Jobs returned to run the company he had cofounded more than two decades earlier, it was worth $3 billion—less than a tenth of the value of Germany-based Siemens, then (and still) one of the world's great industrial conglomerates. Now, after another two decades, Apple is worth not only more than Siemens but also more than the entire, combined DAX index of the thirty leading companies in Germany, Europe's largest economy.

One of the lessons of history, though, is that no company can stay on top forever. In a study of the longevity of more than thirty thousand public firms over a fifty-year period, our colleagues at the BCG Henderson Institute and researchers from Princeton University found that "businesses are disappearing faster than ever before."[22] Some, however, manage to defy the odds of failure by successfully focusing on profitable growth. In effect, they focus on the bottom line and the top line at the same time. In a separate study, the BCG Henderson Institute found that while most companies perform poorly during a downturn, some 14 percent increase sales growth *and* expand profit margins.[23]

Doing this isn't easy. It requires finding new sources of competitive advantage. Apple and other Big Tech companies have found that suppliers are a rich source of competitive advantage and that an advanced procurement capability is a powerful instrument for extracting significant value from those suppliers. But no company—not even Apple—has *fully exploited* the extraordinary value from its supplier network.

It is to show CEOs how they can do this that we have written this book.

• • •

Profit from the Source is structured around three main parts that focus on the three essential building blocks of a revitalized company that puts suppliers at its core and empowers its procurement professionals to extract the maximum possible value from them. The first part focuses on what *the CEO* must do to change. As with so many things, if the CEO doesn't get behind something, it won't happen. The second part focuses on what *the company* must do to change. It is our contention that if CEOs don't change their company, if they don't fundamentally reshape it by putting suppliers at the heart of everything, then they won't be able to deliver their strategic vision and achieve enduring competitive advantage. The third part focuses on what *the company's ecosystem*—the network of suppliers—must do to change. We argue that if CEOs don't change the way their company interacts with suppliers, then they won't be able to exploit the rich potential of procurement to help create products and services that not only cost less but are also more innovative, higher quality, sustainable, faster to market, and generally lower risk.

To help CEOs deliver these changes, we have identified a set of ten practical principles that draw on Boston Consulting Group (BCG) research and our—and our BCG colleagues'—firsthand experience working with some of the world's leading companies. But these are not hard-and-fast principles. If some are followed but others not—that's fine. There is *no company in the world* that is following all ten principles and exploiting the full potential of an advanced procurement capability. On the other hand, those companies that follow some, if not all, of the principles do outperform the market. In a proprietary BCG survey of the 150 top companies in the S&P 500 commissioned for this book, we found that only 35 percent have a chief procurement officer—or equivalent—on the leadership team. Yet strikingly,

FIGURE I-1

Companies with procurement chiefs on leadership teams outperform the market by roughly 130 percent

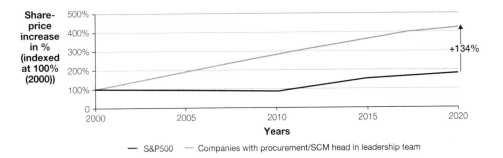

Source: BCG Analysis, S&P 500.

those fifty companies outperformed the market by 134 percent in the twenty-year period from 2000 to 2020. (See figure I-1.)

The first principle, which relates to the first building block (how *the CEO* needs to change), is: *Start at the top. Make your suppliers and your procurement function leadership imperatives.* We recommend that the CEO cultivate a corporate mindset that helps the company as a whole see the most important suppliers as vital partners in the future success of the company and procurement as an essential transformative and strategic value creator rather than simply a transactional and administrative function. We also recommend that the CPO be given a seat at the table, and a new strategic mandate that puts procurement where it should be—at the heart of the business. If they do these things, CEOs will start to make a significant, positive difference to the fortunes of their organization.

The next few principles relate to the second building block (how *the company* needs to change). The second principle is: *Treat your suppliers as friends. Forge new dynamic relationships with your most important suppliers.* All too often, the relationship between buyers and suppliers is antagonistic, with companies engaging in a kind of arm-wrestling match as they try to negotiate deals. We have found that those companies that work *with* each other—rather than *against* each other—have a vastly more fruitful, mutually beneficial relationship: the buyer can expect to double its money, while the supplier can expect to expand its business. Here, we introduce what we call the 360° program, where the CEOs of companies write to the CEOs of their top suppliers and invite them to join a select group, deliver savings up front and, in return, receive a wraparound package of business support. This delivers fast and enduring results—for companies and suppliers—because the conversation is elevated to the CEO level. This makes procurement *personal*, it makes it *strategic*, and ultimately it *makes it matter.*

The third principle is: *Empower your "shoppers." Put your procurement team at the very heart of your product life cycle—from ideation to postproduction.* Many companies developing new products involve their procurement experts only when they need to negotiate deals with the suppliers of the necessary components. That's too late. In our experience, companies that involve the procurement team from the beginning (that is, when the design engineers and product marketers start formulating their ideas for a new offering) create products that are lower cost, higher quality, more innovative, more sustainable, and faster to market.

The fourth principle is: *Go Bionic. Create a procurement function that combines the virtues of human creativity and digital technology.* Typically, a company's procurement function is staffed by deskbound administrative types who are skilled at closing deals that have already been approved by other executives farther up the corporate hierarchy— design engineers, for instance, or product marketers. But for the procurement function to be fit for the new, expanded purpose, CEOs need to retool it in two specific ways: with new digital technologies and with employees who could one day become CEOs themselves.

The remaining set of principles relates to the third building block (how *the company's ecosystem* needs to change). The fifth principle is: *Cut costs—fast. Demand up-front double savings from your top suppliers and double down on the rest.* Companies often get bogged down in protracted negotiations with their biggest suppliers as they try to extract significant savings in a timely manner. Here, we elaborate on our alternative approach—the 360° program—which we introduce in chapter 2. We also show how companies should deal with their other, less strategically important suppliers (we'll call them B and C suppliers). They should treat them more firmly and remind them who calls the shots in the relationship.

The sixth principle is: *Dream big together. Achieve breakthrough innovations by pooling R&D resources with your suppliers.* CEOs are facing increasing pressure to offer products that dazzle with their originality. But doing this, year after year, is difficult. What many CEOs don't realize is that their company's suppliers can help them. They, too, invest in R&D, and they know what a company's competitors are up to. We have found that those companies that collaborate with their suppliers codevelop innovations that give them first-mover advantage in the market.

The seventh principle is: *Settle for perfection. Deliver unbeatable quality by joining forces with your suppliers to wage a war on errors.* Even as CEOs double down on costs and set aside funds for innovation, they cannot afford to compromise on quality. They need to set a goal of zero defects that applies to every stage of the product life cycle—from design through production and distribution—and collaborate with suppliers to achieve it. When customers are unhappy, they don't point the finger at the supplier, even if the supplier is at fault—they point the finger at the company. In our experience, quality issues are less likely to occur when companies build mutually beneficial alliances with their key suppliers.

The eighth principle is: *Share your tomorrows. Become truly sustainable by allying with your suppliers to meet environmental, social, and governance (ESG) standards.* Consumers are prepared to reward companies that make sustainability a central part of their mission. Equally, they will punish those that fail to live up to their promises. Companies that find new ways to work with suppliers in order to develop sustainable products and services and to protect against the reputational damage caused by broken promises stand to prosper in an ESG-conscious world.

The ninth principle is: *Get quicker, faster—as one. Go twice as fast by collaborating with—not competing against—your suppliers.* In the era of Amazon-style same-day delivery, when customers expect instant gratification, a new "creed for speed" has been developed by senior executives. If companies are to achieve this, they must work closely with their suppliers to reconfigure the procurement process, redesign the supply chain, and reengineer the product-development process.

The tenth principle is: *Anticipate the inevitable. Halve your risks by working with your suppliers to predict the unexpected.* No one can say they weren't warned about the likelihood of a global pandemic. Most of the risks that a company will face do not fall into the category of so-called black-swan events. A trade dispute, a viral epidemic, a product failure, a cybersecurity breach, a tsunami—these are all predictable. So, how should CEOs prepare? Among other things, they need to gather intelligence from suppliers, develop deep knowledge of their supply chains, and understand that the next crisis is not an "if" but a "when."

• • •

Taken together, the three building blocks and ten practical principles constitute a blueprint for how CEOs can extract extraordinary value from their suppliers by empowering their CPOs and procurement professionals to drive ample new bottom-line—and top-line—growth.

More than this, they constitute a manual for radical change. If CEOs want to break away from the pack, if they want to fulfill the dreams they have for their company, if they want to leave a legacy of success, then they should follow the tried-and-true recommendations in *Profit from the Source*.

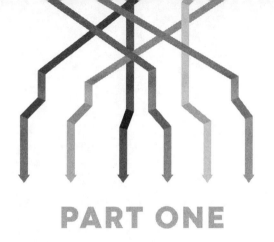

PART ONE

How *You* Need to Change

1

Start at the Top

Make Your Suppliers and Your Procurement Function Leadership Imperatives

t is astonishing that CEOs pay so little attention to their suppliers. In our view, they should spend more time not only thinking about their suppliers but also getting actively involved in the work of their CPO and procurement professionals. If their companies are to draw the full benefits from suppliers, then CEOs should follow our first principle: *Start at the top. Make your suppliers and your procurement function leadership imperatives.* But it isn't sufficient simply to issue a new set of instructions to employees: even in the most hierarchical, top-down organizations, the CEO's edict travels only so far. So beyond this, CEOs should take two very specific actions.

First, they should cultivate a new corporate mindset, one that helps the whole company see the most important suppliers in a new light—as vital partners in the future success of the company—and procurement as an essential transformative and strategic value creator rather than simply a transactional and administrative function. Second, they should give the CPO a seat at the table and a new strategic mandate that puts procurement where it should be—at the heart of the business. If they do these things, CEOs will make a significant, positive difference to the fortunes of their organizations.

These are commonsense things to do, given the amount of money companies spend on suppliers and the amount of value they could extract from suppliers if they empowered their procurement professionals. Yet the fact is that few CEOs really get the importance of suppliers—and the importance of procurement as the function responsible for the company's relationships with them. Partly, this may be because there are few CEOs who have served as CPOs or completed a tour of duty in the procurement department of a major institution at some point in their careers. One of the few prominent former CEOs who are procurement veterans is A.G. Lafley, who served as a supply officer in the US Navy during the Vietnam War. In 2000, when he became CEO of Procter & Gamble for the first time, he unveiled his new strategy of collaborative innovation, setting "a goal that half of new product and technology innovations [must] come from outside P&G."[1] In other words, right from the outset, he gave procurement, as the function responsible for facilitating the collaborations with external suppliers, a central role in the future of the company. Among contemporary CEOs, there is Apple's Tim Cook, of course, but also Volkswagen's Ralf Brandstätter (and his predecessor, Herbert Diess, who is now chairman of the German automobile giant and who was BMW's CPO earlier in his career).

But it is not necessary to have served as a CPO to champion the importance of both suppliers and an advanced procurement capability. Indeed, it could be argued that a CEO who has not been schooled in the old way of doing procurement is best placed to transform the function in new and invigorating ways. Certainly, when we are asked to identify a CEO who prioritized procurement by cultivating a new corporate mindset and giving the CPO a fresh mandate, we point to someone who was not a procurement specialist.

His name is John F. "Jack" Smith.

The House That Jack Built: How GM's CEO Transformed the World's Biggest Industrial Company by Transforming the Procurement Function

On Tuesday, April 7, 1992, Jack Smith was starting his first full day as president of what was then the world's biggest industrial company, General Motors. The day before—on his fifty-fourth birthday—he had been handed responsibility for transforming the company's operations after some of the nonexecutive directors on the board had staged a coup that saw the ousting of the old guard. Ordinarily, it would have been a moment for celebration. The GM job was one of the most coveted jobs in the corporate world—a step away from the position once held by the revered Alfred Sloan, one of the true business greats, who ruled GM for more than thirty years: from 1923 to 1946 as CEO and from 1937 to 1956 as chairman.[2]

But for Jack Smith, there was no time for celebration. He had work to do.

GM was a wounded corporate behemoth facing the once unimaginable prospect of financial oblivion. For most of the time since its founding, in 1908, GM had dominated the automobile industry, with iconic brands such as Buick, Cadillac, Chevrolet, GMC, Oldsmobile, and Pontiac. Now it was close to bankruptcy. The previous year, GM had racked up losses amounting to nearly $11 billion. Jack Smith's job was to, as he put it, "stop the bleeding."

It was a giant responsibility. On his shoulders rested not only the future of every one of GM's 750,000 employees but also the future of the US economy: GM employed one in every five of the factory workers in the country. Not only that, but every job GM created led to five more jobs in the wider economy, in companies that supplied the carmaker with parts and components, provided its customers with car loans, and served its workers in the factories across the country.

In these circumstances, Smith might have been expected to call in his chief finance officer or his chief strategy officer. But no. Instead, the first thing he did was put a call in to the headquarters of Opel, GM's German subsidiary in Russelheim, a town a few miles south of Frankfurt. The man who took the call was Ignacio López, who was known for his forceful personality. The two men talked for a few minutes, and in that time, Smith offered López the newly created post of vice president of worldwide purchasing.

It marked the beginning of modern corporate procurement.

• • •

Smith's call, though seeming to come out of the blue, was in fact many years in the making. Back in 1986, Smith was running GM Europe, with responsibility for Opel and Vauxhall, the British car brand. By then, he had earned a reputation as "a process guy," someone who focused more on how the product was made and less on the product— the car—itself. A GM lifer, he had started out at one of the company's captive suppliers, Fisher Body, as a payroll auditor. Working at the factory in Framingham, just outside of Boston, he spent his time counting car body parts, and over time acquired a deep understanding of the company, from the factory floor all the way up to the executive suite.

Soon after taking the GM Europe job, Smith started to hear good things about the cost-cutting work of a young engineer at the Opel factory in Zaragoza, in the northeast Spanish province of Aragon. One day, Smith decided to visit the factory, meet López, and see for himself what was going on. What he found transformed the way he thought about carmaking. "It was a defining event," Smith later said.[3]

Visiting López's office, Smith was startled to find that the whole room was littered with different parts of a Corsa, a midmarket "super-mini" and one of Europe's best-selling cars. What on earth was López doing? As Smith quickly discovered, López was conducting what would now be called a teardown, completely dismantling the car, inspecting the components, and searching for ways that GM could cut its costs without compromising quality. López reported that he had identified ways to reduce the cost of making each Corsa by 600 deutsche marks, or about $770 today. Smith was so impressed that he offered López a new job at Opel's headquarters in Russelheim, as head of the firm's purchasing operation. Within weeks of arriving, López was making his presence felt at the venerable German carmaker.

Opel was actually founded in 1862 as a manufacturer of sewing machines. But Adam Opel's sons switched the company's focus to transport—first bicycles and then, starting in 1899, cars. In other words, it was older than GM, which bought Opel in 1929 and, during Sloan's remarkable tenure as CEO, turned it into the first German carmaker to build more than 100,000 cars in a year. But by the time Smith assumed control of GM's European division, Opel's best years were behind it. In the period 1983–1986, GM Europe reported annual losses of between $228 million and $372 million.[4] Opel's failings were a big part of this.

It was clear to Smith that he needed to shake things up, hence López's appointment.

From the start, López, who hailed from Spain's Basque region in the north, adopted an aggressive, combative style with GM's suppliers. An outsider in a cozy world where suppliers often wined and dined Opel's decision-makers in order to secure lucrative deals, López was a disruptive force. Not content with shaving two percent of a supplier's contract, he demanded dramatic cuts of twenty percent. When the suppliers protested or refused, he did two things. First, he launched a bold program of "global sourcing" and sought competitive suppliers from around the world. Suddenly, the local German suppliers who had built an easy, comfortable, and indeed lucrative relationship with Opel were being forced to compete for business with rivals half a world away.

Second, López introduced a new efficiency initiative called the "program for the improvement and cost optimization of suppliers," or PICOS for short. He sent crack teams of manufacturing and operations experts to suppliers with the task of finding out how the parts and components were made and how they could be made more cheaply and more quickly, without compromising quality. Of course, the suppliers could have refused to cooperate with these experts—but if they did so, they risked losing the contract with Opel.

Indeed, many of Opel's traditional suppliers did not like López's actions. They were used to keeping their methods a closely guarded secret. Now they were being forced to share this information or face losing their GM contracts. They pushed back. They branded López "the Russelheim Strangler" and the "Basque Bully." But all the while, Smith stood by his procurement mastermind, protecting him, providing him with cover. And why wouldn't he? The cost-cutting initiatives were having a dramatic impact on GM Europe's profitability. In 1987, the division made a net profit of $1.3 billion—its first profit since 1982, when the reported number was a paltry $6 million.

The following year, when GM Europe was on its way to delivering another impressive financial performance, Jack Smith was whisked back to Detroit, where he was appointed executive vice president of international operations. López stayed in Europe and continued his good work: GM Europe's net profit increased to $1.8 billion in 1989 and $1.9 billion in 1990.

Then, in April 1992, López got the call from Smith to come to Detroit. Suddenly, GM's American suppliers were in his sights.

• • •

When López arrived in Detroit, he let it be known that times were changing. In a highly symbolic move, he ceremoniously switched his watch from his left wrist to his right wrist and said he would not move it back until GM had recorded record profits in North America. His loyal procurement executives—the people he called "warriors" because they were engaged in a battle to put GM back in the black—followed his example and strapped their watches on their right wrists. Also, they followed what he called a "warrior diet," having been given copies of his forty-four-page health pamphlet titled *Feeding the Warrior Spirit*. This diet banned fattening, sugary, junk food and prescribed fruit, vegetables, and rice. It was all part of López's attempt to change the modus operandi. Never again would purchasing managers be permitted to conclude deals with suppliers over long, languid lunches. They would be lean in every sense of the word.

Not surprisingly, López became a kind of cult figure. But although his eccentric actions attracted the interest of the media—and underscored the fact that procurement was no longer a shadowy back-office function with limited strategic importance—his smart organizational reforms attracted the ire of GM's long-standing suppliers.

First, he centralized the procurement operation, creating one office where previously there had been twenty-seven offices. Until then, suppliers had been able to strike different deals with different procurement managers, and some of the managers were more scrupulous than others. Sometimes, personal relationships had counted for more than price and quality, with the result that GM might end up paying three times as much as a rival for a car seat, a steering wheel, or some other critical component.

Second, López built on the success of his aggressive supplier cost initiative and sent efficiency teams to all of GM's main suppliers across the United States. Some, such as Rockwell International, pushed back and pulled out of joint initiatives. Others launched a backdoor campaign, appealing to Smith and GM's board. The animosity that López stirred among suppliers was perhaps best summed up by the astute observer James Womack, a Massachusetts Institute of Technology professor and coauthor of a book about Toyota's legendary lean production practices, *The Machine That Changed the World*. "I've been watching for headlines in the European press: 'Car Bomb Gets GM Executive: Supplier Charged,'" Womack commented.[5]

But Smith stood firm, and when López was called to address the board and explain his actions, he was reportedly given a standing ovation. The fact that he was on course to save the company a staggering $4 billion no doubt helped to persuade the nonexecutive directors to give López their enthusiastic backing. As things turned out, it wasn't only GM executives who were impressed by the work of the CPO. Back in Germany the newly installed chairman of Volkswagen, Ferdinand Piëch—whose grandfather Ferdinand Porsche, one of the greatest designers in automobile history, had designed the iconic VW Beetle—was watching the transformative impact López was having on GM.

News that VW was taking an interest in López soon reached the ears of Jack Smith. So, in January 1993, two months after being named CEO of GM as a result of another boardroom coup, he persuaded the board to give López a promotion to vice president for the whole company, not just the North American division. But that didn't stop the rumors, nor the conversations between López and VW. Piëch quickly offered the job of VW CPO to López, who accepted it.

But Smith considered López so important to GM that he fought back, offering him the elevated post of president of the North American business—in effect, his number two. This was sufficient to make López waver. He did verbally accept Smith's offer, but on the day when Smith called a press conference to announce López's promotion, López boarded a private jet to Germany, and started his work at VW.

Smith didn't let López go quietly. GM filed a lawsuit against VW, claiming that López had taken corporate secrets with him to the German giant's headquarters in Wolfsburg, east of Hanover, in the north of the country. The matter was finally settled out of court, after VW accepted López's resignation and agreed to pay GM $100 million in damages and buy GM parts and components worth $1 billion.[6]

This was perhaps scant compensation, given that López had helped VW deliver significant savings from suppliers. But Smith's struggle to hold onto López and then to make VW pay for his departure demonstrated his belief in the importance of procurement, and this was again underlined when he appointed Rick Wagoner, GM's rising star and Smith's future successor, as the company's new CPO.

Why CEOs Should Aspire to Be "The Jack Smith of the 2020s"

The story of Jack Smith is instructive for any business leader. He was given the daunting responsibility of delivering the turnarounds of GM Europe, and then of GM North America, and then of the entire company, and he delivered, every time. This was because he turned to what he called his secret weapon: the CPO and the procurement function. Although Smith was not a procurement specialist, he understood the value that the function could offer, and he was ready to cultivate a new corporate mindset and give the CPO a seat at the table and a wide mandate for change.

Of course, nearly thirty years on, the world has changed, and CEOs cannot expect to have the same impact simply by reprising Smith's actions. He was narrowly focused on the bottom line and cutting costs, whereas today a sophisticated procurement capability can be used to deliver top-line growth. But by drawing inspiration from GM's former CEO and elevating the role of the CPO, today's CEOs can have a transformative effect on their companies.

Cultivate a new corporate mindset

In the vast majority of companies, suppliers are a second thought and procurement is a back-office function with little or no strategic involvement. If this is to change, as we think it must, then companies will need to start viewing them both very differently, and the only way to change perceptions is for the CEO to take personal responsibility for cultivating a new corporate mindset. But how, exactly, should CEOs achieve this? By leading from the front and taking very tangible, visible actions at an *individual* and *institutional* level.

At an individual level, CEOs should start spending about 25 percent of their time thinking about suppliers and participating in procurement activities. In practical terms, this means that they should allocate part of each day to nurturing personal relationships with the CEOs of their companies' top suppliers and meeting the leaders of companies that are not yet on their roster of approved suppliers but that show some promise of strategic potential. Also, they should get to know the CPO and the other procurement professionals—their work, their preoccupations, their passions. It is striking that Jack Smith went out of his way to meet and spend time with Ignacio López, who at the time was a little-known industrial engineer working far from the main centers of GM activity.

At an institutional level, CEOs should consider making suppliers—and by extension the procurement function—one of the top agenda items at board meetings on a regular basis. (This will send a clear message to the rest of the executive team.) The CPO should be invited to join the CEO's inner circle so that they can contribute to and be consulted on the strategic direction of the company. In many companies, the CPO is an administrative figure, reporting to someone in the senior executive team. This makes little sense. By cutting the CPO out of the high-level strategic conversation, companies risk squandering valuable commercial intelligence that comes from their relationship with suppliers—in particular, news about competitors' current and future products, information about up-to-the-minute trends, and the latest thinking on faster, better, and safer ways to source and make products.

Again, it is striking that Smith gave López an important role on the strategy board of GM's North American business. He rightly understood that if it is to be effective, the procurement department needs to be transformed from an *instruction-taking* to a *decision-making* function. Moreover, after López's departure, he appointed someone—Rick Wagoner—who could, and eventually did, succeed him in the top job. This is critical. If CPOs are to merit a place in the CEO's inner circle, they must be powerful corporate figures in their own right, people who can command the respect of their fellow executives. They may or may not have previous procurement experience, but they must certainly have the personality to challenge the status quo, foster disruptive thinking, deliver radical change, and one day run the whole company.

We often recommend that to underscore the CPO's authority, CEOs should make them a direct report, as Smith did with López. Also, if possible, they should consider installing the CPO in an office next to or near their own. You can tell a lot about CEOs by looking at the company they keep and the people they keep close by their side.

Give the CPO a seat at the table and a new strategic mandate

In most companies, the role of the CPO and the procurement team is limited to negotiating the terms and conditions of contracts with suppliers that have already been agreed with the company's product engineers and manufacturers. Those companies would do well to learn from the pioneering work of Jack Smith all those years ago. When Smith gave Ignacio López a new strategic mandate after watching with amazement how he deconstructed an Opel Corsa and worked out how it could be reconstructed more cheaply without compromising quality, he transformed the role of procurement. Even so, he was still focused on cost reduction. Today, with a new and different set of challenges, CEOs should take a leaf out of Jack Smith's book and once again give the CPO a seat at the table and a new strategic mandate. This time, however, the mandate should not be focused on cost reduction but on *profitable growth.*

Indeed, unless companies are facing imminent bankruptcy, then CEOs should always be focused on profitable growth—namely, expanding the existing business by maximizing the core and pursuing adjacent opportunities at the periphery. When Smith was digging GM out of its multibillion-dollar hole, he really had no option other than to focus the whole company on slashing costs. His stroke of genius was to give his brilliant CPO a strategic role. It was not, however, a pain-free decision. It came with some significant downsides. First, a strategy based on cost cutting is necessarily short term. At some point, you cut to the bone, and then you can't cut any further. Second, it often requires brutal tactics. López's uncompromising "warrior" approach was deeply resented, and some observers have suggested that it inflicted long-term damage on GM's relationships with key suppliers. On the other hand, times were different then and if López had not taken such a tough approach, it is very doubtful that the suppliers would have changed their ways.

Nowadays, CPOs should, more often than not, foster a collaborative relationship with their most important suppliers. This is because a mandate focused on profitable growth is necessarily long term and future focused. CPOs cannot afford to burn too many bridges. Of course, there are still times when they must take a López-style hard-bargaining approach, not least because even as they pursue profitable growth, they must continue to pay attention to the bottom line through smart cost-reduction strategies.

But profitable growth—paying attention to the top line—requires companies to tap several other sources of competitive advantage besides cost reduction. Specifically, they are: innovation, quality, sustainability, speed, and risk reduction. On each of these, the CPO can and should be allowed to help deliver for the company.

But this raises a question: Why should the CPO and the procurement function be given such an elevated role in the company?

It is a fair question.

The answer lies in the way companies are starting to—and eventually will all have to—organize themselves. As we explained in the introduction, if you go back one hundred years to the days of Henry Ford and the Model T, what was then the world's most successful company was vertically integrated, making virtually *everything* itself. Even thirty years ago, GM was substantially organized this way, making 70 percent of everything that went into its cars. Now the world's most successful companies—Apple and the other technology giants—are organized very differently. They make virtually *nothing* themselves. They are, in effect, the consumer-facing, brand-owning centripetal force at the core of a business ecosystem. Right from the start, they have understood one thing: they don't have a monopoly on wisdom. As a result, they have sought to collaborate with other companies—suppliers—that are best-in-class at what they do. These top suppliers have many customers, they are not beholden to any one company (even one as powerful as Apple), and they bring their own value to the partnership. Working together, companies and suppliers are stronger, more agile, more innovative, and more profitable.

Never has this approach been more essential than it is now. Such is the pace of change, such is the avalanche of existential crises, that many companies will simply not survive unless they work collaboratively with the select few suppliers who are the best in the world

at what they do and have enormous strategic potential. And this ne-
cessitates an expanded mandate for the CPO, since it is the CPO's
job to orchestrate this complex network of suppliers—the supplier
ecosystem—and, ultimately, ensure that the company offers the right
product with the right innovation from the right suppliers.

It is now often said that all companies will have to become technology companies in the future, if they are not so already. Usually,
this is a statement of the obvious: in a world where almost everyone
on the planet is connected via the mobile internet—with some 5 billion of the 5.7 billion adults on earth possessing a mobile phone,
and more than 80 percent of American teenagers owning an Apple
iPhone—companies that are not driven by technology just will not
survive.

But we think there is an additional point to be made: all companies will have to organize themselves in the same way that technology
companies do now. And that means CEOs must make procurement
their top priority. At most companies, if you want to get something
unusual done, you turn to the head of engineering or the head of
manufacturing. At technology companies, you turn to the CPO and
the procurement function.

They hold the keys to the engine that really drives the company
and its future.

Conclusion

Leadership is key. Any transformation must start at the top. As we'll
show in the next three chapters, CEOs must then use their powers
to drive through major changes in three critical elements of their organization's business: the way the company interacts with its suppliers, the way the CPO and other procurement executives interact with

the company's other functional leaders in the course of creating new products and services, and the way the procurement function operates on a daily basis.

 ## Notes for the CEO

Key Takeaway

If you want to realize your dreams for your company, you should put suppliers at the core of your business. They can give you an edge over your rivals by helping you tap all the key sources of competitive advantage: cost savings, innovation, quality, sustainability, speed, and risk reduction.

Key Strategy

Take a leaf out of Jack Smith's playbook: make the CPO and procurement your secret weapon (because they own the corporate relationship with suppliers). Elevate the role of the CPO. Take personal responsibility for doing this. Don't delegate it. Make it a leadership imperative.

Key Tactics

- Cultivate a new corporate mindset (to change the way your company thinks about suppliers and procurement).

- Lead from the front. Make it your personal mission. Spend 25 percent of your time thinking about suppliers and participating in procurement activities. Meet the CEOs of your suppliers—and your potential future suppliers.

- Challenge your suppliers. See which ones are ready and willing to enter a deeper and more meaningful relationship through what we call a 360° program.

- Consider appointing the CPO on day one. Select someone who can challenge the status quo, foster disruptive thinking, and deliver radical change and who shows the potential to one day succeed you in the top job.

- Give the CPO a seat at the table. Bring them into your inner circle. Be visible about this. Install them in an office next to or near yours.

- Give the CPO a new mandate. Instruct them to focus on profitable growth rather than just cost reduction. Let them help shape the corporate strategy, not just support it.

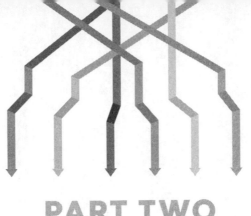

PART TWO

How *Your Company* Needs to Change

2

Treat Your Suppliers as Friends

Forge New Dynamic Relationships with Your Most Important Suppliers

Visit most companies, and you'll find that the interaction between buyer and supplier is essentially a transactional tug-of-war. The buyer tries to squeeze as much profit as possible from the supplier, who in turn tries every way possible to limit the negative impact on its profit margin while still retaining the buyer's business. But it's all a charade: the supplier sets an artificially high starting price and agrees to a program of cuts that gives the illusion the buyer is getting a good deal. For its part, the buyer's procurement team receives plaudits—and bonuses—for seemingly squeezing the supplier.

The buyer-supplier relationship could be so much more valuable to both companies if only they worked *with* each other rather than *against* each other. The often dysfunctional dynamic between buyer and supplier is the result of the way procurement departments are organized. Today's products are extremely complex. They comprise thousands of components and all kinds of raw materials—collectively called commodities—that are supplied by companies based around the world. On one level, then, it makes perfect sense for the procurement team to have specialist commodity managers whose job is to negotiate deals with the suppliers of particular commodities. If anything were to go wrong—if, for example, there were an interruption in the supply of an engine or a chassis or even a windshield wiper— the whole enterprise could be negatively affected. As Peter Hasenkamp, former head of supply-chain strategy for the Tesla Model S, once put it: "It takes 2,500 parts to build a car, but only one not to."[1]

But there is a downside to how procurement teams are organized. Many suppliers have become so large that they often provide companies with a broad range of commodities. For example, take Bosch, the world's biggest car-parts supplier. It makes everything from batteries and brakes to spark plugs, steering systems, and throttle devices. This often means that car companies have several different commodity managers negotiating separately, and in an uncoordinated way, with Bosch's executives. As a result, the CEOs of the car companies are relatively powerless to drive change within their organizations. If they want to drive down costs, for example, they have to get multiple managers to conduct multiple negotiations across multiple commodities. The process is slow, cumbersome, and ultimately ineffective.

Surely there must be a better way? Yes, there is. Buyers should focus less on the commodities and more on the suppliers. As our second principle states: *Treat your suppliers as friends. Forge new dynamic relationships with your most important suppliers.* Of course, some friends are closer than others, and buyers should distinguish between different types of suppliers. As we will now show, one way to do this is to use what we call the 360° approach, which focuses on the biggest and most important *current* suppliers—those who account for the largest proportion of a company's procurement budget. The other way is the performance/potential approach, which classifies not only *current* suppliers but also possible *future* suppliers according to their performance and strategic potential.

These two approaches are intertwined. The 360° approach should be viewed as a stepping-stone between old-style commodity-focused procurement and new-style supplier-focused procurement.

The Cost Savings Solution: The 360° Program Approach

The number-one task of the procurement function is to generate cost savings. The 360° program offers a proven way of doing so—and doing so fast. Companies can achieve significant cost reductions when they demand up-front savings from their biggest suppliers in return for exclusive access to a wraparound package of business support (hence the 360° name).

We developed the 360° approach in our work with big technology companies. In 2012, we were asked to help one of the world's biggest computer manufacturers cut its $35 billion annual bill for suppliers—and quickly. For the previous twenty years, it, along with other personal-computer companies, had enjoyed solid double-digit growth and the consequent financial resources to invest in ambitious efficiency and innovation programs. But with the advent of smartphones and tablets—Apple's iPhone in 2007 and the iPad in 2010 were the game-changers—the PC industry had started to slide toward stagnation.

Although the computer giant wanted to cut costs, it did not want to compromise its carefully cultivated relationships with its most valued suppliers. We knew that we couldn't recommend the classic approach to cutting costs. Back then (and sometimes even today), the typical procurement project began with a detailed baseline analysis of the power dynamic between the company and its key vendors. Who was more powerful? How could the company extract savings commitments from the suppliers over whom it wielded greater power? The trouble with this approach was that the results did not usually affect the balance sheet for at least six months. And the computer company was in a hurry—it needed to see results *now*. In the computer business, the product life cycle is less than two years. The top executives couldn't afford to wait six months for the savings to hit the bottom line.

We were forced to think in a new way, fast. If we didn't act quickly, this multimillion-dollar client would take its business elsewhere. Under pressure, we went back to first principles. What, we asked ourselves, is procurement really about? During an all-night brainstorming session, we found ourselves talking about the very first market traders—the people who bartered in the ancient bazaars of Babylon. It was Adam Smith, the high priest of capitalism, who observed in *The Wealth of Nations* that mankind's "propensity to truck, barter, and exchange one thing for another" lies at the heart of business enterprise, giving rise to "the division of labor from which so many advantages are derived."[2] Building on this, we concluded that when all is said and done, procurement is a fundamental business activity—perhaps the most fundamental. It's about dealmaking between two people or two parties: the buyer and the seller. And the price they negotiate for goods and services reflects the shifting balance of power between the age-old economic forces of supply and demand.

But how could we apply this knowledge today? How could we use it to ensure that the computer company's executives got what they wanted so that we could retain them as our client? Our conclusion: We had to make procurement *personal*. We had to make it *strategic*. Above all, we had to *make it matter*.

From these insights, we recommended several practical steps to the company.

To make procurement personal, strategic, and matter, we first had to elevate the communication to a higher level. Ordinarily, the business of procurement is conducted at an operational level by commodity managers (at the buyer company) and account managers (at the supplier company) who have limited decision-making authority. We recommended that the computer company's CPO reach out to the CEOs of the supplier companies and begin a one-on-one dialogue. That made it personal.

But which suppliers should the CPO reach out to? Clearly it wasn't practical for the CPO to communicate directly with the CEOs of all the firm's many thousands of suppliers. Nor was it logical. In our experience, the top twenty to forty suppliers—those we call the A suppliers—account for 50 percent of a typical company's procurement budget. Accordingly, our second recommendation was that the CPO focus exclusively on these suppliers. That made it strategic and made it matter.

It also raised the question: What should the CPO say to the CEOs of the A suppliers? There was no point going into a detailed and protracted discussion about each and every commodity. We recommended that the CPO step back, take a big-picture view, and ask the CEOs for an up-front commitment to double savings. Only once this commitment had been made should the CPO offer something in return: the opportunity to strike a new, collaborative relationship between the two companies that would not only boost their profits but also increase their pipeline of innovations, reduce their carbon footprint, and develop other beyond-cost projects.

There was one more issue to address: How should the CPO get the conversation started with the CEOs of the A suppliers? Back in 2012, we recommended writing a good old-fashioned letter. Today, we have found a letter still works. The best letters typically include the following:

- An explanatory opening statement on why higher savings are needed—and why now

- A clear, straightforward request for a commitment to deliver double savings

- A list of the benefits of participating in the 360° program

- An invitation to propose collaborative projects that would help the supplier become more profitable

The letters should be personalized. So if a company has forty A suppliers, then the CPO should produce forty individually crafted letters.

Sometimes suppliers don't immediately "get" the 360° program. After years of having played tug-of-war with the buyer company, they can find it hard to adjust to the idea of a more collaborative relationship. In these cases, it's important to be clear about what the company is offering them so that they have no doubt about the benefits of saying yes and the implications of saying no. We recommend something along the following lines: "I am going to dedicate substantial resources to the 360° program. My intention is to help you become more profitable and grow your business with us. But remember, if you don't take me up on this offer, these resources could be deployed to audit everything you are doing and help grow your competitors' business. Ultimately, the choice is yours. We would love it if you chose to collaborate with us."

Sometimes we find that even those suppliers who say yes may find it difficult to propose collaborative projects that would help them become more profitable. It's as if Aladdin, granted his every wish by the genie, has no idea what more to ask for. We usually recommend that the CPO orchestrate brainstorming sessions with the supplier CEOs and their teams. After some back-and-forth, it is usually possible to identify joint projects that will help the suppliers improve their financial performance and their ability to deliver double savings.

These practical steps sound simple. But when we first proposed them, they heralded nothing less than a paradigm shift, promising to turn traditional procurement on its head. For a start, they signi-fied the end of procurement as a purely operational function: by con-ducting the dialogue at the highest level, procurement would have a crucial strategic, decision-making role in the future of the company. Second, they reversed the traditional sequence of procurement: by being placed in the driver's seat, the computer company would see the benefits of a cost-cutting exercise from the very beginning of a new deal with the suppliers—not at the end. Third, they countered the belief that procurement is a zero-sum game: by making sure that the computer company collaborated on projects designed to enhance its and its suppliers' profit margins, we showed that procurement could be a win-win game.

The 360° approach, which focused the computer company's at-tention on the relatively few suppliers who accounted for half of its procurement budget, resulted in lower costs within weeks of imple-mentation. What we didn't know then is whether or not the 360° ap-proach would lead to companies creating a new set of close, cozy, noncompetitive relationships—the kind that Ignacio López fought so hard to overturn. Our experience since then shows that the very opposite happens. Companies introducing the 360° program quickly become used to receiving double savings from their suppliers—and come to expect them year after year. And suppliers deliver for two reasons. One, the deeper relationship between customer and supplier that is forged within a 360° program allows for more attention to de-tail, and this helps them drive down costs and reap other benefits. Second, the top companies put in place robust mechanisms for keep-ing suppliers on their toes. In the tech industry, for example, quarterly business reviews with suppliers are commonplace. Suppliers receive blunt feedback on their performance against such key indicators as time, cost, quality, innovation, and sustainability. They are measured against absolute and relative standards. In follow-up reviews, suppli-ers have to report their progress. Since their quarterly performance informs decisions about future business, they tend to be diligent in finding ways to deliver cost savings.

What we also didn't know when we worked with the computer company is whether or not this approach would work for companies in nontech sectors. Typically, technology companies are innovative, ready to experiment, and ready to take a leap of faith. They are usually led by executives who are bold, rational, fast decision-makers and left-field thinkers prepared to shake things up.

Toward the end of 2018, the CPO of one of the world's leading carmakers, Advanced Luxury Vehicles (ALV), asked us to help him make a fast cut in the company's procurement budget.* The challenges ALV faced were similar to the challenges faced by the technology companies we had been helping for the past six years. It needed to find $500 million of savings . . . within three months.

This is how the 360° program worked for ALV.

How Advanced Luxury Vehicles ran its 360° program

Headquartered in central Europe, ALV produces not only its eponymous car but also several other marques—the sleek status symbols of millionaires throughout the automotive era. Founded more than a century ago, it has managed to change with the times; today, it is responding to the challenges presented by a new age of electric vehicles, self-driving cars, and ride-sharing. One of the executives playing a key role in this transformation is ALV's chief procurement officer. Let's call him Bernhard Schmidt.

Schmidt is not your traditional CPO. Appointed only a few months before we met him, he has spent most of his working life in manufacturing—first at a major car supplier and then at ALV's various European factories. As a result, he has an insider's perspec-

---

* For confidentiality reasons, we have changed the company's name.

tive on both carmakers and their suppliers—how they think, what makes them tick, and what they want from each other. So when we sat down with Schmidt, we felt pretty sure that he would welcome unconventional thinking. And as we talked, this feeling was confirmed. Schmidt saw the factory not just as the place where cars are assembled but also as the last stop on the car's journey to the customer. When he ran one of ALV's factories in Europe, he saw it as his responsibility to ensure that the car came off the assembly line in perfect condition for the customer. What most people saw as noisy, oily, mechanical, and inward facing—the manufacturing function—Schmidt saw as customer oriented and outward facing. This is precisely how we see the procurement function. It needs to be viewed not as a backroom, administrative function but as strategically important, customer oriented, and outward facing.

The task Schmidt faced was monumental. When he was picked to be CPO, with a seat on ALV's board, his mission was to help leverage the supplier network, given that it was becoming increasingly important to the company. But by the time he began his new job, Schmidt was confronted by a more immediate challenge: to close a savings gap of $1 billion in three months. He already had plans to save $500 million. Now he needed to find a further $500 million of savings. The massive savings gap was caused by three main factors, none of which were of ALV's making, but all of which severely affected the company. First was Brexit, the impending departure of the United Kingdom, one of ALV's primary markets, from the European Union. Second was US President Donald Trump's trade war not only with China but also with the EU. Unusual for European carmakers, ALV has one of its biggest factories in the United States, which mostly makes big, expensive SUVs that are largely exported to China. Third was the fact that after ALV had spent millions in making the world's most efficient diesel engines, the diesel-emissions scandal curbed customer interest in diesel cars.

How could Schmidt possibly close the $500 million savings gap in a mere three months? As at most companies, ALV's procurement department is structured according to commodities—the five thousand or so parts and components used to build the typical premium vehicle. There were some sixty commodity managers, each of whom takes responsibility for negotiating with suppliers for the delivery of their collection of commodities. Inevitably, some managers are better negotiators than others. Regardless, whenever ALV wanted to drive down costs—or increase savings—it had to work through each of the managers. It made for a slow, cumbersome, and generally unsatisfactory process.

In light of this, we recommended a 360° program focused on ALV's A suppliers. Designed to deliver results quickly by building or expanding on Schmidt's personal connection with the CEOs of ALV's most important suppliers, this program expected participants to make an up-front commitment to cut costs—and thereby deliver double savings. In return, ALV would offer a wraparound package of support, including teaching the suppliers how to improve their profitability across all facets of their business—from manufacturing and procurement to engineering and inventory management.

This was different from anything that had been tried before in the automobile industry. But Schmidt liked the idea, and he gave the plan the green light. To start, he sent letters to the top executives at ALV's thirty biggest A suppliers, who together accounted for 50 percent of the company's procurement budget. Each letter was crafted with the particular recipient in mind. Schmidt compared the task to penning a thoughtful, carefully worded Christmas card. In some cases, he spent an entire weekend refining the minute details of the letters.

Among the first executives to respond positively was a supplier that had already promised savings amounting to $50 million. After reading Schmidt's letter and conducting follow-up conversations, the CEO committed to double the savings—offering an astonishing

$100 million, or 10 percent of the total savings ALV was looking to make in just one quarter. As a quid pro quo, ALV agreed to a phased program of support relating to the supplier's own particular manufacturing challenges. This started with providing the supplier with practical help to integrate its recent acquisition—a US-based producer of car safety equipment. If all went well, ALV would give the supplier the exclusive opportunity to participate in a codevelopment research project into next-generation battery technology.

It is important to remember that each of the top suppliers must be offered a tailor-made 360° program. In the end, twenty of ALV's thirty A suppliers agreed to partner with ALV. One was a Shanghai-based company, among the world's largest suppliers of car seats and interior designs. The firm's general manager signed up to the program with alacrity, not least because he regarded the partnership as an opportunity to influence and be influenced by a leading automobile brand.

Originally, the Shanghai supplier promised to deliver more than $10 million of savings. But after accepting the challenge of doubling the savings, the company made an up-front commitment to deliver over $26 million in savings. In the spirit of reciprocity, ALV offered, among other things, to run workshops to help the supplier improve its profitability, to engage in an exclusive strategic dialogue so that senior Chinese executives could interact with ALV's top management, and to launch an innovative collaboration program designed to develop the "interior of the future." To seal the deal, Schmidt attended a signing ceremony, which was conducted with great fanfare, in China. There he handed the supplier's top executive a personal commemorative booklet in which he summarized the key features of the 360° program and noted that this was just the beginning of a partnership designed "to make an important contribution to the future sustainability of our companies."

By striking a new, collaborative relationship with ALV's biggest suppliers, Schmidt was able to deliver $1 billion of savings in three months. He also seeded the idea within ALV that supplier-focused procurement could be used to extract value from sources of competitive advantage beyond mere cost savings.

Beyond Cost Savings: The Performance/ Potential Approach

The 360° approach provides a fast, effective way of focusing on the most important current suppliers for the purposes of cutting costs and collaborating on other urgent issues, such as reducing carbon emissions. It is a stepping-stone on the path to collecting all the potential benefits of a newfound relationship with suppliers. Essentially, the 360° approach draws on what can be considered a *lagging* indicator: the list of the buyer's biggest suppliers as defined by their share of the company's procurement budget. If CEOs are to find sources of competitive advantage beyond savings, they should draw on forward-looking, *leading* indicators. To help them do this, we have developed the performance/potential approach. It allows companies to plot the position of each of their suppliers on a chart according to two factors: their performance and their strategic potential.

In our estimation, only around 5 percent of a company's suppliers are top performers offering real strategic potential. But they should occupy 95 percent of a CEO's—and, by extension, a CPO's—time. These suppliers, which form a critical cluster, fall into three main categories, and they require companies to approach them in different ways.

One category of suppliers is those that often serve several rival companies in the same sector. So, on one hand, they don't offer much opportunity for differentiation. On the other hand, if a CPO can *influence* them in such a way as to secure exclusivity—even for a short time—they stand to benefit substantially. This is precisely what

Ocean Victory Corporation, one of the world's premier defense companies, is trying to do.*

Another category of suppliers includes those that offer potentially game-changing products or services but often require a significant investment of time, money, knowledge, and other resources in order to build the capabilities to meet a company's needs. Companies and other organizations that can *invest* in these suppliers, and help them overcome challenging performance issues, can reap significant rewards. One organization that has engaged with its suppliers in this way is NASA, the US space agency. As we will show, its relationship with SpaceX, the space startup founded by Tesla CEO Elon Musk, is a classic example of how to get the most out of a supplier with high strategic potential.[3]

The third category of suppliers in the critical cluster—and the most valued—includes those that are handpicked and rarely number more than four or five for companies with, say, one thousand suppliers. Typically they deliver top performance *and* possess high strategic potential. Companies that *integrate* these suppliers into their business by building a mutually beneficial, multiyear, exclusive relationship—a partnership with a capital *P*—can enjoy a competitive edge over their rivals. This is the kind of relationship that Apple has nurtured with Taiwan Semiconductor Manufacturing Company (TSMC), the world's largest contract manufacturer of computer microchips.

Let's look at how companies are dealing with these different categories of suppliers, starting with Ocean Victory Corporation (OVC).

How to influence your suppliers—the story of Ocean Victory Corporation

Headquartered on Germany's Baltic coast, OVC has a distinguished history of naval design and construction dating back to the

---

* For confidentiality reasons, we have changed the company's name.

nineteenth century. Today it builds warships and submarines for several of the world's most powerful navies. Increasingly, OVC's primary customers—government defense departments—want to buy vessels that can be used for a variety of purposes, from participating in armed conflict and protecting commercial trading fleets to countering terrorism and drug trafficking and conducting disaster-relief missions.

As a result, OVC has started to change the way it works with, and ultimately influences, suppliers. In the past, it collaborated with relatively few suppliers, who proceeded to establish a monopoly position in OVC's supply chain. This approach has become increasingly problematic. For a start, the world's navies are beginning to demand greater innovation that will put them one step ahead of potential enemies in a changing world of naval warfare. Also, these customers want greater value as they deal with competing pressures on public finances.

To satisfy these customers, OVC decided to increase the number and variety of potential suppliers it invited to participate in the competition to provide vital parts for its next-generation warships, frigates, and submarines. Starting in 2020, it began holding what it called technology conventions—a combination of expert conference, brainstorming session, and selection platform. OVC wanted to build relationships with suppliers who could give it first-mover advantage. It was signaling its willingness to be a launch customer for new innovative technologies.

As the Covid-19 pandemic continued, potential suppliers gathered at OVC headquarters for a series of socially distanced workshops. They shared their ideas for new technological solutions, talked with OVC's procurement and engineering executives about the latest industry trends, participated in confidential selection meetings, and heard directly from defense procurement officials and other OVC customers about what they were looking for. It was a clever carrot-and-stick strategy. For new suppliers, the carrot was multifaceted: the chance to share the burden of creating new innovations, the opportunity to become one of OVC's strategic partners, and rare access to OVC's customers. For existing suppliers, the stick was the risk that they might lose their lucrative, and often long-established, contracts.

Using the technology conventions, OVC began its search for suppliers who offered innovative thinking on everything from standardized floor plates to more-differentiating features of the warships and submarines, such as engines, steering systems, and, above all, fuel cells. New hydrogen-powered fuel-cell technology presents OVC with a way to build nonnuclear submarines that could appeal to some of the largest navies. For decades, the US Navy has relied exclusively on nuclear-powered submarines. But there have been calls for it to consider air-independent propulsion systems of the kind OVC is developing.[4]

When discussing different features of ships and submarines, OVC deliberately kept its specifications general and nonspecific so that suppliers would be encouraged to be as creative and innovative as possible. On the technological front, OVC's CPO and the procurement team were looking for better technical solutions, fewer production difficulties, and increased reliability, among other things. On the financial front, they were looking for a lower purchase price as well as lower development, production, operating, and maintenance costs.

The technology conventions proved beneficial in several ways—and ensured that OVC was able to influence a diverse range of suppliers and better serve its customers. Incumbent suppliers were forced to raise their game when it came to creativity and cost—or lose out to hungry rivals. New suppliers were given a chance to dislodge longtime incumbent suppliers who failed to participate in a meaningful way. And all the suppliers, new and old, were exposed to the customers and their needs as they had never been before. In other words, they were obliged to come up with customized solutions.

Through the simple mechanism of a technology convention, OVC managed to exert significant influence on suppliers. It pitted one supplier against another in a very visible way, and in a particularly smart move, it enrolled the end customers—the world's navies—in the selection process. The suppliers had to impress not only the OVC executives but also the defense procurement officials who hold the purse strings *and* the officers who would pilot the ship or submarine.

As expected, not all of OVC's existing suppliers were able to deliver what was asked of them. Indeed, OVC estimates that, as a result of the experimental conventions, one-third of suppliers will be new. It believes this level of turnover will breathe new life into its products and help the company meet its stated goal of becoming "the most modern naval company in Europe."

How to invest in your suppliers— the story of NASA and SpaceX

To understand NASA's approach to SpaceX, we have to go back to February 1, 2003. Just before 9:00 a.m., as *Columbia*, the oldest of NASA's reusable space-shuttle orbiters, was reentering Earth's atmosphere, it burst into flames, breaking into pieces and killing all seven astronauts aboard. The tragedy led to NASA's decision to work with private companies in a radically new way.

Like NASA's Apollo program, which had put the first man on the moon in 1969, the space shuttle—officially the Space Transportation System—was a triumph of American engineering and business collaboration. Several companies had been involved in the construction of Saturn V, the rocket that took Neil Armstrong to the moon, including Boeing. Boeing was once again NASA's main subcontractor for the space shuttle after acquiring Rockwell International, the aircraft manufacturer that had won the original $2.6 billion contract to build the world's first reusable orbiter in 1972.[5] But for all its success, the space-shuttle program did not fulfill its loftiest ambitions. Built to fly twelve missions every year, *Columbia* flew just twenty-eight times in twenty-two years. There were several reasons for this. One was that NASA's budget kept shrinking, as new presidents chopped and changed priorities, leaving the organization with reduced funds for repeated missions. Another was that flight costs kept spiraling upward, as repairs, maintenance, and refurbishment increased the price of sending seven astronauts and twenty tons of cargo into space to an unaffordable $1 billion. That meant a large chunk of NASA's budget was being consumed by routine missions to the International Space Station, reducing the amount of money available for NASA's primary objective: "to discover and expand knowledge for the benefit of humanity."

To get back on track, NASA created the Commercial Orbital Transportation Services (COTS) program in 2005. The goal was to start what it called "the engine of competition" and engage with private companies in a new way so that they could build the affordable spacecraft needed to undertake routine missions to the Hubble Space Telescope and the International Space Station. In the past, NASA had designed its spacecraft, paid subcontractors like Boeing to build them on a cost-plus basis, and kept ownership of the vehicle. In other words, it paid all the costs of designing the spacecraft and all the expenses incurred by private companies while building the spacecraft (plus an additional incentive), and retained ultimate responsibility for the program. Under COTS and the associated Commercial Resupply Services program, this changed. NASA began issuing general specifications for the spacecraft, leaving private companies with the challenge of designing them. It also began awarding fixed-price contracts, thereby transferring the costs of delays and other problems to the private companies. And it let the private companies keep the spacecraft and all associated intellectual property.

In 2006, NASA put the contract out to tender. It planned to award contracts to two companies that would compete with each other to be first to demonstrate their space-transportation capabilities. In all, NASA received twenty-one proposals. SpaceX, a California-based, privately owned commercial startup not yet four years old, was one of two successful bidders, beating out better-known, publicly listed and government-funded companies. NASA tasked it with building a rocket powerful enough to take crew and cargo to the International Space Station following the anticipated retirement of the space-shuttle fleet in 2010. The time frame was challenging. So, too, were the commercial terms. Since NASA wanted the companies to have skin in the game, SpaceX was required to provide matching funding for the space agency's investment of nearly $396 million. In the end, SpaceX raised $454 million from investors, including the US Air Force and the governments of Canada, Malaysia, and Sweden.[6] The other company awarded a contract—Oklahoma-based Rocketplane Kistler—failed to raise sufficient matching funding, and its contract was awarded to Orbital Sciences Corporation (now owned by Northrop Grumman).

After its early fundraising success, however, SpaceX suffered a series of setbacks that imperiled its future. From 2006 to 2008, it tried, and failed, three times to launch its relatively small Falcon 1 rocket. Founder Elon Musk was poised to admit defeat. But a fourth launch, in September 2008, was an unquestionable success, making SpaceX the first private company to put a liquid-fueled rocket into orbit. It vindicated Musk's commitment to space exploration, and it vindicated the dogged determination of NASA's procurement team, which had defied the skeptics questioning the controversial strategy of working with private companies in this way.

A few months later, SpaceX was awarded a $1.6 billion contract to undertake twelve cargo missions to the International Space Station over the next eight years. Coming so soon after the first successful demonstration of the Falcon 1 rocket, this appeared to be an extraordinary vote of confidence in SpaceX. But it reflected the increasingly close working relationship between NASA and the company. NASA invested billions of dollars in SpaceX; and also time and expertise. The COTS program authorized a transfer of knowledge accumulated by NASA since its creation in the late 1950s. SpaceX gained access to the secrets of many of NASA's technologies, giving it a signal advantage over its commercial rivals. This bequest has been compared to the time when the US Defense Department handed over one of its inventions—the internet—to the private sector.[7]

NASA's gamble paid off. In 2012, SpaceX—having developed its more powerful Falcon 9 rocket and Dragon cargo capsule—became the first private company to dock a spacecraft at the International Space Station. For NASA, the price tag for developing this capability was approximately $400 million, a fraction of the $4 billion it estimated it would have spent doing everything in-house.

Two years later, NASA gave SpaceX another vote of confidence. After the final space-shuttle flight touched down in 2011, the United States was dependent on its old Cold War rival, Russia, to send American astronauts into space, on missions powered by the Soyuz rocket—for the princely sum of $90 million per person. To avoid the perpetuation of this situation, NASA sought proposals from companies willing to power crewed missions to the space station. If its astronauts were going to get an Uber-style lift into space, then at least the service should be American.

In the end, NASA's procurement team awarded the contract to two companies: SpaceX and Boeing. Boeing's contract was more lucrative—$4.2 billion versus SpaceX's $2.6 billion.

From then on, the two companies engaged in friendly but competitive rivalry, and it was the relative newcomer that reached the finish line first. In August 2020, two NASA astronauts, Bob Behnken and Doug Hurley, completed the first US-crewed mission to the space station in nearly a decade, paving the way for the first operational mission in November 2020.

Among the game-changing technologies pioneered by SpaceX, and designed to reduce costs radically, were the reusable rocket booster and the reusable crew-capable Dragon capsule. NASA specified *what* it wanted—a vehicle that would take astronauts and cargo to space—but it did not specify *how* SpaceX should design and build the vehicle. This gave SpaceX significant room to maneuver, and gave Musk the opportunity to ask his brilliant engineering team a simple question: How many people would fly across the Atlantic if, at the end of the journey, the airplane was scrapped?

No one, the team responded.

Exactly, said Musk.

And so the team set to work developing a reusable rocket. The result was an affordable price tag: $60 million for every SpaceX mission rather than $1 billion for every space-shuttle mission.

Such is the faith that NASA has in SpaceX that it is extending its contractual relationship beyond the routine transportation of astronauts and cargo to the International Space Station. In 2020, the space agency awarded SpaceX the contract to provide cargo transportation services for Gateway, a planned new space station that will orbit the moon and support humankind's sustainable, long-term return to the lunar surface. Using the company's Falcon Heavy, the world's most powerful rocket operating today and the biggest since Saturn V, SpaceX will take 3.4 metric tons of pressurized cargo and 1 metric ton of unpressurized cargo to the station. The precise details of the commercial deal have not been disclosed, but it's safe to say that SpaceX, once a wild card in the space-exploration business, has fully justified NASA's bold investment approach to procuring the services of the private sector.

How to integrate your suppliers—the story of Apple and Taiwan Semiconductor Manufacturing Company

Apple's timeline includes most of the important dates in the tech company's evolution—its launch in 1976, the first Apple Mac in 1984, the first Apple laptop in 1989, the first iPod in 2001, the first iPhone in 2007, the first iPad in 2010, the first Apple Watch in 2015. Missing, however, is July 1, 2013, which should be added. It's the date when Apple began one of its most important, and potentially game-changing, supplier relationships—with Taiwan Semiconductor Manufacturing Company (TSMC).[8]

When Apple launched the iPhone, in 2007, its microprocessor was designed by UK-based Arm and manufactured by Samsung Electronics, the South Korean conglomerate. In 2010—a year that saw the launch of the iPad and the first iPhone to have FaceTime video calling—the company introduced the first Apple-designed microprocessor: the A4. Developed by the specialist team that Apple acquired when it paid $278 million for P.A. Semi, a California-based semiconductor business, the microprocessor was based on Arm architecture and, once again, manufactured by Samsung.

But by 2013, Apple and Samsung were becoming deadly rivals in the smartphone market, with the more affordable Samsung Galaxy providing stiff competition for the iPhone. It was an accepted part of global business that companies could be frenemies—at once friends and enemies. But as Apple was ramping up production to meet the demand for its new products, it was keen to diversify suppliers in a way consistent with what Tim Cook has called the company's "long-term strategy of owning and controlling the primary technologies behind the products we make."[9] The CPO and the procurement team went in search of a second microchip manufacturer.

Apple was already familiar with the cluster of computer manufacturers in Taiwan—its main assembler, Foxconn, is headquartered there. Before long, Apple alighted on TSMC, and the timing of its approach was good. TSMC had significant spare capacity after the swift decline of Nokia, the Finnish company. Once the world's biggest mobile-phone company—with a market share of 49.4 percent in 2007, the year that Apple launched the iPhone—Nokia had seen its fortunes collapse. By the first half of 2013, it commanded just three percent of the market.[10]

Since Samsung had a contractual lock on production, TSMC could not start making Apple-designed chips until July 2014.[11] But thereafter, it became increasingly integrated into the Apple supply chain. TSMC was able to put its newfound steady income stream to good use, investing in advanced technology that would eventually bring the two companies even closer. Specifically, TSMC focused its R&D effort on building its capability to manufacture five-nanometer microchips, spending $10 billion on a technology designed to increase the speed and reduce the energy consumption of computers, smartphones, and other consumer electronics.[12]

TSMC did not have to wait long for a new, and unexpected, opportunity to integrate further with Apple. In 2015, Intel, the world's largest semiconductor business, introduced its latest product: Skylake. Apple, which had partnered with Intel since 2006, put the new processor in its latest models: the 2015 iMac and the 2016 MacBook and MacBook Pro. It was a disaster. Angry customers, including normally loyal fans, took to social media. There was nowhere for Apple to hide.[13]

Apple had already been considering designing its own microchips following the success of the Apple-designed chips in the iPhone, iPad, and Apple Watch.[14] Also, the company was acutely aware of how unequal its relationship with Intel was: Apple relied exclusively on Intel for its computer microprocessors, whereas Intel's Apple business accounted for only 5 percent of Intel revenues.

The Skylake debacle was the final straw. It forced Apple to accelerate plans to launch its microprocessor and find a manufacturer to make it. TSMC was the obvious partner. Unlike Intel, which designs and manufactures microchips, TSMC focuses solely on manufacturing (in industry jargon, it's a "foundry"), and along with Samsung, it's the best in the world at what it does. After years of investment—made possible by the steady income stream from Apple—TSMC was able to manufacture the much vaunted five-nanometer microchip containing sixteen billion transistors. This put it years ahead of Intel, which at the time of writing was still producing ten-nanometer microchips. The company whose legendary CEO Andy Grove famously said "only the paranoid survive" had dropped the ball.

In November 2020, Apple unveiled the first products with its own computer microprocessor—the M1—manufactured by TSMC. Also, it booked out most of TSMC's capacity for producing five-nanometer microchips, a procurement tactic that ensured its rivals wouldn't catch up anytime soon.[15]

Once upon a time, computer companies were happy to have the "Intel inside" sticker on their products. It was a stamp of quality, and it meant that they could compete on other factors—price, look and feel, and applications. Now, thanks to the integrated partnership between Apple and TSMC, they have to compete on the performance of the humble microprocessor. Apple computers with the M1 chip reportedly allow users to watch twenty hours of video on a single charge—twice the length of computers powered by the latest Intel microprocessor.[16]

Apple's carefully nurtured relationship with one of its suppliers may help the world's fourth-largest PC maker capture an even greater slice of the global market.

Conclusion

According to procurement orthodoxy, the best way to get savings is to focus on the commodities embedded in any product or individual product category. If you can itemize commodities and categories, and hand responsibility for their management to specific executives, you can bring down costs. But this can be short term and destructive, leading to buyers and suppliers fighting each other for a share of the profits. A better way forward is for buyers to build constructive relationships with suppliers at the highest strategic level. When they do, magic happens: they cut costs and grow the business pie for their mutual benefit. But as we'll show in the next chapter, it is essential that the voice of the supplier is listened to throughout the life of a product. That means giving the CPO and the procurement team, the people responsible for the company's relationship with suppliers, a much bigger role in the company.

 Notes for the CEO

Key Takeaway

To draw the maximum value from your suppliers, you need to distinguish between the most important and the rest, treat them as friends and partners, and forge new dynamic relationships with them.

Key Strategy

Make procurement personal and strategic, and make it matter. Instruct your CPO to focus on suppliers—not commodities. Get them to focus 95 percent of their time on the 5 percent who constitute your biggest and most important suppliers.

Key Tactics

- Identify your most important A suppliers and invite them to join an exclusive 360° program. Establish a one-to-one dialogue between you or your CPO and the CEOs of the top suppliers. Begin by sending an individually crafted personal letter.

- Identify potential future suppliers who could help you transform your business. Categorize them according to two dimensions: their performance and their strategic potential.

- Focus on a critical cluster of three types of suppliers:

    o Those you can *influence*

    o Those who offer you potentially game-changing products if you *invest* time, money, knowledge, and other resources

    o Those who can offer you the edge in your competition with rivals if you *integrate* them into your company

3

Empower Your "Shoppers"

Put Your Procurement Team at the Very Heart of Your Product Life Cycle—from Ideation to Postproduction

S peak to most CPOs, and they say that they and their procurement teams are invited to get involved in new product development only when it comes to negotiating with suppliers. This is way too late. We think they should not simply be *involved* in the process, they should be given *central responsibility* for the entire product-development process, from ideation to postproduction. This is what we mean when we say that the CEO should give the CPO a fresh mandate.

But what does this mean in practice? In our work with companies, we often talk about the importance of empowering the procurement function. Specifically, we say that procurement should "own the product life cycle." To put it another way, the CPO and the procurement team should be there when the design engineer picks up a pencil to start sketching out ideas for a new product, and they should still be there when the last product rolls off the factory production line. When we explain the practical implications of giving the CPO a fresh mandate, we sometimes get puzzled looks from CEOs. Are you serious, they say? Why should we give the CPO so much power and influence? Given the traditional view of procurement (as an administrative function) and the conventional position of procurement in the corporate hierarchy (low down), this incomprehension is entirely to be expected. There are many senior executives who regard the CPO and the procurement team as merely the company's "shoppers," to quote one senior director of a FTSE 100 company who described them to us this way.

This view is short-sighted.

When the CPO and procurement team participate in every critical stage of a product's evolution—from concept development and the award of supplier contracts to the start of production and through the end of production—they can significantly lower costs *and* ensure that the company benefits from the accumulated knowledge and expertise of suppliers in a way that generates value across five other sources of competitive advantage: innovation, quality, sustainability, speed, and risk reduction.

Before we look at how the CPO can dramatically influence the development of products, let's first look at how things are done at most companies.

How Products Are Made, and Why This Is a Costly Problem

Today, most companies do not involve procurement executives in the early developmental stage of a new product. Generally, what's known as "concept development" is the preserve of two functions: design engineers, who are responsible for creating a product that works, and product marketers, who are responsible for ensuring the product is something that customers will want to buy. The CPO and the procurement team tend to get involved only after the product's design and associated specifications have been pretty much "frozen."

At that point, they are instructed to start negotiating the most cost-efficient contract with suppliers. This is not easy. As often as not, the design engineers have drawn up the product specifications with particular suppliers in mind—typically, those they have worked with before. They do this for two main reasons. First, they often have personal relationships with these suppliers, relationships they have built over many years. As they explain: "Why should we go looking for new suppliers when we know our existing suppliers and they have given us good service in the past?" Second, they are almost always under time pressure and focused entirely on meeting the deadline for the start of production. So they are usually reluctant to go through the lengthy process of selecting and onboarding new suppliers.

The reluctance of engineers even to entertain the idea of enrolling new suppliers was something that Ignacio López, General Motors' CPO, tried to combat nearly forty years ago. But it still happens—and it hampers the procurement managers as they try to strike the best possible deals for their company. No matter their skill at driving the hardest possible bargain, procurement managers' hands are ultimately tied by decisions made earlier, and they can do little more than tweak the small print of a preagreed contract.

When a contract is finally signed and sealed, the CPO and the procurement team can theoretically move to other things, confident of a job well done. In practice, however, they can't. Most of the time, the price they agreed to with suppliers starts to creep upward as soon as the ink is dry. Indeed, by our calculation, the average "cost creep" between the time when a company awards a contract to a particular supplier and the start of production is an astonishing *seven percent*.

At any time, that's a shocking waste of money. But in today's challenging climate, it is unaffordable.

Why does it happen, and so often?

One reason, as we have said, is that the design engineers too often develop a product's specifications with only one or two favored suppliers in mind. Their primary focus is making a product that works—not one that is cost-effective. This potentially leaves the company at the mercy of the preferred supplier, who can exercise a kind of monopolistic power. Another reason is that, although product designs are supposedly frozen when suppliers are awarded contracts, they almost always require further tweaks, and suppliers sometimes use even the slightest modifications as an excuse to revise their prices upward.

There is a third reason, too. Procurement managers typically award contracts to the lowest bidders, and they get plaudits—and bonuses—for conducting a tough negotiating round. When costs creep up, as they almost always do, the managers can absolve themselves of any blame, since the costly tweaks and narrowly defined specifications are not of their making. For their part, the suppliers making implausibly low bids in order to win the contracts know that they will be able to increase their prices as the product is modified in the months ahead of launch. Indeed, it is an extraordinary fact that during the lifetime of a product, most companies *never* actually pay the supplier what was agreed on when the contract was signed—they generally pay more. In other words, the contract is really not worth the paper it is written on.

To explain what's really going on, we like to use a chart showing the full extent of a product's life cycle (see figure 3-1).

At one end of the straight line at the top is a diamond dot marking the beginning of the process—the concept-development stage ("kickoff"). At the other end is another dot marking the end of the process—the EOP, or end of production. In between, there are dots for the awarding of the contract and the SOP, or start of production.

FIGURE 3-1

Procurement at some companies often focuses on price at contract award

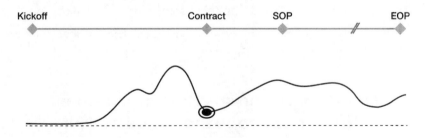

Below that line is another, representing the cost of the project. For the first part of the chart, the cost line stays flat, and consistent with the top-down cost target set by the company's CFO. It does so because the design engineers are, at this early stage, focused exclusively on developing the concept. The cost of the project is the last thing on their minds. As the product starts to take shape, the engineers make their first cost estimates, and it is at this point that the cost line curves sharply upward. On the face of it, this looks bad. But in the engineers' view, that's not their problem—that's a problem for procurement, which will be tasked with sorting it out later.

When the procurement managers are finally invited to participate in the product-development process, their focus is on choosing the supplier that offers the lowest possible price. It is then that the fun and games—or, if you like, the deceptions—begin. As we show in our chart, the procurement team can bend the cost curve down as low as they like. But it's little more than a conjurer's trick. We liken it to pulling a rubber band at one end: the other end, representing the real (and unalterable) cost of making the product, won't fundamentally change, and in time, the rubber band will spring back to its original, correct, position.

It should be said that by acting as they do, the CPO and procurement team are being perfectly rational. They are incentivized to negotiate the best possible price at the contract-award stage, and that's what they do. But they are doing their company a disservice.

Fortunately, as several companies have found, there is a better way.

From Start to Finish—How Procurement Can Really *Shape* the Future of Your Product (and Your Company)

The delayed involvement of the CPO and the procurement team is a manifestation of the fact that most CEOs generally ask them to play a secondary role: to *support* the business strategy and focus on cost reduction. As we have said, in our view, CEOs should give them a fresh mandate that allows them to play a primary role: to *shape* the business strategy and focus on profitable growth. By definition, this means that they should be involved from the very beginning of every new product launch—not halfway through, as they typically are today. But when they do participate in this way, they should no longer be confined to using all the *commercial*, tough-talking negotiating tactics in the book. Instead, they should be able to leverage a much larger toolbox of *technical* and other tactics and strategies for driving down costs and driving up value.

The first step on this journey is the creation of a cross-functional team.

The cross-functional team

When a company embarks on the long journey toward the launch of a new product, the CFO usually sets the cost target, which is generally based loosely on a mixture of historical data (the cost of previous products), the projected selling price, and the desired profit margin. This top-down cost target provides the benchmark for the design engineers and the product marketers who take the lead in the development of the product. But the target is rarely met. This is because the design engineers and product marketers are not really incentivized to ask the right questions. For the design engineer, the key question is: Can we create a product that works? For the product marketer, the key question is: Can we create a product that consumers want to buy?

By giving the procurement manager a bigger role, and by making the product-development process a three-way conversation on a cross-functional team, CEOs can instantly transform the economics of their company's product pipeline. Right now, the procurement manager's key question is: Can *I* negotiate the lowest price from the supplier (even though I know it will go up before launch day)? But when the procurement manager becomes part of the conversation and they are given a strategic role, their key question becomes: Can *we* develop the right product with the right innovation from the right suppliers? Inevitably, cost is part of the equation that makes the product "right." But so are several other factors. Is the product too complex (and therefore difficult to make)? Does it have too many features (more than the customer actually wants or needs)? Is it sufficiently innovative? Is it appropriately sustainable? Are the suppliers the best in the business (or are they just the ones that the design engineers are comfortable working with)? How does it compare to the competitor's product?

In a way, it is astonishing that simply by changing the conversation, by getting everyone in the same room to ask and answer different questions, CEOs can change the fortunes of their company and achieve profitable growth. But that's exactly what we have seen happen when the CPO and the procurement team are given a central role in a cross-functional product-development team.

The experience of Alexander Dennis, the world's biggest maker of double-decker buses, is instructive.

• • •

The Scotland-headquartered bus and coach manufacturer has a storied history. Now owned by the Canadian bus and coach company NFI Group, Alexander Dennis can trace its roots back to 1895, when the Dennis brothers started building bicycles, before graduating to motor cars (1901), buses and vans used by Harrods department store (1904), and fire engines (1908).[1] Today, more than half of the buses on UK roads are made by the company, including the iconic London red bus. Globally, some twenty-five thousand people take a ride on one of its buses every single day of the year.[2]

In 2015, when we started working with the company, it had already seen several years of record organic sales growth through international expansion. There was a desire to do the same for profitability, particularly through procurement, given that 70 percent of costs were in the materials that the company bought.

As a result, we recommended that Alexander Dennis launch a procurement-performance program to bring the latest best practices from different industry sectors and apply them to improving the bottom line and addressing the issue of product complexity. With more than four thousand different parts going into a finished Alexander Dennis vehicle, product complexity could be a real challenge to manage cost-effectively.

We also recommended that senior executives give the procurement team more decision-making authority in the product-development process. Why? Simply because we were convinced that this would help the company design a product that considered not only factors relating to engineering and the "look and feel" favored by product marketers responding to consumer demand but also practical factors relating to production and distribution.

You might ask: What do procurement managers know about production and distribution? Wouldn't they be skilled in the fine art of negotiation rather than the science of materials, manufacturing, and mass production? Actually, on the Alexander Dennis procurement team, there were (and still are) procurement engineers who had in-depth knowledge of supplier material specifications, manufacturing processes, potential sources, and costs.[3] They were trained engineers who also, by virtue of their close association with suppliers, had access to the very latest trends, creative ways to design and manufacture products, and innovative materials.

Alexander Dennis's senior executives listened to our advice and created a cross-functional project team with a new set of roles and responsibilities for the engineering, product-marketing, and procurement functions. The CPO and procurement managers participated in product strategy and product development along with the engineering and marketing teams. They helped initiate and validate the concept, developed specifications, brought market feedback into the discussion, refined the prototypes, and stayed with the project right to the end. The result was a more cost-effective and streamlined product-development process, one that reduced time to market and improved profitability in line with the company's goals.

• • •

The cross-functional team is really critical to the success of any product, so it is important that it be set up in the right way. If it is cross-functional in name only, if the old hierarchies are allowed to persist, then it won't work. Of course, the design engineers and the product marketers—those executives who have historically dominated the product-development process—will need to be incentivized to work collaboratively with their procurement colleagues. Equally, the procurement managers will need to earn the respect and trust of the design engineers and product marketers by giving them fresh ideas on product features, new materials, and consumer needs, from their conversations with suppliers.

In our experience, the best way to get the most from these teams is to keep them small, remove any residual hierarchy, and give the members some shared workspaces so they really can collaborate together. Also, CEOs should consider creating one overall team that takes responsibility for the product from start to finish, and several smaller "sprint" teams that focus on specific tasks in an agile way and for a limited time only. By doing this, CEOs can inject repeated bursts of energy into a product-development process that can extend from months to years.

The technical and tactical toolbox

When the CPO and procurement team join a cross-functional product-development team, they can start deploying several levers for doubling cost savings and doubling the value of one or more of the other sources of competitive advantage: innovation, quality, sustainability, speed, and risk reduction. In our experience, there are five levers that can have a material impact on the company. In no particular order, they are: teardowns, should-cost analysis, consumer clinics, structured supplier questionnaires, and big data analysis. These are *technical* levers—as opposed to the *commercial* levers normally used by procurement managers when they negotiate with suppliers. If the CPO and procurement team are going to make a real impact, it is important that CEOs allow them the right to use these levers, which are normally reserved for use by design engineers and product marketers.

Let's look at each of the levers in turn.

A teardown and a should-cost analysis really go together. A teardown is where a procurement engineer completely dismantles a product, breaking it into its constituent parts. In a sense, it is nothing new. Nearly forty years ago, it was an extraordinary teardown of an entire automobile that brought Ignacio López to the attention of Jack Smith. Since then, teardowns have become an established lever in the procurement toolbox—and have certainly become more sophisticated, with procurement experts able to draw all kinds of insights from the process: what parts are necessary (and, of course, unnecessary), what materials are used (and could be replaced by cheaper but equally effective versions), what complex mechanisms can be simplified.

Once they have dismantled a product, the procurement team can begin their should-cost analysis. As the name suggests, this analysis involves determining what a product *should* cost, based on everything from the constituent materials, the labor, any overhead, and the profit margins. Again, like teardowns, this tool is nothing new. Although some companies had begun experimenting with this approach after the Second World War, should-cost analysis really only came into common use in the late 1960s, after being adopted by the US Department of Defense, which was then under the direction of Robert McNamara, the former Whiz Kid who, as we described earlier, transformed the fortunes of Ford Motor Company before being tapped for the job of Secretary of Defense by President Kennedy.

In 1967, McNamara grew alarmed at the spiraling cost of the new F-111 fighter jet. In particular, the price of each TF30 engine had skyrocketed from $279,000—the price originally quoted by aerospace manufacturer Pratt & Whitney—to $750,000. Gordon Rule, one of the US Navy's procurement chiefs, was ordered to find out what was going on. "We don't want you to approach this on the basis of what it will cost," he was told by officials in the Department of Defense. "We know what the company said it will cost. We want you to get in there and tell us what these engines 'should cost.'" Rule pulled together a team of forty people who spent weeks at Pratt & Whitney's plant in Hartford, Connecticut. They determined that the entire TF30 contract should cost $100 million less than Pratt & Whitney was charging the government. It gave the government grounds for renegotiating the contract.[4]

These days, when procurement experts do participate in the earliest stages of a product's development and conduct should-cost analyses based on the raw materials and core components provided by suppliers, they can, by our calculation, lower the contract price from an average of 8 percent above the should-cost price to an average of 5 percent above the should-cost price. This amounts to a significant saving.

But they can deliver even greater value if they conduct two other types of teardown: one on competitor products and one on the products of companies in other, adjacent sectors. One carmaker we worked with conducted a very revealing teardown of a competitor's car seats. It dismantled the whole seat, reviewed the different components, examined the materials, and even conducted a geometric analysis to determine the seat's comfort features. From this, it identified twelve places where costs on its own seats could be shaved: from €1.50 by simplifying the back cover and €2.52 by changing the interior material in the headrest to €5.61 by redesigning the seat structure and a massive €21.33 by replacing the leather on less visible areas of the seat with cheaper leatherette. All told, the procurement team was able to identify savings of €55.89 per seat—making the new seat more than 15 percent cheaper.

As well as teardowns and related should-cost analyses, the procurement team can ensure that the views of customers and suppliers are taken into account during the product-development process. You might think that product marketers, whose job it is to ensure that the company creates products that customers want, would take responsibility for reflecting the views of customers. Yet time and time again, we find that companies overengineer products, adding features that customers do not want and that push up costs. In other words, it sometimes seems that product marketers aren't doing their job, and aren't having the necessary impact on their company. To address this, we recommend that the procurement team introduce some much needed discipline into the process.

The classic method of doing this is to organize formal customer clinics. Here, companies invite anywhere from three hundred to one thousand customers to participate in the review of a new product. Typically these clinics, which can be convened at the concept stage and the later prelaunch stage (or both), are held at a central, high-security location (no smartphones or cameras are permitted) and last for two to six hours. In the wake of the Covid-19 global pandemic, and also because of cost issues, some companies started looking at ways to replicate the face-to-face sessions with a mix of video conferencing and virtual-reality technology. Either way, the goal is to establish whether or not the new product meets the customers' technical, functional, and emotional needs. From quantitative and qualitative interviews, the procurement team can determine what features are necessary and should come as standard, and what features are just "nice to have" and should come as optional.

Just as the procurement team can ensure that the voice of the customer is heard, they can ensure that the voice of the supplier is heard, too. They, of course, are the owners of the company's relationship with suppliers, and you would expect them to do this. But because procurement typically joins the product-development process so late, the suppliers' voice is rarely heard in a way that can meaningfully influence the new product. As we have seen, companies that run a 360° program do listen to their suppliers, but there is no reason why all companies shouldn't listen—and learn—from their suppliers. Often, supplier companies have good ideas for how buyer companies could achieve savings and improvements by selecting different materials, reducing complexity, or stripping out unnecessary parts. All it takes is for them to be asked for their views in a structured way.

Those companies that do this typically put a procurement manager in charge, giving them the responsibility for proactively soliciting the views of suppliers—either by sending out questionnaires or holding workshops—and then overseeing the review process. Once the ideas are collected, they can be filtered; sent for assessment by a team of engineers, manufacturing experts, and sales and marketing executives; and if accepted, incorporated into an implementation schedule.

There is one other lever that we have found increasingly useful in the constant battle to cut costs and generate value from all the potential sources of competitive advantage: big data analysis. It is commonly said that data is the "new gold" or the "new oil" fueling the global economy of the future.

Many companies have access to vast lakes of data, which are expanding by an estimated 2.5 quintillion bytes every day.[5] As well as product-related data, companies can draw on other types of data—including online search records, credit-card data, sales data, and geo-location data (showing where people spend their time). Yet too often, they fail to fully exploit a crucial asset that is getting more valuable every single day that their customers use their products.

These five different levers can be used separately or, more usefully, together to deliver double savings. One company that has done this with great success is Dell Technologies.

• • •

A few years ago, Dell's procurement managers began analyzing the company's classic tower as part of a cross-functional team. To begin with, they conducted a teardown of the product. This helped them identify two striking design features of the computer: one, it had a heavy, twenty-five-liter metal chassis for encasing the electronics; and two, there was a series of complex fitments requiring eighty rivets and screws inside the machine. From an engineering perspective, these features were not problematic—after all, the computer *worked*. But, from a procurement perspective, there were all sorts of problems. For a start, the size of the tower's chassis meant that only the largest suppliers were able to handle its manufacture, and whenever they suffered operational issues (as they often did), Dell's whole production line was held up, adding to the cost and cutting into the company's profits. Also, the weight of the tower made the cost of distributing it as air freight prohibitively high. Finally, the complexity of the product was a problem, because sourcing all the different components was slow work that created delays and drove up costs.

So the procurement team's teardown was very effective for uncovering these problems—although, of course, it would have been even better if they had participated in the early development of the product and therefore helped the company avoid making the costly design decisions in the first place. Separately, they commissioned a market-research study that found that 80 percent of consumers did not really want many of the features designed into the product—in particular, six PCI express (PCIe) slots for connecting the computer to other devices.

With this feedback, the engineering team went back to first principles and designed a computer that took account of supply-chain logistics and consumer need. The result was an affordable computer with a powerful central processing unit (CPU) housed in a simply designed plastic chassis that was much smaller, at just two liters. Paint, cabling, and unnecessary PCIe connector slots were nowhere to be seen. By shrinking and simplifying the computer, Dell was able to consider a broader set of suppliers who could handle its manufacture, including microfactories located closer to consumers. This was important because it meant that Dell could deliver its products more quickly. In the past, small plants were a necessarily costly option, because they did not enjoy the economies of scale of larger plants. But now that the newly designed computer cost less to make—more than 30 percent less—Dell could afford to select small plants, get the product to the consumer in double-quick time, and still enjoy significant savings.

Also, Dell could be confident that it had designed a computer that consumers really wanted and that, because it was light enough to be transported by air, could be delivered in a timely way.

Vigilance for the entire lifespan of a product

Very often, the procurement team's job is considered done after they have awarded the contract to a particular supplier and production has begun. In fact, the job is only half done at that point, and the procurement team needs to remain vigilant until the very end of production. (For some products, such as automobiles, fighter jets, and medicines, this can be many years.) Why do we say this? All the evidence suggests that suppliers routinely find ways to make the product more efficiently (and therefore more cheaply) and do not necessarily pass on any of the savings to the buyers. They are able to make products more efficiently for a number of reasons. Partly, it is the natural learning curve at work—the more we do something, the better we get at doing it. Also, they try to boost their profit margin by looking for clever ways to cut costs—either through using different materials, removing redundant components, or developing more-efficient tools and machinery. In addition, they can sometimes benefit from exogenous factors that are outside of their control but that deliver savings—such as swings in foreign-exchange rates and the price of raw materials.

Advanced Luxury Vehicles, whose real identity we have disguised and whose approach to its top A suppliers we described in chapter 2, has an end-to-end focus so that it does not miss out on benefiting from the cost savings achieved by suppliers. The company's procurement function has a large team of cost engineers, 250 in all, who are tasked with carrying out teardowns of suppliers' products not only before the start of production but also at various intervals after production has begun. What they try to do is recalculate the true cost of the product. One way they do this is by simply weighing the product and comparing the result with the weight as listed in the original design specifications. From this examination, ALV can determine if a supplier has found some new, lighter-weight materials or has simply removed certain parts that do not affect the product's performance. Another way the cost engineers work out the true cost of the product is by taking account of currency fluctuations as well as changes in the highly variable price of steel and other raw materials (changes that can be used to justify disproportionately high price increases). From this analysis, ALV can establish if their suppliers have benefited from shifting prices—and failed to pass on any of the savings.

By conducting this kind of product review, ALV is able to close the gap between the contract price and the price as it escalates after the awarding of the contract, with each new modification ordered by the design engineers and product marketers. Typically, ALV uses the information to recoup any excess costs—either through a lump-sum repayment or a renegotiated contract—and to develop more-effective and more-efficient products in the future. Of course, not every company can afford to retain an in-house team of specialist cost engineers. This, however, need not prevent companies from doubling down on costs after the start of production. There are several types of external providers that can supplement the company's own cost engineers, though these too are another kind of supplier.

The New Procurement Economics— Why the "Toyota Way" Is Being Superseded by the "Tesla Way"

You may wonder why we have spent so much time showing you how companies can reduce costs by giving a greater role to their CPO and procurement team. Surely the lean approach pioneered by Toyota (and documented in one of the greatest business books of all time, *The Machine That Changed the World*) solves the problem of creating reliable and affordable products in a timely way without having to raise the profile of procurement within the company?

There is no doubt that over the past fifty years, Toyota's lean approach has helped the company deliver on three of the most critical dimensions for any business—time, cost, and quality—while growing market share. The Japanese car giant has built its worldwide business on the back of its reputation for reliability. "We put quality at the heart of everything we do," the company often states, and when the immensely popular BBC TV program *Top Gear* decided to put a Toyota truck to the test, it was not found wanting. The Toyota Hilux was dumped into the sea, flattened by a caravan, dropped from a great height, thwacked by a wrecking ball normally used to knock down buildings, and set on fire—and yet it was still able to be driven away from every abuse.[6]

How has Toyota managed to do this? The company recognizes the central importance of suppliers. It does this by creating fixed—rather than flexible—relationships with suppliers. As detailed earlier, one of the key features of the Toyota Production System is *keiretsu*, a corporate network in which Toyota retains a significant minority stake in key suppliers. This keeps the suppliers in Toyota's orbit and determines how they interact with the carmaker during the product-development process.

These favored suppliers work with Toyota in a very collaborative way, with Toyota and the supplier designing the product together (whether it's a seat or a steering wheel or some other commodity) and making key financial decisions together (there is no squabbling over the costs, the price, or the share of the profits). The whole process is overseen by a senior engineer—a *shusa*, or chief. It sounds almost utopian. Certainly, as a result of this, Toyota manages to avoid many of the downsides we often see in US and European companies: poorly designed or faulty components that need reengineering or remaking; costs that rise in an unexpected, uncontrolled way; interrupted manufacturing schedules; and even delayed product launches.

But there is one great downside of Toyota's approach: its fundamental conservatism. In recent years, Toyota has looked leaden-footed, its loyalty to suppliers who performed well in the past now looking like something of a liability. When European automakers introduced PC-influenced entertainment and navigation systems, Toyota hung on to old-fashioned knobs and switches. It briefly caught the zeitgeist with its low-carbon, hybrid vehicles, launching the Prius back in 1997. But it has been slow to embrace fully-electric vehicles.

There is no doubt that the combination of *keiretsu*, which ensures strong partnerships with a few selected suppliers, and *kaizen*, which ensures continuous incremental improvement, has served Toyota extraordinarily well over the past fifty years. But we no longer live in a world of predictable, steady-state change. Those days are over. Now what's required in our world of unexpected and turbulent change is a new approach that not only delivers affordable and reliable products in a timely way but that also delivers products that are fizzing with innovation. We believe that by letting the CPO and the procurement team own the product life cycle, CEOs can deliver precisely this.

In chapter 6, we will show how some companies are achieving *breakthrough innovations* by pooling their R&D resources with those of their suppliers. But here, we want to show how CEOs can transform the trajectory of their business with cutting-edge innovations if they put the CPO and procurement team, and through them the suppliers, at the heart of the product-development process.

It is something that Tesla is starting to do.

• • •

In July 2020, Tesla overtook Toyota as the world's most valuable automaker. It was a seminal, and richly symbolic, moment. Toyota had
sold more cars than Tesla—10.46 million versus 367,200 in the year to
March 2020. It had also posted higher annual revenues—$282.2 bil-
lion versus $24.6 billion.[7] Yet Tesla, founded in 2003, was deemed
by shareholders to be worth more than the Japanese giant, founded
in 1937. So what's driving this extraordinary valuation? It is investors' belief that Tesla will dominate the future of the electric-vehicle
market—which means effectively the future of the entire automotive industry, since the days of the combustion engine are numbered
(with several countries, including Norway, France, Germany, the
United Kingdom, India, and Spain, already committed to banning
or restricting sales of new petrol and diesel vehicles over the next
two decades).[8] And why do investors think this? It is because Tesla
is far ahead of Toyota and its other rivals in terms of product range,
production capacity, and innovative technology—and one of the big
reasons for this is Tesla's approach to suppliers and the associated capability of procurement.

Now, on the face of it, Tesla may not be the first company that
springs to mind when the word *procurement* is mentioned. It has
made some well-publicized missteps, with faulty products, delayed
launches, and other setbacks. (In January 2021, for instance, just a
week or so after Elon Musk overtook Amazon founder Jeff Bezos
as the world's richest man in the Bloomberg Billionaires Index, the
US National Highway Traffic Safety Administration ordered Tesla to
recall 158,000 cars with faulty touchscreen displays deemed to pose
a safety risk.[9]) Yet procurement plays a central role in the remarkable
story of Tesla's innovative machines. This ranges from the development of the seemingly humble wire harness—the collection of cables
connecting a car's power and computer systems—to the creation of

an unquestionably cool proprietary motherboard that provides the "brain" of the autonomous vehicle.

Elon Musk has long had the ambition to build not only *autonomous* vehicles but also *automated* factories. As he once put it, he wants to build "the machine that builds the machine." He hoped to achieve this with Tesla's Model 3, which was launched in 2017, but he encountered repeated production problems. In particular, his factory robots struggled to manipulate the wire harness, even though this had been designed to be lighter and shorter than the one used in the previous generation of cars. In the old Model S, the wire harness was an extraordinary 3 *kilometers* in length. In the Model 3, this was shortened to a more manageable 1.5 kilometers. But evidently this was still too long. So, the product-development team, comprising engineers, manufacturers, and procurement specialists, went back to the drawing board.

It is a feature of Tesla's approach that the company has cross-functional teams that, as Tesla puts it, "operate with a nonconventional philosophy of interdisciplinary collaboration." Each individual member of the team "is expected to challenge and to be challenged, to create, and to innovate."[10] Procurement managers are responsible for the sourcing, manufacturing, and production of all the "components intrinsic to the successful operation of the organization." In particular, they are expected to "influence product manufacturability, testability, and supply chain responsiveness."[11] Working together, Tesla's cross-functional product-development teams devised a new wire harness for the next-generation Model Y vehicles that began their rollout in 2020. Designed to be installed by robots, the harness is just one hundred meters in length, has a rigid structure (rather than the flexible structure that was so hard for robots to deal with), and has fewer components. The changes have transformed the manufacturability of Tesla cars.

In a parallel move, the cross-functional teams developed a new underbody structure for the Model Y. The previous Model 3—like most cars on the road today—had an underbody made from seventy or more stamped steel parts that were spot welded, laser welded, riveted, and glued together. As this short description suggests, making such an underbody is a laborious, time-consuming process, and mistakes often slow everything down and lead to rising costs. To address this, the Tesla teams devised a new underbody composed of just two die-cast parts made from aluminum. Because the underbody was simpler to make, and lighter too, Tesla was able to enjoy significant savings. By our calculation, the new underbody delivered a 10 percent cut in production costs, a 20 percent cut in direct labor costs, and a 30 percent cut in the amount of factory floor space needed to install the underbody in the new vehicle.

The wire harness and the underbody are things that customers never see, and those customers probably only benefit insofar as the Tesla vehicle is delivered on time (since the company keeps most, if not all, of the cost savings generated by a simpler, easier-to-make automobile). Something else that customers never see is the Tesla motherboard, but they definitely benefit from this in a very tangible way, and once again procurement has played an important role in the development of the proprietary product.

Most automakers install minicomputers to support their vehicles' entertainment features, navigation functionality, and smartphone connectivity. But since they have not traditionally considered these electronic control units to be part of their core competence, they have generally been happy to buy them off-the-shelf from the main automotive suppliers, including Bosch, Continental, ZF Friedrichshafen, and Harman International, a subsidiary of Samsung. With the transition to electric vehicles, however, this view is starting to change. Electric vehicles, as well as autonomous vehicles, require more-powerful computers, and some companies are realizing they need to develop market-differentiating solutions. Accordingly, they no longer rely on the big one-stop-shop suppliers. Instead, they are developing a network of specialist suppliers orchestrated by the procurement team, and taking charge of the final assembly. For instance, Volkswagen has created an independent software unit, CARIAD, with five thousand coders and other IT experts. Currently, it relies on suppliers for 90 percent of its digital platforms. By 2025, it expects this to fall to 60 percent. Similarly, Daimler is building a team of software developers to produce more of its own technology, and it is developing a supplier network that includes Nvidia, the US chip maker, and Microsoft, which provides cloud computing.[12] In a sense, these companies are following the practice of some of the big technology assemblers, such as Dell, HP, and Lenovo. But there is one automotive company that is going much further. It is taking a leaf out of the Apple procurement playbook and developing its own custom-built silicon microprocessors.

That company is Tesla.

It is an extraordinary fact that Apple extracts two-thirds of the profits from the global smartphone industry even though it has only a 12 percent market share and even though it does not actually make the iPhone.[13] So, what does it do? Above all, it controls what is known as "the entire stack": it designs everything in the iPhone, right down to the silicon chip that makes the phone "smart," and it works with specialist suppliers who are commissioned to make, or assemble, the iPhone. A hundred years ago, Ford dominated the automotive market by *owning* the entire supply chain. Today, Apple dominates the smartphone market by *controlling* the entire stack through its ownership of the fundamental intellectual property and its skilled management of suppliers.

Tesla is trying to do the same. It understands that if you own the IP, you can control the stack, and if you control the stack, you can grow market share and capture a greater proportion of the profits. More specifically, it understands that if you design the silicon microprocessors inside the computers that power the new generation of electric cars, you will dominate the market. There are four features that will determine the success of an electric car: one, its range (how many miles it can travel with one charge of the battery); two, the effectiveness of its advanced driver-assistance system (which includes autonomous-driving functions); three, the sophistication of its telematics (which provide the automaker with data on the vehicle's performance); and four, the quality of its augmented-reality experience (which relies on cameras, GPS, and radar to scan the road and project navigational information on to the windscreen). The last three of these depend on the silicon chip. If you can differentiate here, you can differentiate in the marketplace.

So, in 2016, Tesla created a team of top silicon experts (many of them former Apple engineers previously involved in the development of the A4 and A5 microprocessors that powered some of the early iPhones as well as the first iPads), and had that team design the first custom-built computer for autonomous vehicles. The result was Hardware 3.0: a computer designed to control the new generation of electric cars. We have conducted a teardown of this computer. There are four motherboards: two that control the vehicle's infotainment system, one that controls the Wi-Fi connectivity, and one that controls the autopilot system. Only one of these is fully outsourced—the infotainment processor board, which is supplied by Intel. The rest are designed by Tesla, although the general infotainment board and the Wi-Fi boards have silicon chips supplied by NXP Semiconductors (a Dutch-American company) and Intel, respectively. The truly innovative board is the one that controls the autopilot system, and it contains Tesla's very own silicon chip.

This chip is game-changing in three ways. First, it is more effective than off-the-shelf silicon chips, since it permits a reaction time faster than any human being can achieve (less than one hundred milliseconds). In other words, if a pedestrian were to step in front of the car when the autopilot function was activated, the car would stop more quickly than a driver-controlled car would. Second, it is more efficient than off-the-shelf products, since it has a minimal impact on the life of the electric battery (and therefore on the potential driving range of the car). Third, it costs less: Tesla's previous autopilot board, which was part of the company's Hardware 2.0 computer and contained four microprocessors (which were supplied by Nvidia and the German semiconductor company Infineon Technologies), cost Tesla about $280. By designing the new autopilot board, Tesla was able to cut the number of processors from four to two, cut the number of suppliers from two to one (Nvidia and Infineon were dropped and replaced by Samsung, which was commissioned to manufacture the processor), and cut the cost from $280 to $190.

Tesla began the rollout of its Hardware 3.0 in 2019. And with news that it was collaborating with the US software company Broadcom and TSMC on Hardware 4.0, its stock-market fortunes rose. The world was still in lockdown because of the Covid-19 pandemic, but Tesla's approach, with procurement playing a key role in the reconfiguring of the company's relationships with suppliers, helped Tesla top the *Financial Times'* ranking of one hundred companies that defied the gloom and prospered during the pandemic. As the *FT* observed: "Investors believe its technology is years ahead of its competitors."[14]

It is indicative of the impact Tesla is making that Apple, the company that inspired its shift toward controlling the entire stack, is once again reviving plans to launch its own Apple-branded electric car, in partnership with a mainstream automaker as the supplier. This is just the kind of extraordinary development that is possible when the CPO and the procurement team are involved in the product-development process from the get-go.

Conclusion

CEOs can transform the fortunes of their company if they put their suppliers at the core of their business and, as a practical reflection of this, give the CPO and the procurement team a new mandate that puts them at the heart of the product life cycle. But for this extension of power and responsibility to be effective, CEOs must oversee a radical overhaul of the procurement function, because right now in most companies, that function is not fit for so elevated a role.

 Notes for the CEO

Key Takeaway

If you want your suppliers to have a bigger role in the fortunes of your company, you need to empower your CPO and procurement function.

Key Strategy

Give your CPO central responsibility for your company's product life cycle—from ideation to postproduction.

Key Tactics

- Create a cross-functional product-development team. Give your CPO a leadership role. Get them to change the conversation.

- Allow your CPO to use the full range of technical and tactical levers—teardowns, should-cost analysis, consumer clinics, structured supplier questionnaires, and big data analysis.

- Get your CPO to stay vigilant to the very end of the product life cycle. Make sure your company shares in the savings achieved by your suppliers.

- Ask your CPO to develop deep supplier networks that give you the freedom to develop your own product components.

4

Go Bionic

Create a Procurement Function That Combines the Virtues of Human Creativity and Digital Technology

Martin Ashborne, CPO of Apex Motors, one of the world's largest automakers, stared intently at the PowerPoint slide that we had just presented him, his eyes darting from side to side as he tried to take in the significance of what the featured chart was telling him.*

On the x-axis were the words *procurement focus*, with a scale running from "cost reduction" to "profitable growth." On the y-axis were the words *procurement mandate*, with a scale running from "supporting the corporate strategy" to "shaping the corporate strategy." In the lower left corner was Apex Motors along with their rival automakers. But we could just as easily have inserted the names of companies from any number of sectors—most CEOs instruct their CPO to focus only on reducing costs and supporting the corporate strategy.

* For confidentiality reasons, we have changed his name and that of the company.

FIGURE 4-1

What good looks like in procurement

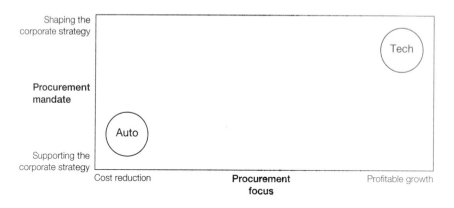

Source: BCG.

Most CPOs in Ashborne's shoes might have been content with what they gleaned from our chart: after all, it showed that Apex Motors was like pretty much every other automaker. But Ashborne was far from happy. All he could see were the companies in the top right corner of the chart. It was clear that these companies took a very different approach to suppliers. Their CPOs had evidently been instructed to focus on generating profitable growth and shaping the corporate strategy. (See figure 4-1.)

If there was a glimmer of light for Ashborne, a new high-level recruit charged with helping the CEO turn the company into the Apple of the automotive industry, it was this: the chart showed not only the current position of Apex Motors (and, by implication, how much work Ashborne needed to do to create a world-beating procurement function) but also what was possible and what he needed to do next. Apex Motors' CEO had instructed Ashborne to focus on generating profitable growth and shaping the corporate strategy. The CPO realized that to carry out these instructions he needed to rebuild the procurement function so that it was fit-for-purpose.

A few days after our presentation, Ashborne told us his plans. He had resolved to create a procurement function that would focus on reducing costs while forging mutually beneficial supplier relationships to do three things: one, develop innovations that could drive Apex Motors' profitable growth; two, establish sustainability initiatives that could make the automaker a world leader in the reduction of CO_2 emissions; and three, introduce advanced warning systems that could safeguard the company's supply of critical components in uncertain times. When Ashborne asked us what we thought he needed to do to achieve these goals, we recommended that he follow our fourth principle: *Go bionic. Create a procurement function that combines the virtues of human creativity and digital technology.*

The word *bionic* first entered the popular lexicon in the mid-1970s, with the blockbuster TV show *The Six Million Dollar Man.* Former astronaut Colonel Steve Austin was endowed with superhuman powers as a result of being rebuilt with bionic implants after suffering life-threatening wounds in a crash. At Boston Consulting Group, we use the term *bionic* to describe a company that blends the power of technology with the power of human ingenuity, creativity, judgment, empathy, curiosity, and intuition.[1]

To create a bionic company, CEOs have to radically retool their procurement function in two ways: one, they must focus on what we call the human dimension by hiring the CPO and instructing them to staff the function with people who bring different skills and a different mindset to the job of procurement; and two, they must focus on the digital dimension by investing in a raft of new digital technologies for the business of procurement.

Let's look at these two different features of the new-model procurement function, starting with the human dimension.

The Human Dimension

In any corporate transformation, even a digital one, the people should come first and the technology second. So where should the CEO start? The first appointment CEOs should make on day one of the job is the new CPO. Get that right, and they can significantly improve their own chances of success. After that, they should instruct the CPO to recruit a new generation of procurement professionals.

Choosing the ideal CPO—what the CEO needs to look for

Sitting at the top of the procurement function's hierarchy, the CPO should have all the hallmarks of a future CEO: the strategic vision to run a business that must be transformed by new technology and new people, the dynamism and leadership skills to drive through challenging transformation programs, the collaborative working style to influence the executives heading other business functions, and the thick skin to make decisions that may be unpopular.

When talking to CEOs about potential CPOs, we stress the importance of looking for what we call "catalytic" leaders: people who don't give orders from on high but who instead get to know their staff as individuals, encouraging them, enabling them, energizing them. We urge CEOs to look for people with resilience. Delivering change in a company is hard, and the task of shifting the procurement function from a supporting role to a shaping role should not be underestimated. Even though CPOs should be driving the CEO's own change agenda forward, they will nevertheless encounter plenty of pushback from competitors and colleagues. Time and time again, they will have to demonstrate that they and their function are indispensable in every facet of business. Even if the CEO gives the CPO a seat at the table, no one will automatically hand them anything on a plate. Indeed, they may have to fight to get a seat at the table—and they will almost certainly have to fight to keep it.

Once they have appointed their CPO, CEOs should give them the green light to hire a new generation of procurement professionals: highfliers who are comfortable negotiating face-to-face with suppliers, making choices between suppliers, and striking deals. These star recruits should challenge conventional wisdom and pose the difficult questions. CPOs should create an in-house red team that stress-tests product proposals, looks for flaws in their reasoning, and picks them apart—in other words, a team of indispensables.

This caliber of employee is usually attracted to jobs in corporate finance, technology, and marketing. To recruit them, the CPO needs to overturn the reputation of the procurement function as a dead end for ambitious, innovative people. At Apex Motors, Martin Ashborne is doing this by turning the procurement function into a springboard for future leaders.

He wants the procurement function to be, as he puts it, "the place to be."

How to turn the procurement function into "the place to be" for a team of indispensables

The CPO will need to attract new recruits who have very different skill sets from those who currently staff the typical procurement functions. We estimate that only 30 percent of *operational* buyers— those deskbound staff who carry out such mind-numbing administrative tasks as checking purchasing requisitions, filling out purchase orders, and transferring data to invoices—will be necessary in the new-model procurement function. They will have to be retrained to use robots, which can complete the tasks more quickly, more cheaply, and with fewer mistakes. By reducing the number of operational buyers by 70 percent, CPOs will be able to shrink the size of the procurement function and reinvest the savings in a recruitment and retraining program.

Most *strategic* buyers will still be needed, but they will have to broaden their skill set. The ideal strategic buyer is a diplomat, a strategic thinker, an implementation coach, a negotiator, an analyst, and a data miner–cum-researcher. Three of these roles require human skills: as diplomat, the strategic buyer must interact on a personal level both with the leaders of the company's other business functions (e.g., engineering, marketing, operations, and legal) and with the most important A suppliers; as strategic thinker, the buyer must bring their experience to the broader discussion about the company's future direction; and as implementation coach, the buyer must develop ways to persuade the people in other functions to drive through promised savings and other value-generating commitments. Three of the roles require strategic buyers to be experts in digital technology: as negotiator, the buyer must draw on the power of AI; as analyst, the buyer must expect to increasingly rely on digital technology over the next five years; and as data miner or researcher, the buyer must expect to become almost exclusively reliant on digital technology.

To help existing employees make the shift, CPOs must give them the time, space, and resources to get up to speed, especially if they are to become the go-to experts on specific categories or products. At Apex Motors, Ashborne is creating a procurement academy, or corporate university, unofficially known as "the Harvard of procurement," to train both recently hired and existing procurement professionals in the new skills they need. Everyone will be expected to use and understand data analytics; many team members will also be required to exhibit a range of soft skills—a capacity for empathy, for example, to foster relationships and resolve conflicts.

Another way of attracting top talent is to offer high-potential employees the chance to work in regions of the world where they can develop their knowledge, get close to key suppliers, and serve as the firm's eyes and ears. That's what General Motors did when it established its automotive procurement arm in Israel. The unit taps into Israel's technological expertise, and works closely with the firm's advanced technology center, also based in Israel, which is exploring a host of cutting-edge technologies to address big issues, including autonomous vehicles, cybersecurity, user experience, and smart mobility. As Gil Golan, executive director of GM's technology center, observed: "We are in a race, a race to find talent and partnerships that will help us move from Auto 1.0 to Auto 2.0."[2]

CPOs will need to create a raft of other new roles to support the new, digitally powered procurement function. These include researchers, superforecasters who can advise on future risks, master data engineers, AI programmers who update the new-style negotiation tools, and robotic-maintenance engineers who keep the automated procurement show on the road. Where should companies look for these new recruits? Wherever talent resides. CPOs could hire strategists from the military, sustainability experts from campaign organizations such as Greenpeace, innovative technologists from computer companies, and data scientists from NASA. The challenge is a formidable one. Headhunting firm Odgers Berndtson predicts "an international battle for talent," as companies strengthen their procurement capability.[3]

The challenge is not just recruitment and retraining. The influx of digitally proficient employees will have implications for how CPOs organize their procurement function. We recommend they divide the function into three distinct groups. One group is the digital creators. Accounting for about ten percent of procurement employees, these are the AI geeks—the master data specialists, robotics engineers, and software programmers responsible for building the AI negotiation coaches, supplier radar systems, and other tools required to make sense of what data scientists call data lakes. Also, they include the digital change agents—the people whose sole task is to persuade buyers to "buy in" to the digital transformation. The second group is the digital core, comprising the strategic buyers who will use the latest technology to extract value. The third group is the digital users—primarily the operational buyers who have a basic understanding of the robotic technology that will increasingly execute many of their currently manual functions.

• • •

Hiring people who can harness the power of digital technology to develop market-leading insights that will give a company an edge is a critical factor for success. The procurement function should include specialists who are leading authorities in their area—the go-to experts hired for their knowledge and experience.

One company that has created a market-leading business on the back of its procurement experts is voestalpine. You may not have heard of this Austrian company, but it is one of Europe's few consistently profitable steel companies. It owes some of its extraordinary success to the way it approaches procurement, hiring dedicated experts in metallurgy, machinery, telecommunications, and several other specialty areas.

An early cornerstone of voestalpine's success was (and remains) its ability to make high-quality steel from the kind of iron ore (with low iron content) that is readily available in Austria. This metallurgical process, which was developed decades ago, offers a classic example of how procurement and production can be successfully linked together. Ever since then, voestalpine has built on this achievement by fostering a mutually beneficial collaboration among production technology, procurement, and suppliers.

Today, voestalpine has a dedicated unit of twenty to thirty procurement specialists who focus on the procurement of iron ore and other raw materials. Also, as the company has expanded beyond

steelmaking and into the related businesses of processing and technology, it has developed its pool of procurement experts in a variety of specialist disciplines. For example, in addition to its five-hundred-plus purchasers in different business units, it now has a team of about ten companywide "lead buyers" who each take charge of the procurement of specific indirect goods and services, such as IT, telecommunications, cranes, machine tools, and chemicals.

Using their expertise, these lead buyers and other procurement specialists, as well as those in the raw-materials unit, play an important role in the innovations that voestalpine codevelops with some of its major suppliers. Among the most important of these innovations is what voestalpine calls "greentec steel": the manufacture of high-quality steel using low- and zero-carbon-emission production processes.[4] The company has developed an industrial-scale process for carbon-neutral steel and secured the intellectual property rights to the process from the European Patent Office. To accelerate the development of such future-oriented and specific value-adding procurement capabilities—not only coinnovation and green procurement but also digitalization—voestalpine is providing employees with further specialist training at its purchasing power academy.

What can companies learn from voestalpine's experience? With its emphasis on experts and excellence in procurement, the Austrian company offers a model for the new generation of CPOs: to build a function that is so critical to the future of their company that other leaders in the business automatically give them a seat at the table.

The Digital Dimension

Getting the human dimension right is 70 percent of the challenge facing CEOs as they instruct their CPO to retool the procurement function. To get the digital dimension right, they should invest in technology that *automates* most of the menial administrative tasks carried out by the procurement team. By doing this, they can, by our calculation, expect not only to achieve productivity increases of 30 percent to 50 percent but also to free up as much as 50 percent of their procurement professionals to work on more-strategic and higher-value tasks. After making this investment, CEOs should invest in technology that *augments* the capabilities of the CPO and the procurement team by enhancing their decision-making when negotiating deals with suppliers, by facilitating fast and effective collaboration across the company and beyond, and by helping them deliver greater value.

We have identified four multipurpose technologies that should be top of the list for CEOs revamping their procurement function: robotic process automation (to help automate tasks in order to reduce the size of the workforce, improve efficiency, and accelerate dealmaking); big data and advanced analytics (to crunch raw data in order to make more cost-efficient and value-enhancing decisions); artificial intelligence and machine learning (to enhance the work of employees, including their core activity of negotiating with suppliers); and blockchain technology (to verify product legitimacy and origins, thereby eliminating inspection and certification costs).

Let's look at the experience of some companies that have benefited from these technologies.

Automation and digital transformation

The first essential technology for the new-model procurement function is robotic process automation (RPA). RPA technology allows companies to dramatically transform the laborious purchase-order process by automating nine out of ten tasks. It can also reduce the time it takes to process invoices and onboard new suppliers. It can do all this while reducing the size of the workforce by as much as

70 percent. By our estimation, one robot can do the work of four people.

One company whose procurement function we have helped automate in this way is National Grid, one of the world's largest publicly listed utility companies, which provides electricity and gas for all of the United Kingdom and for twenty million people in the northeastern region of the United States. National Grid has developed a digital strategy to create frictionless processes in order to deliver energy in a safer, faster, and easier way than ever before. As part of this, CPO Vivienne Bracken is leading the global procurement function's digital makeover.

As a first step, National Grid—which spends around £5 billion on procuring a vast range of nonproduction goods and services (everything from connections for new offshore wind farms to ink for thousands of office printers)—conducted a review of the way it contracts with suppliers. Focusing on the core UK business, the company examined 2,500 active contracts created and managed by 318 people (both in-house staff and external employees), including 546 contracts that accounted for more than half the spending with suppliers. This review uncovered several practices or "frictions" that needed urgent attention: there was suboptimal collaboration between the procurement and legal teams working on the same contract; there was limited access to basic contract information, spend data, or supplier performance data; and there was no common process for creating contracts (so individual employees were left using their own initiative).

Following the review, National Grid addressed these issues by devising a strategy that included streamlining the contract process (there is no point building a new technology platform on top of a broken process), purchasing the best digital tools, and training the procurement staff. There are three main goals: one, to make all contracts 100-percent compliant (contracts containing errors, inconsistencies, and other faults lead to costly delays in the completion of deals with suppliers); two, to achieve a 30-percent efficiency gain (allowing staff either to handle more contracts or to be redeployed on other, more value-added activities); and three, to reduce the cost of purchased goods and services by an incremental 3 percent. National Grid calculates that by creating a digital process for contracting with suppliers, it could save a potential £60 million per year and reallocate some 146,000 lost hours of labor—the equivalent of more than ten years of a working life—toward more value-added activities.

To streamline the process, National Grid is creating a library of standardized templates for contracts. Given that contracts can run hundreds of pages, this will save time—and therefore money. Also, the company is changing the way that contracts are managed: optimizing and negotiating the terms and conditions (which could generate savings of 15 percent); reclaiming overpayments and rebates (which could, where appropriate, slice 7 percent off the supplier's bill); making adjustments for inflation or fluctuating commodity prices (a potential savings of 4 percent); and exercising the right to volume discounts (a potential cost reduction of 3 percent).

As it does this, National Grid is putting in place the digital tools it needs to automate the contract process. Fortunately, it did not need to go out and buy a new digital system to do so—it already uses one supplied by SAP Ariba, the California-based subsidiary of German software giant SAP. Instead, it chose a specific AI solution—a product from DocuSign that enables everyone working on contracts to search, filter, and analyze them—that could interface with its existing system. With this capability, National Grid will be able to establish what data scientists call the single source of truth: a central hub that contains all the contract templates, all the information on existing contracts, and all the data relating to the spending on and performance of suppliers. Also, procurement managers will benefit from a kind of Google Alert that prompts them when they need to take a particular action (renew a contract, claim a rebate, etc.).

National Grid's biggest challenge is getting procurement managers to change the way they work. Too often, companies invest in new digital tools but fail or "forget" to invest in the people who will use the new technology. Three years ago, National Grid attempted to transform the way it created and managed supplier contracts. The effort had limited success, however, because the company was unable to change work practices. Even in the best of times, old habits die hard. Back then, the chosen approach wasn't geared toward fundamental change: participation was optional, there was no complementary training program, and the overriding theme was "business as usual." This time, National Grid is making participation mandatory, providing ample training, and underscoring the fact that the initiative is part of the wider digital transformation of the procurement function.

National Grid's digital transformation is a work in progress, but all indications are that the RPA technology will have the desired impact. The company has already reduced some of the risks of noncompliance, which can include statutory and legal penalties, reputational damage, and the costs of righting a wrong. Also, it has generated a significant portion of the projected cost savings of £60 million per year and started to recover some of the procurement function's lost time and redirect it toward more-strategic, value-added activities.

Big data, advanced analytics

It is widely recognized that data is becoming the new oil fueling the modern global economy.[5] Whoever owns data—more specifically, whoever can make sense of it—stands to prosper. If companies do embrace automation, as most will over the next few years, they will become owners of vast treasure troves of information—the data lakes—that can be plumbed to generate savings and new sources of value. We have become used to the language of massive computer storage power—megabytes and gigabytes. But these are poised to be replaced by even larger numbers. According to the World Economic Forum, it is projected that the world will be creating 463 *exabytes* of data every day by 2025. That is the equivalent of the data stored on some 212 million DVDs.[6]

This is giving rise to some big questions: Who owns the data within the company? Who is responsible for extracting the value the data contains? Standing at the confluence of several rivers of corporate data, the CPO and the procurement function are positioned to own the data—or at least to make a critical contribution to the way it is collected, interpreted, and used to augment the capabilities of executives and drive future growth.

Much of the data collected by companies is not used. A recent study found that, on average, more than half of a company's data is "dark data"—unquantified and untapped.[7] To extract the ideas and insights locked inside this data, the CPO should invest in a multi-purpose technology that has come to the fore with the evolution of enormously powerful computers to make sense of, or crunch, big data: advanced analytics. With this technology, CPOs can shine a light on the dark data, recognize patterns in vast and complex data sets, draw commercially valuable conclusions, and make decisions. Importantly, this technology operates in a purely rational way. Unlike people, it is not swayed by conscious or unconscious biases, although it can be undermined by inconsistent and incomplete data.

Using advanced analytics, we have helped a variety of companies find cost savings by improving the strategic development and practical implementation of their procurement plan of action. Advanced analytics can help with make-or-buy decisions, since it requires only a few clicks on the computer keyboard to cluster information on the costs of different options. It can also help identify suppliers who underperform and overcharge, by creating a scatterplot that shows suppliers who are outliers when it comes to unacceptably high defective rates (usually expressed as parts per million, or ppm) and product prices.

One of these companies is Global Car Corporation.*

• • •

Global Car Corporation, one of the world's biggest and most recognizable automotive companies, has a procurement function with two thousand people who manage the company's relationship with four hundred thousand suppliers around the world. To optimize the organization of this complex network, it has embarked on a wide-ranging digital transformation. One of its first initiatives was to get a better understanding of the costs of the machined parts purchased from suppliers for its trucks and buses division. Every year, this division sells nearly five hundred thousand vehicles, and it therefore has an enormous demand for axles, brakes, and gear systems as well as engines and drivetrains. To get a handle on the costs of all these parts, the procurement team collected data from fifteen million production orders across twenty global sites, specification data for more than one million parts, and invoice prices from more than 250,000 invoice records. With computers crunching this raw data, the company found that some suppliers had not passed on preagreed discounts over the previous three years. Armed with this information, procurement executives were able to renegotiate with those suppliers and realize cost savings of 10 percent.

This early success prompted GCC to expand its deployment of advanced analytics technology across the procurement function. For example, buyers can now make calculations so that they don't overpay for nonproduction-related goods and services such as machinery

* For confidentiality reasons, we have changed the company's name.

for factories. It's often hard to establish the "true" price for, say, the robotic arms used in GCC's state-of-the-art factories that manufacture its luxury vehicles. One supplier might quote one price, while a second supplier might quote a different one. Of course, the buyer will choose the lowest price. But who's to say whether that's the "right" or "fair" price for the equipment? Perhaps even the lowest price on offer is too high? Our analysis suggests that buyers tend to accept the lowest offer without investigating whether or not they should demand an even lower price. This haste is principally due to their being overwhelmed by the number of so-called price-plausibility checks they have to carry out. Some of these checks get done; some don't.

Now, however, buyers have the advanced analytical tools to help them.

GCC has started routinely collecting data from a range of internal and external sources. All the spend data and contract data are housed in its central buying system. It puts this information alongside data on the volume and price of every previous order, which is stored by Newtron, a German-based trading platform for completing deals with suppliers. In addition, GCC's procurement team conducts should-cost analysis, which provides a useful guide, although on its own, it doesn't reflect what the market might pay for a product. Finally, GCC adds into the mix data from external sources, including Bloomberg and the Economist Intelligence Unit.

As a result, GCC has been able to conduct regular price-plausibility checks on orders worth less than €2.5 million, giving buyers more time to focus on bigger orders; detect significant price deviation; challenge suppliers' quotes; and generate savings of three to five percent.

AI, or augmented intelligence

The most powerful of the new digital technologies—one with the potential to transform a company's prospects—is AI. Ordinarily, the *A* stands for "artificial," but we prefer to think of it as standing for "augmented." AI can enhance the work of the procurement team, helping them not only generate significant savings but also find other sources of competitive advantage. One task where AI is proving particularly useful for procurement executives is the all-important negotiations with suppliers.

Several companies have benefited from using our proprietary AI coaching tool. At most companies, the CPO and procurement team resort to the same set of negotiation tactics that they have always used: for example, an auction, where they look for the lowest bidder, or a tender, where they invite bidders for the contract and review the offers against several different factors. But there are many more tactics available to executives. By using only a few, the CPO is leaving a lot of money on the table—by our estimation, as much as five percent. Our answer to this problem is an AI-powered coaching tool that uses game theory to come up with the best go-to-market negotiating tactics and an advanced machine-learning algorithm that improves the advice with every new deal.

A negotiation is, by definition, a dialogue between a buyer and a seller. To a significant degree, it is also a trial of strength influenced by the economics of supply and demand.

We use the analogy of chess—and the chessboard, with its sixty-four squares—to help procurement executives think through their options when negotiating with suppliers. In the book *The Purchasing Chessboard*, the buyer is presented with different ways to reduce costs and increase value, depending on the balance of power with the supplier.[8] Now, with game theory and AI technology, it is possible to lay out the options with greater precision and increased speed.

Game theory is the science of strategic interactions pioneered by the Hungarian-born American mathematician John von Neumann (who, incidentally, played a key role in the top-secret Manhattan Project that developed the first atomic bomb). Rooted in mathematics, psychology, and behavioral economics, game theory assumes that people seek to maximize their benefits in a rational way. One of the classic applications of game theory is when military leaders engage with opponents after burning their own boats. This has happened on many occasions throughout history: the Arab leader Tariq ibn Ziyad burned his boats before capturing what is known today as the Rock of Gibraltar in AD 711; William, Duke of Normandy, did it before winning the Battle of Hastings and becoming king of England in 1066; and the Spanish conquistador Hernán Cortés did it before taking control of the Aztec empire in 1519. In each case, they faced an overwhelming force, but they changed the odds in their favor by undertaking a seemingly self-defeating, irrational act. By burning their boats, the leaders conveyed two messages: the first, to their opponents, that they were ready to fight; the second, to their own soldiers, that there was no going back.

How does this relate to suppliers and procurement? By following the rules of game theory, buyers in the procurement function can predict and influence the decisions and actions of suppliers—and thereby achieve significant savings. This means taking four steps: one, securing an advantageous position (to do so, it is not always necessary to burn one's boats); two, assessing potential scenarios; three, modifying the approach with each new piece of information; and four, moving swiftly to close the deal within small windows of opportunity.

As we'll now show, we have built these steps into an AI tool for a number of companies.

• • •

Dynamo Power Group (DPG) is one of the world's leading suppliers of engines and propulsion systems for powering submarines and frigates, passenger ships and ferries, mega yachts, and even nuclear power plants.* Although it is a specialist subsidiary of a multinational aerospace and defense company, DPG has its own suppliers. We got involved when the CEO instructed the CPO to generate savings as part of the procurement function's contribution to the firm's ambition to improve the overall cash position by an extra £1 billion by 2020.

We recommended the creation of a bespoke AI negotiation coaching tool. To start, we conducted a review of the procurement function's approach to negotiations. In our work with other companies, we have found that buyers frequently resort to the same set of negotiating tactics—regardless of the unique characteristics of a particular negotiation. For instance, one global industrial company relied on face-to-face negotiations 40 percent of the time and a mix of tendering and face-to-face negotiation 37 percent of the time. The buyers also did not adequately prepare for negotiations, making only limited use of either should-cost analyses or other commercial tactics (38 percent of the time) or product-specification benchmarking and other technical tactics (17 percent of the time). DPG had a similar reliance on a set of favored negotiating tactics, and we knew that the AI negotiation coach could help the company's buyers by providing them with a significantly larger tool kit. In the case of the global industrial company, the AI negotiation coach led to a reduced reliance on face-to-face negotiation (down to 10 percent from 40 percent of the time) and an increased focus on commercial preparation (up to 81 percent from 38 percent of the time) and on technical preparation (up to 70 percent from 17 percent of the time).

After the review, we helped DPG develop an AI negotiation coach tailored to the types of negotiation its buyers conducted on a day-to-day basis. The first step was building on game-theory principles to create what we call a decision tree. To do this, we held a series

* For confidentiality reasons, we have changed the company's name.

of workshops for the buyers of different kinds of raw materials and components used in the manufacture of the company's engines. In each workshop, which lasted two to three hours, we drew a decision tree on a whiteboard the length of an office wall. The tree started with an instruction: Enter baseline spend, and enter savings target. This was followed by a question: Is this a new go-to-market opportunity or an optimization within an existing relationship? If the answer was "a new go-to-market opportunity," it was followed by another question: Do you have a clear and complete specification of the product or service? If the answer was "an optimization within an existing relationship," a different question followed: Is this the only supplier who can provide this product or service? Each answer was followed by a yes-or-no question.

By the end of the workshop, the whiteboard was a maze of boxes and lines, but when buyers followed the logical course of a decision, from left to right, they came to a clear recommendation on the best course of action. As a second step, this information was plotted on an Excel spreadsheet and subsequently coded into an algorithm for the AI negotiation coach. Over the course of the next few months, the tool refined its recommendations as it learned in real time from the buyers' actual decisions. This resulted in the buyers using a broader range of negotiating tools and, most important, achieving significant savings. There was another benefit too: the procurement function, so often viewed as a dull administrative operation, started to be seen within the firm as a cool, smart, tech-savvy center of excellence.

• • •

Dynamo Power Group built a bespoke AI negotiation coach from scratch. But this isn't an absolute necessity. Heidelberger Druckmaschinen, the world's largest maker of printing presses, approached us when it was facing a squeeze on its cash flow. Could we help find some savings? Yes, we could. There was no time to develop a bespoke AI negotiation coach. So, instead, we recommended the use of a ready-to-go version that could deliver significant savings—and quickly.

We focused on approximately sixty buyers at Heidelberger, each of whom took responsibility for around ten suppliers who together accounted for around €750 million per year. The task was to reduce this figure by about €20 million. Initially, we held a series of supplier days, where ten or more rival suppliers were invited to a one-day event, given a briefing on the company's strategic vision and the value of the suppliers' particular products, and sent away with an offer of closer cooperation in return for significant savings. After this, we turned to the AI negotiation coach for guidance on which suppliers to focus on and which negotiation tactic to use when the final bidding process got underway.

Then the data for each supplier was fed into the negotiation tool's algorithm. Very quickly, the AI negotiation coach determined that Heidelberger's buyers should focus on 299 suppliers—roughly half the overall number of suppliers. Also, it made a series of specific tactical recommendations to the buyers. The top-ranked negotiation recommendation was face-to-face negotiation, followed by the supplier day, the classic auction (so often chosen as a default option by buyers), and the parallel negotiation, where two or more suppliers are invited to the company's headquarters, hosted in separate rooms (each supplier is unaware that the others are also there), and engaged in a simultaneous discussion (where the buyer moves from room to room, challenging each supplier with the lower offers received by other suppliers, until there are no more concessions).

Significantly, the AI negotiation coach focused not only on the negotiation itself but also on the commercial and technical preparation that buyers should undertake before engaging with suppliers. The top three commercial recommendations were negotiation simulations (buyers prepare their scripts and conduct a full dress rehearsal before stepping into the negotiation room), war gaming (buyers and their teams plan each move and countermove in precise detail and work out their best approach), and should-cost analyses. The top three technical recommendations were supplier plant visits (buyers carry out a thorough inspection of a factory and look for possible ways to extract savings), cost-out conventions (buyers invite suppliers to present them with clever ways to take cost out of specific, high-volume products), and adjustments of specifications (buyers relax some of the technical demands so that suppliers have more room to develop cost-effective solutions).

It's important to emphasize that the algorithm gives recommendations—not orders. The AI negotiation coach is precisely that: a *coach*. Its purpose is to deliver savings by encouraging buyers to step outside their comfort zone and challenge conventional thinking. Its purpose is *not* to turn them into automatons. In the realm of buying and selling, experience still counts for a lot, but there is no question that decision-making can be enhanced with the help of computers.

For Heidelberger, the proof came with the results. In one or two cases, the buyers did not negotiate any savings from the suppliers, but in most cases they did. Indeed, in a few spectacular cases, the savings ran into double figures.

• • •

AI can not only help CEOs deliver significant savings, it can also help them tap other sources of competitive advantage. Swift Post Logistics (SPL), one of the world's largest courier companies, has used AI and machine-learning technology to support its sustainability strategy.*

---

* For confidentiality reasons, we have changed the company's name.

It wanted to ensure that its suppliers met the high standards that it set for itself and shared its values. Given that it has more than two hundred thousand suppliers operating in more than two hundred countries, this was never going to be easy. To help SPL, we collaborated on the creation of an AI-powered, cloud-based supplier risk-management tool, the supplier sustainability radar, which identifies high-risk suppliers and recommends strategies for mitigating risks—and does so in a fast, efficient, automated way.

Building the tool required gathering critical data from a variety of sources: information manually collected by the procurement team from questionnaires and visits to suppliers, facts and figures held on both the company's and suppliers' enterprise resource planning systems, and material stored in the databases of institutions such as the United Nations, the Organization for Economic Cooperation and Development, and the International Labor Organization. After this, the data was aggregated, the algorithm was built, and the procurement team was able to have a risk score based on a series of variables, such as location, financial health, and industry.

When it came to environmental risks, for example, the radar was fed information on 242,000 suppliers. Of these, 140,000 suppliers were subject to further analysis, with the radar dividing them into different risk clusters. This led to special focus given to 7,000 suppliers. By the end of the process, 357 suppliers were identified as high risk and requiring dedicated attention. For each supplier, the AI tool recommended one of thirteen specific actions designed to mitigate the risks. These ranged from communicating with suppliers about the importance of risk issues, giving them SPL's supplier handbook, and adding liability clauses to supplier contracts, to sending personalized letters demanding improvement, conducting a formal supplier audit, putting the business relationship on hold, and immediately terminating the relationship.

With this AI solution, the courier company has been able to meet the challenge it set itself: to work only with suppliers that share its values.

Conclusion

With a radically retooled procurement function that forges dynamic new relationships with suppliers and plays a central role in the life cycle of a company's products, CEOs will be able to face today's challenges with fresh optimism. For starters, they will be able to relieve any cost pressures. And they will be able to tap into several other sources of competitive advantage. But as we'll explain in the third part of *Profit from the Source*, CEOs should instruct the CPO and procurement team to follow six powerful principles in order to extract maximum value from the company's suppliers.

Notes for the CEO

Key Takeaway

If you want to change the relationship between your company and your suppliers, you need to radically retool the procurement function so that it is fit-for-purpose.

Key Strategy

Give your CPO the resources to create a bionic procurement function that combines the virtues of human creativity and digital technology. Make the procurement function "the place to be" in your company. Invest in new technology, but focus on your people first—otherwise your transformation will stall.

Key Tactics

- Pick a catalytic leader as your CPO—someone who can encourage, enable, and energize the procurement team.

- Retrain a new generation of strategic buyers. Attract star talent by offering elite, Harvard-style training and foreign postings.

- Recruit a broad range of support staff, including superforecasters, master data engineers, AI programmers, and robotic-maintenance engineers.

- Invest in the full range of digital technology: robotic process automation, big data and advanced analytics, AI and machine learning, and blockchain technology.

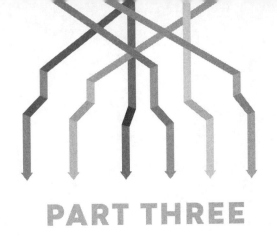

PART THREE

How *Your Company's Ecosystem* Needs to Change

5

Cut Costs—Fast

Demand *Up-Front Double Savings* from Your Top Suppliers and Double Down on the Rest

The pressure on CEOs to cut costs never goes away. In a crisis, such as the one triggered by the Covid-19 pandemic, the pressure is existential: to ensure the survival of the company. But even in good times, CEOs face pressure to cut costs so that they can free up resources to expand into new markets, create new innovative products, or conduct mergers and acquisitions. In such moments, CEOs look to the CPO. In their eyes, the CPO was put on earth to deliver cost savings first.

The trouble is that the way CPOs are expected to deliver cost savings is limited—and ultimately damaging for the company. In most companies, as we have shown, the procurement teams get involved in the product-development process only at the relatively late negotiation stage. By then, many of the costs are already baked into the product, leaving the CPO with only limited opportunity to reduce the price of goods and services provided by suppliers.

Not surprisingly, with their options for making an impact so constrained, some CPOs engage in hardball tactics and treat all suppliers in more or less the same way regardless of their importance to the company. Although this might work in the short term, it most definitely does not work in the long term. Ultimately, it turns procurement into an unproductive, zero-sum game of cat and mouse—where the CPO (the cat) is constantly trying to catch the supplier (the mouse), who is doing everything it can to find clever ways of shaving costs (and keeping the proceeds) while meeting the specifications of the commissioned product as set out in the contract. In some cases, this aggressive approach persuades strategically important suppliers not to work with the buyer company. General Motors' Ignacio López transformed the business of procurement in many positive ways, but his combative approach to negotiation left GM having to spend time and effort mending broken relationships with suppliers long after he had departed the company.

We have made it clear that the best way to generate cost savings is to give the CPO central responsibility for the entire product-development process, from ideation to postproduction, so that costs are not crystallized too early and so that the procurement team can develop mutually beneficial relationships with the most important suppliers. But given that the A suppliers number only between twenty and forty at even the biggest companies, how should CPOs handle all the other suppliers, who can number in the thousands? What should the company's overarching approach to cost savings be?

At Toyota, the buyers and the suppliers—who are selected on the basis of their past performance record and their relationship with the company rather than on the basis of a competitive tender—work together to determine the cost and price of specific car parts and a fair distribution of the profit.[1] This approach certainly keeps a lid on costs—but it also keeps a lid on innovation, because it limits the range of new suppliers that companies work with. This is a significant downside of Toyota's approach. As an alternative, we recommend that CEOs follow our fifth principle: *Cut costs—fast. Demand up-front double savings from your top suppliers and double down on the rest*. It is an approach that draws inspiration from an Italian economist operating at the turn of the twentieth century: Vilfredo Pareto. It allows companies to cut costs fast and, at the same time, build relationships with suppliers who can help them tap several other sources of competitive advantage.

Back in 1896, Pareto observed that 80 percent of Italy's land was owned by 20 percent of the population. Since then, the Pareto principle, which is now sometimes known as the 80/20 rule, has become an axiom of business management, with strategists reporting that 80 percent of sales come from 20 percent of customers. We have found that the Pareto principle can also be broadly applied to suppliers.

In our experience, some 85 percent of a global company's procurement expenditure goes to the top 120 to 240 suppliers of commodities, components, and other goods and services (depending on the size of the company). The remaining 15 percent goes to the legions of other suppliers spread around the world. It therefore stands to reason that the CPO should focus disproportionately on the top suppliers. This is why we recommend that companies divide their suppliers into three distinct categories: A suppliers, who account for about 50 percent of the procurement budget; B suppliers, who number one hundred to two hundred and account for about 35 percent of the budget; and C suppliers, who constitute the most numerous group of providers (often numbering several thousand) but who account for only about 15 percent of the budget.

Having separated suppliers in this way, companies can then begin to tailor different customized strategies for each of these three different types of vendor. We will now look at two companies that treat their suppliers in a nuanced, variegated way: Advanced Luxury Vehicles (ALV), the company we introduced in the chapter on "treating your suppliers as friends," and Malleable Containers Group, one of the world's leading manufacturers of sustainable, flexible packaging for the consumer and pharmaceutical sectors.*

How to Approach A Suppliers

A suppliers consume a disproportionate percentage of a company's procurement budget and by definition have a disproportionate impact on a company's prospects, so it stands to reason that they should be treated differently. Both ALV and Malleable Containers Group, a relatively small, privately owned company whose revenues amounted to €1.5 billion in 2020, use the 360° program. It might be assumed that the Pareto approach is a solution designed exclusively for big, powerful companies like ALV, with the corporate muscle to wrestle powerful suppliers into submission. But actually, the experience of Malleable Containers shows how even small companies can secure cost savings from their much bigger suppliers.

Malleable Containers, based in central Europe, may be relatively small, but it has a presence in more than twenty countries and its products are in high demand, since it makes the packaging for consumer goods and medicines produced by some of the biggest companies in the world. In other words, it occupies an important place in the supply chain of those companies, and as a result, it has real leverage in the market. Malleable Containers' investors were especially attracted by the fact that it is likely to benefit from a number of megatrends that could lead to a growing demand for an increasing array of types of packaging. These trends include urbanization, the growth of the middle classes, and the increased consumption of single portions (requiring more but smaller packages).

* For confidentiality reasons, we have changed the company's name.

We were approached to help Malleable Containers' business leaders achieve cost savings when they were dealing with some specific challenges. Consumer buying habits were starting to change, with a growing appetite for simpler products with simpler packaging. For example, the fad for fruity yogurt with matching colorful packaging was being supplanted by a new fad for healthier, plain, natural yogurt with matching plain packaging. Also, there was a growing preference for sustainable products, and Malleable Containers' reliance on laminated foil packaging, which is notoriously hard to recycle, put the company at a disadvantage. While it had taken steps to address this—opening a factory for making recyclable flexible packaging as part of its plan to offer 100-percent recyclable packaging by 2025—it needed to do even more to create the financial headroom for investing in new machinery that could make the new styles of packaging and for delivering on its promise to shareholders.

To generate the extra funds, Malleable Containers' business leaders decided to look for significant cost savings. To achieve them, we suggested that the CEO strike up a one-on-one dialogue with the CEOs of some of its suppliers, including such giants as Dow Chemical. At first, our suggestion was received with a degree of skepticism. Why would some of the busiest CEOs on the planet bother to reply to the CEO of a relatively small firm? Nevertheless, just before going on holiday, Malleable's CEO fired off personal emails to his counterparts at about forty A suppliers—and thought no more about it. But within days, his executive assistant was buzzing his cell phone. She was anxious to reach him because several CEOs had gotten in touch and *wanted to talk*. Malleable Containers may be a dot on the global corporate landscape, but the CEOs saw an opportunity to get some direct feedback from one of *their* customers.

Malleable Containers set about realigning its relationship with these A suppliers, developing a reciprocal 360° program that offered a package of benefits and preferred trading terms in return for up-front savings. As ALV had found, not every A supplier signed up to the 360° program; and even with those that did, there had to be some tough talking. For example, one of Malleable Containers' major suppliers of aluminum had to be told very firmly that some of its share of business would be distributed to other aluminum suppliers if it did not lower its prices.

In the end, that supplier did lower its prices, and a sufficient number of A suppliers agreed to give Malleable Containers what it wanted: double savings.

How to Approach B Suppliers

The approach to B suppliers has to be quite different than the approach to A suppliers, because B suppliers are more numerous, yet they account for a smaller proportion of the procurement budget— which indicates that they are less important to the company. Typically, we say that whereas the approach to A suppliers should be all about the *suppliers*, the approach to B suppliers should be all about the *categories*. Also, the approach should be less about fostering a mutually beneficial relationship and more about striking the best financial deal. In this regard, it is worth noting that Apple, which has led the world in the way it has forged partnerships with its most important suppliers, is nevertheless resolutely focused on squeezing out all unnecessary costs from suppliers. The job of Tony Blevins, Apple's vice president of procurement, is reportedly to "stare down suppliers and slash prices to the bone."[2]

At ALV, the two hundred or so B suppliers were each assigned to one of about sixty of its procurement managers—specialists in a diverse range of categories, including headlights, bumpers, steering wheels, and car seats. The managers, with a vested interest in the performance of the suppliers, took responsibility for negotiating the terms of all the contracts in their particular category. To ensure that they got the best deals for ALV, we trained them to use a wide range of negotiating tools when conducting tricky contract talks. Traditionally, procurement managers use only a small handful of negotiating methods when trying to strike a deal with suppliers. As a result, they usually end up paying way too much, leaving on average between three and five percent of money on the table. As we showed in chapter 4, we have developed an AI negotiation tool, powered by artificial intelligence, that allows procurement managers to decide which negotiating methods to use, when to use them, and how to use them. With these kinds of tools, ALV was able to double the level of cost savings that B suppliers had previously been willing to offer.

Malleable Containers followed a similar plan as it doubled down on what it called "category optimization." It identified 118 suppliers that ranged across eleven categories, including film and resins, chemicals, paper, logistics, packaging, and insurance. A target price cut was worked out, and then suppliers were invited to make competitive bids to keep their business and also, if they so wished, win business from rival suppliers. The message went out: everything was up for grabs. Then Malleable Containers' procurement managers engaged in direct negotiation, or in some cases coordinated online auctions, before finally selecting the suppliers.

Not all of the suppliers were amenable to Malleable Containers' demands, but the company managed to strike new deals with several suppliers, delivering savings of about 3 percent, which amounted to several million euros.

How to Approach C Suppliers

The bulk of ALV's cost savings—$470 million—came from the A and B suppliers. But a significant sum—$30 million—also came from the thousands of C suppliers who are so often overlooked by CEOs, and who commonly fly under the radar because they are so numerous that they are cumbersome to deal with. Although they accounted for a relatively small proportion of the company's overall procurement budget (as they do for all companies), they represented a significant opportunity for a company looking to cut costs.

We recommended that ALV appoint a single caretaker procurement manager to oversee the entire group of C suppliers. Such a complex task would have been impossible for one person without the help of a digital tool. ALV used what we call the AI haircutter tool, which determines the optimal savings target for each supplier. With this information, the executive was able to demand a required price cut (there was no negotiation), get feedback within a certain number of business days, and draw up an escalation plan if the supplier refused to comply with the price cut or threatened legal action against ALV, as sometimes happens.

At first, a significant percentage of these C suppliers refused to make the requested price cuts: 15 percent of those receiving $20 million to $30 million in business from ALV rising to 67 percent of those receiving $5 million or less. Eventually, however, most agreed to make the price cuts, as they came to realize that they really might lose ALV as one of their clients. For the price of a single caretaker executive's salary, ALV got its remaining cost savings, and hit the overall target of $500 million.

Malleable Containers took a similar approach to its C suppliers. In all, it has around nine thousand suppliers. The company selected the three hundred most important—those it was paying at least €150,000 per year—and sought to generate significant enough savings from them to pay for investing in new types of packaging. As with ALV, Malleable Containers used the AI haircutter tool. This helped its procurement managers determine not only the appropriate price cut for each supplier but also the appropriate tone to take in their letters to suppliers. Rather than sending them letters personally signed by the CEO (as the company had done with its biggest suppliers), Malleable sent C suppliers automated letters from a middle-ranking procurement manager, but tailored them according to certain criteria provided by the AI haircutter tool. If, for example, the supplier was sited close to Malleable Containers and enjoyed a long-standing relationship, then the tone of the letter was friendly. If, on the other hand, the supplier relied on Malleable Containers for a large percentage of its business but had not offered any cost savings over the previous five years, then the tone of the letter was firm and uncompromising. Also, the AI haircutter tool advised on different cultural nuances, depending on whether the supplier was headquartered in Europe, Asia, or North America.

In all, the AI haircutter tool makes an assessment based on twelve variables. Of these, seven are critical: (1) your company's share of the supplier's revenue, (2) the amount of savings delivered by the supplier over the past three years, (3) how many competitors the supplier has, (4) where the supplier is headquartered, (5) whether the supplier is headquartered close to your company, (6) how many years the supplier has worked with your company, and (7) the size of the supplier in terms of revenue. The rest are optional: (8) the risk of the supplier going bankrupt, (9) the potential for codeveloping innovative products, (10) the quality of your company's relationship with the supplier, (11) the supplier's capacity to increase volume production, and (12) the quality of the supplier's parts and components.

Malleable Containers' central procurement team sent out their price-reduction request letters, drawing on a selection of ten different templates as recommended by the AI haircutter tool and translating them into different languages, as appropriate. But it was the buyers located in the forty factories scattered across Europe who followed up with the local suppliers and reported back to the central team. Every week, there was a conference call with the buyers in the local factories, and this was how the central team could keep up the pressure. The strategy worked: the cost-reduction program delivered savings of nearly 4 percent from these C suppliers.

Conclusion

Every CPO must put cost savings at the top of their agenda. After all, if they don't deliver these economies, then they will have zero credibility with the CEO. But smart CPOs make cost savings the starting point, not the end point, of an enduring reciprocal relationship with suppliers that can deliver enormous value for their company and the suppliers. They understand that, in the future, the most successful companies will constitute the nexus in a thriving corporate ecosystem, collaborating with a variety of suppliers in mutual pursuit of profitable business. Costs are part of the conversation, but as we will show, they are not the whole story.

➡ Notes for the CEO

Key Takeaway

If you want to achieve a goal of double cost savings, you need to find a new way of collaborating with your most important suppliers.

Key Strategy

Instruct your CPO to demand an up-front commitment to deliver double savings as a condition of a new partnership. Remember: no double savings, no deal.

Key Tactics

- Coach your CPO to implement the Pareto principle. Get them to divide your suppliers into three groups (A suppliers, B suppliers, and C suppliers).

- Take personal charge, with your CPO, of your A suppliers (those that account for about 50 percent of your procurement budget).

- Ask your CPO to put your category managers in charge of demanding cost savings from your B suppliers (those that account for about 35 percent of your procurement budget). Give those managers an AI negotiation coach tool.

- Have your CPO appoint a caretaker executive to oversee all your C suppliers (the rest of your vendors, who despite numbering several thousand, account for only about 15 percent of the budget). Give the caretaker an AI haircutter tool to automate the price-cut recommendations.

6

Dream Big Together

Achieve *Breakthrough Innovations* by Pooling R&D Resources with Your Suppliers

nnovation drives change, boosts productivity, and sparks growth. But companies are finding it harder and harder to develop game-changing new technologies. In the United States, the telltale sign of this is the decelerating rate of productivity growth, which has historically been generated by innovation. From 1948 to 1973, output per hour grew at an average rate of 3.3 percent per year. Over the next twenty years, it slowed to 1.6 percent. There was a brief acceleration from 1995 to 2004, when it bounced back to 3.2 percent. But the following eleven-year period—which was marked by the global financial crisis—saw the growth rate drop to 1.2 percent. Today, it is lower than it was one hundred years ago.[1] Some economists, such as Larry Summers, contend that the world is entering an era of secular stagnation.[2] Others, such as Robert Gordon, are gloomier still, arguing that the century of innovation from 1870 to 1970, which witnessed the emergence of electric lights, motor vehicles, air travel, telephones, radio and television, and other transformative inventions, won't be repeated.[3]

We are not so pessimistic.

Throughout human history, need has been a driver of innovation. As the saying goes, necessity is the mother of invention. Today, the need for companies to innovate is stronger than ever. Consumers have an insatiable appetite for new things. According to one report, the number of new packaged goods unveiled every year has grown thirtyfold over the past fifty years—and now exceeds thirty thousand products.[4] And while the pace of globalization may have slowed, a globalized approach remains necessary for companies hoping to adapt their products and services for new and different markets.

Another factor is the speed of technological change and the speed with which new technology is adopted by consumers: it means that companies must necessarily be constantly thinking about the next innovation. Even before the Covid-19 pandemic, the accelerating speed of new technology was breathtaking. It took fifty years before fifty million consumers picked up a telephone receiver. By contrast, it took twenty-two years for the same number of consumers to use a TV. For computers, mobile phones, and the internet, the time frame was fourteen years, twelve years, and seven years, respectively.[5] With the start of the pandemic, in March 2020, there was a further acceleration as the world staged an unprecedented migration online. That this was going to happen was clear from the beginning of the global health crisis. In April 2020, as the world started to adapt to the language of lockdowns, companies closed their offices, and employees began working from home and staying connected via Microsoft Teams, Zoom, and other videoconferencing platforms. As Satya Nadella, CEO of Microsoft, noted at the time: "We've seen two years' worth of digital transformation in two months."[6]

But need and speed are not sufficient for successful innovation. There are two other critical elements: funding and the willingness of people to collaborate for their mutual benefit. Over the years, companies have found different ways to harness these other elements. AT&T created Bell Labs, which attracted gifted researchers (including several who won Nobel Prizes for their work at the laboratories) and which benefited from significant funding because of the company's government-guaranteed telephone monopoly.[7] More recently, companies have collaborated with, and in some cases acquired, startup companies that had originally secured resources from venture capitalists. Procter & Gamble, which has been committed to working with innovative suppliers since the days of A.G. Lafley, is one such company. "It's a fact," the P&G notes, that "collaboration accelerates innovation. In an increasingly connected world, the biggest business wins come from working together."[8] The company positions itself as a business that has "the heart of a start-up and the resources of a global corporation." It has an investment arm, P&G Ventures, with a mission to "identify big consumer problems that aren't being met today and look for business and technology partners to help solve them."[9] It also has an external partnerships program, Connect + Develop, for finding patent holders and other innovators who can help the company develop new products and processes in a range of business categories—everything from beauty and grooming and home care to packaging and manufacturing.[10]

Today, it's the big technology companies that offer the best model for achieving breakthrough technology. As we've said, they don't actually *make* anything. Yet they are the most successful, the most highly valued, and the most innovative companies in the world.

How is this possible?

The answer is that they follow our sixth principle: *Dream big together. Achieve breakthrough innovations by pooling R&D resources with your suppliers.*

The Secret of Buyer-Supplier
Product (and Process) Development:
Demand-Driven Innovation

In the heyday of Bell Labs, some brilliant, albeit eccentric, scientists pursued blue-skies research that delivered an astonishing array of innovations, including the transistor, the solar-powered battery cell, the laser, cell phones, communications satellites, and Unix and C, the technologies that form the basis of most essential computer operating systems and languages. Some of these innovations were useful for AT&T; some were subsequently exploited by other companies. The model of the proprietary innovation hub was adopted by other companies. In many cases, however, they too failed to commercialize some of their most striking innovations. Xerox, for example, founded the Palo Alto Research Center, where some very relevant innovations—laser printing and electronic paper, among others—were developed.[11] But it also came up with inventions that the company did not commercialize effectively. For example, its researchers built the first personal computer—the Xerox Alto—with the first mouse, Ethernet connection, and graphical user interface (GUI). "Xerox could have owned the entire computer industry," Steve Jobs once said. But the company's managers were too focused on the success of its copying business. "Basically, they were copier-heads: they had no clue about a computer and what it could do," Jobs said (Apple exploited the GUI technology).[12] Similarly, Kodak funded one of the most industrious R&D facilities—one that registered some 19,576 US patents between 1900 and 1999. But the company missed the opportunity to be the first to commercialize the digital camera, which one of its engineers invented in the mid-1970s.[13]

The big trouble with these innovation hubs was that they were *producer driven.* Unconstrained by costs, the scientists were free to explore and come up with brilliant ideas and inventions, for which the company either found a commercial use or failed to. There is, of course, a place for producer-driven, blue-skies R&D, but that place is probably a college campus. Like the big tech companies, we think corporate R&D should be *demand driven.* In other words, it should be focused on meeting the demands, satisfying the needs, and solving the real-world problems of consumers and society at large.

What are those demands, needs, and problems? One way to find out is for the sales and marketing function to ask consumers. But it isn't sufficient just to ask consumers for their views and listen to what they have to say. It is also necessary to analyze what they actually *do.* In the Internet of Things era, it's possible to know which product features consumers use (and which therefore could be further developed) and which features they don't use (and which therefore could be removed, reducing costs).

But for companies to create a stream of innovations, they need to do more than simply listen to the voice of the consumer. As Henry Ford once reputedly said: "If I had asked people what they wanted, they would have said 'faster horses.'"[14] So, what else do companies need to do? In our experience, they need to listen to two other voices if they want to speed ahead of their rivals by *anticipating* the next wave of innovations.

• • •

One of the two other voices that help companies predict the next innovations is what we call the voice of society. This voice is expressed through a welter of data on environmental, social, and governance (ESG) factors. The shifts in public and political opinion on a range of issues—including carbon emissions, human-rights abuses, social inequality, and gender disparities—have to be tracked and taken into consideration as companies begin their product-development process. Public opinion is notoriously fickle, and liable to sway this way and that without much warning. By contrast, political opinion, and the policy that turns it into action, is more predictable. We know, for instance, that several countries have announced dates for when they will ban the sale of cars with internal-combustion engines, starting with Norway in 2025. This gives companies a time frame for developing electric cars.

Listening to the voice of society is a powerful way of identifying the kinds of innovations that consumers may demand in the future. Another way to do this is to listen to what we call the voice of the product. Of course, there are several products that literally speak, such as Apple's Siri and Amazon's Alexa. Also, there are many products that have built-in sensors capturing and communicating data about the way they work and the way consumers use them. But we mean the voice of the product in a different, very specific way. If you listen carefully, it is possible to determine two things: one, where your product stands in the developmental cycle and two, how you should innovate to further develop your product or devise a different product. We know this thanks to the work of a brilliant Soviet military engineer named Genrich Altshuller.

In the late 1940s, as the Cold War began, Altshuller, then a young lieutenant, was working for the Soviet navy, helping military engineers secure patents for their inventions. He himself was already an inventor, having secured his first Soviet patent for an underwater breathing device when he was just fourteen years old.[15] During his time at the Caspian Sea Naval Patent Office, Altshuller and his colleagues analyzed more than two hundred thousand patents, and they came up with some astonishing conclusions. First, most of the inventions were not really inventions but rather modifications and enhancements. Second, the inventions were not just random developments; they had evolved from one stage to another in a very steady, predictable way. Third, the inventions were not the product of some creative brain wave—a kind of Archimedean eureka moment; they were the result of a discernible pattern of problem-solving.

Altshuller gave his systematic approach to innovation a Russian acronym: TRIZ, short for *Teoriya resheniya izobretatelskikh zadatch*. Until the collapse of the Berlin Wall, in 1989, and the conclusion of the Cold War, the TRIZ approach was a closely guarded secret. It has since been exported around the world, and it is usually translated into English as "the theory of inventive problem-solving." But it isn't so much a theory as a set of inventive principles that companies can use to plan and advance their programs of innovation. Underlying this set of principles is the belief that problems are best viewed as contradictions that can be resolved without the need to compromise. For example, one of the principles is sometimes called "lemons to lemonade": it refers to the idea that a negative can be converted into a positive. In the military sphere, the classic example of this thinking involves the Russian navy's flagship torpedo: the VA-III Shkval.

The laws of physics dictate that a traditional torpedo has a maximum speed of approximately fifty miles per hour. So how can a torpedo go faster? Russian scientists worked out that if they could put the torpedo inside a bubble, or cavity, of gas, which travels more quickly through water than solid objects, they could build a faster torpedo. Working with this principle, they gave the torpedo a rocket engine, rather than the usual propeller or pump-jet, and channeled the rocket exhaust (in effect, the lemon) to the nose of the torpedo, where water could be vaporized into gas (the lemonade). In this way, they solved the problem of drag in the water; the result is known as a supercavitating torpedo, able to travel a remarkable 250 miles per hour—five times faster than a conventional torpedo.

The Shkval was a game changer, forcing the United States and other military rivals to scramble to catch up. Companies can make a similar jump if they apply TRIZ thinking and listen to the voice of the product. Done right, it can help them establish the direction of their next innovation and the steps they need to take. At its most basic, the TRIZ approach can help companies move up the existing innovation S curve: from making the product work to making it work better, maximizing performance, maximizing efficiency, maximizing reliability, and finally minimizing costs. Applied more ambitiously, it can help companies take a giant leap forward to a new S curve, with a new product or a new process.

• • •

Companies need to pursue demand-driven innovation by listening to the voices of the consumer, society, and the product. Companies often do listen to these voices: the sales and marketing function captures what consumers say and do; the sustainability function gathers crucial ESG data; and the design, engineering, and manufacturing functions monitor the performance of the product. But as often as not, there is no one function that combines all the information from this intelligence-gathering effort and converts it into a program of innovation.

Some might argue that the company's R&D function is best placed to carry out this critical task. However, we think that the CEO should hand responsibility for this to the CPO and the procurement function. In our experience, companies that prioritize procurement and their relationships with suppliers hit upon the best solutions to the problems identified through listening to the voices of the consumer, society, and the product.

Let's turn now to the experience of some of these companies, starting with Apple.

Product Innovation

Although Apple spends more on R&D now than ever before—some $16 billion by the end of 2019—it spends less as a proportion of its annual revenue than either Microsoft or Google.[16] So how does it stay ahead of its competitors? One of the ways is by fostering a culture of collaboration with suppliers—a culture driven by the procurement function and a group of go-to procurement experts, a team of indispensables. These specialists are tasked with knowing everything there is to know about their topic of expertise, immersing themselves in the granular details, and engaging in collaborative debate with their colleagues in other functions and with suppliers. As Joel Podolny, dean of Apple University, and Morten Hansen, a professor at the University of California Berkeley, explain, this reliance on "the judgment and intuition of people with deep knowledge of the technologies responsible for disruption" reflects the fact that Apple is committed to offering consumers the best possible products and competes in markets where the rate of technological change and disruption is high.[17]

Apple's reliance on go-to experts illustrates how one of its greatest, if understated, innovations came about: the unibody chassis, or enclosure, for its notebook computers. A traditional PC notebook enclosure is made from around five to fifteen discrete plastic and metal components that are glued or screwed together. This is problematic, for several reasons. As Apple noted in its patent claim, "enclosures formed from multiple pieces add size, weight, complexity, can be relatively expensive, and can require an excessive amount of time to assemble." Not only this, but they can "have a relatively high probability of failure because the entire enclosure may fail if any single piece fails," and they "can be difficult to recycle and therefore can be burdensome on the environment," because some of the parts are made from nonrecyclable materials.[18]

Apple went searching for ways of producing "enclosures that are more cost effective, smaller, lighter, stronger, and aesthetically more pleasing than current enclosure designs." Given these criteria, Apple's experts determined that aluminum was the perfect material—so they were dispatched to find out more about how to shape it into an enclosure. After talking with the big aluminum suppliers, the experts in the procurement function came back with an answer: computer numerically controlled (CNC) milling machines. These machines were originally designed for making small batches of complex parts, such as the main titanium structure of the F-35 fighter jet. Because they chisel away at a solid block of metal—just as a sculptor chips away at a block of marble—CNC machines are expensive and slow. Repurposing them for manufacturing millions of notebooks was, to say the least, counterintuitive. But it was also typical of Apple's determination to think beyond the obvious.[19]

Apple's aluminum experts urged senior executives to consider using CNC machines. After trials returned encouraging results, the company turned to its top suppliers, tapping into their manufacturing knowledge to find out whether they could industrialize the process. They found a way, and from 2010 onward, Apple started buying up nearly the entire global supply of CNC machines and installing them at the facilities of their suppliers—notably Foxconn and Catcher Technology. By doing this, and by filing a patent claim with the US Patent and Trademark Office, Apple secured the supply chain, which meant its rivals were unable to quickly follow its example when the unibody chassis became a hit with consumers.

It is highly unlikely that without Apple's guidance, its suppliers would ever have come up with CNC machining as a feasible way of making an enclosure. Equally, Apple needed its manufacturing suppliers to figure out how to make aluminum enclosures in large numbers—not just for notebooks but also for desktops, laptops, smartphones, tablets, and smart watches.

Process Innovation

Apple worked with innovative suppliers to refine its successful range of computer *products*. Other companies have done this to improve their *processes*. Siemens Gamesa, for example, has collaborated with Fujitsu, the Japanese IT company, in order to accelerate its program of safety checks on 28,000 wind turbines positioned around the world.

A Spanish-based subsidiary of the German industrial giant, Siemens Gamesa is the world's largest wind-turbine manufacturer and a pioneer in renewable energy. Its wind turbine towers stand as high as 395 feet, and they are fixed with fiberglass rotor blades that are 250 feet long. The blades are the most expensive part of the turbine as well as the most vulnerable due to the extreme loads and weather conditions they are subject to. Carrying out safety inspections is time-consuming and sometimes dangerous work, given that some turbines are located far out at sea or in remote regions. In 2017, the company's senior executives started to wonder whether there was a way to make the job safer, faster, and more effective.

The procurement function was tasked with soliciting the views of suppliers. These external vendors suggested that there could be a workable and cost-effective AI solution. The CPO and the procurement team then conducted a review of companies specializing in machine-learning before proposing an alliance with Fujitsu, one of Siemens Gamesa's longtime suppliers. Together, the two companies developed an AI program, Hermes, for detecting abnormalities in images, and they did so by conducting joint workshops and creating a proof of concept before eventually recommending the program for real-world use. Hermes combines image and signal processing with deep-learning technology and draws on Siemens Gamesa's archive of blade-maintenance data for fifty thousand blades over a twenty-year period.[20]

Siemens Gamesa now has a fleet of drones that can capture approximately four hundred photographic images of a turbine's three blades in just twenty minutes. These images are then uploaded into Microsoft's Azure cloud platform and analyzed using the Hermes AI program: first, they are stitched together (a process that takes seconds rather than hours); then they are cleaned so that the blade is clearly distinguishable from the background of sky, ocean, and land; and then they are scanned for faults using a version of facial recognition, and the faults are classified on a scale of one to five, with a five requiring immediate attention. With this information in front of them, experienced quality controllers conduct a thorough review—a process that takes just one and a half hours (not the six to eight hours it used to take). As Kenneth Lee Kaser, head of supply-chain management at Siemens Gamesa, put it: "Fujitsu's groundbreaking artificial intelligence technology dramatically cuts the time required for an inspection of turbine blades."[21]

The electricity generated by Siemens Gamesa wind turbines stationed off Germany's north coast is conveyed to consumers by several transmission system operators (TSOs), including 50Hertz Transmission GmbH. A subsidiary of the Belgian-based Elia Group, 50Hertz serves northern and eastern Germany, including Berlin and Hamburg, and it is playing a central role in the country's *Energiewende*—a radical and rapid transition from fossil fuels to renewable energy. Germany is projected to be carbon neutral by 2045. To meet this ambitious goal, 50Hertz, along with TenneT, another TSO, is overseeing the building of the SuedOstLink, a 310-mile underground cable for channeling electricity between Wolmirstedt, near Magdeburg, in Saxony-Anhalt, and Isar, north of Munich, in Bavaria.[22]

This is a €5 billion project. The cost of digging the ditches and laying the cables is roughly 20 percent of the overall project budget, which prompted the 50Hertz team to find a cheaper way of doing both rather than the traditional method of breaking the ground with mechanical diggers, laying the cables, and then filling in the holes. With our assistance, the procurement team investigated alternative options. One option is trench sledging, where an excavator creates a trench in front of a trench box that houses the cables and guides them into position. Another is plowing, where a plow pulls the laying machine that feeds the cable into a cavity that closes almost immediately. 50Hertz had already proven the technical feasibility for cable projects in a cooperative undertaking with a supplier a year before. Both technologies help reduce costs by up to 15 percent, because they are less labor intensive and they lay the underground cables more quickly.

There are few suppliers of either technology, so 50Hertz decided to develop a new market of suppliers of the trench-sledging technology. In effect, 50Hertz acted as a supply-market maker: It offered to coinvest with several civil-engineering suppliers to develop the technology to meet the specific requirements of high-voltage cable projects. For the plowing technology, 50Hertz had two other options: partner with a supplier to buy the plowing machines, which cost approximately €2 million each, or coinvest in the development of specialist plow-machine manufacturers. Without these incentives, it's unlikely that suppliers would have been willing to take on the risk of building their own capabilities in this business.

In addition to coinvestment, 50Hertz held out the promise that if these suppliers successfully developed the technology and associated machinery, they would prequalify for the national tender conducted under rules set by the German government. At the time of writing, the codevelopment program for the trench sledging is ongoing.

Product and Process Innovation

One proof that the age of transformative innovations has not passed is the success of the global effort to develop and distribute not just one highly effective Covid-19 vaccine but several of them. This achievement illustrates that when there is the need, the resources, and the willingness to collaborate, companies can achieve remarkable results. Above all, it illustrates the power of a sophisticated corporate procurement capability to deliver transformative change.

In January 2020, news of a previously unknown acute respiratory disease started to emerge from China. Initially, it was unclear whether the virulent strain of coronavirus that caused the disease—SARS-CoV-2—would be a localized epidemic like SARS, MERS, and Ebola.[23] By early March, with rising numbers of infections and deaths across Asia, Europe, and North America, it was obvious that Covid-19 was fast becoming the worst public-health crisis since the Spanish flu had killed as many as fifty million people in the aftermath of World War I. Accordingly, the World Health Organization pronounced Covid-19 a global pandemic.[24]

This caused the big pharmaceutical companies to accelerate their response. The task before them was to develop an efficacious vaccine that could inoculate the world's population of seven billion people. Given that the industry produced only five billion vaccine doses every year for infectious diseases, including influenza, pneumonia, and yellow fever, it was a daunting challenge that was going to take radical, innovative thinking.

Who would win the race to be the first to produce a vaccine?

The front-runners were the world's three biggest vaccine producers: GlaxoSmithKline (GSK), Merck, and Sanofi. In May 2020, after several countries had introduced lockdown measures, Ken Frazier, Merck's CEO, expressed skepticism that a Covid-19 vaccine could be developed in the twelve to eighteen months demanded by politicians. "Our experience suggests those are very aggressive compared to other timelines for getting a safe and effective vaccine," he said.[25] But GSK and Sanofi announced that they were going to call a temporary halt to their ongoing rivalry and combine their proprietary technologies to develop a joint vaccine.

The GSK-Sanofi truce was an extraordinary move. "As the world faces this unprecedented global health crisis, it is clear that no one company can go it alone," Paul Hudson, Sanofi's CEO said. Emma Walmsley, GSK's CEO, agreed: "By combining our science and our technologies, we believe we can help accelerate the global effort to develop a vaccine to protect as many people as possible from Covid-19.[26]

But was this move bold enough? As we now know, the answer is no.

While GSK, Sanofi, and Merck focused on adapting their existing vaccine technologies, pharmaceutical companies with a smaller, or in some cases minimal, presence in the global vaccine business quickly determined that if they were going to make a serious contribution to solving the worst health crisis in a century, they would have to partner with suppliers of innovative, but untested, vaccine technology. This search process was carried out by their external supply experts, the owners of the corporate relationship with suppliers. Pfizer, the world's fourth-largest vaccine producer, partnered with BioNTech, a German life-sciences company with which it was already collaborating on an innovative influenza vaccine. Pfizer's leaders were impressed with BioNTech's farsighted approach. As soon as he had learned of the reports coming from China, Uğur Şahin, BioNTech's Turkish-born cofounder and CEO, ordered his company to repurpose its prototype influenza vaccine technology—known as messenger RNA, or mRNA for short—for a new coronavirus vaccine. Explaining the partnership, Mikael Dolsten, Pfizer's chief scientific officer, said: "We believe that by pairing Pfizer's development, regulatory, and commercial capabilities with BioNTech's mRNA vaccine technology, we are reinforcing our commitment to do everything we can to combat this escalating pandemic as quickly as possible."[27]

As Pfizer announced the collaboration, AstraZeneca—an Anglo-Swedish company that Pfizer had tried to acquire when it pursued a hostile takeover with a $69 billion offer—struck a deal with a team of scientists at Oxford University.[28] AstraZeneca, headquartered in Cambridge, had no vaccine track record, but it was impressed by the work of Sarah Gilbert and her team at the Edward Jenner Institute for Vaccine Research, named after the English physician who pioneered the use of vaccination in the 1790s. Like BioNTech, the Oxford team was working on an experimental vaccine technology (to prevent the spread of Ebola) when it switched to Covid-19.

The Pfizer-BioNTech and Oxford-AstraZeneca partnerships raise the question: Who is the supplier? There is a parity of expertise, with each partner bringing something critical to the relationship. Arguably, Pfizer is the buyer, having previously funded BioNTech's work on influenza vaccines. But it also describes itself as a codeveloper of the Covid-19 vaccine. With the Oxford-AstraZeneca partnership, the university held a lot of the cards, and it insisted that the jointly developed vaccine should be a "vaccine for the world," sold to poorer nations at cost for the duration of the pandemic.[29] AstraZeneca agreed to these terms and conditions—and took responsibility for managing the clinical trials, manufacturing the vaccine, and distributing it around the world.

• • •

It became apparent that Pfizer's and AstraZeneca's decision to work with suppliers was paying off when there were early signs of success. GSK and Sanofi, however, ran into trouble. At the end of 2020, they announced a yearlong delay in the rollout of their vaccine, due to problems in the developmental process.[30] A month later, Merck announced it was abandoning its efforts to develop a Covid-19 vaccine.[31]

But creating an efficacious vaccine was only part of the challenge. Just as essential was the task of creating an efficient process for achieving three objectives: one, delivering a sufficient quantity of ingredients to make a sufficient quantity of vaccine doses (a significant challenge given that a typical vaccine contains as many as 280 inputs that have to be sourced from different places); two, manufacturing the vaccine in a way that meets the highest safety specifications; and three, distributing the vaccine around the world.

The supply chain that AstraZeneca created illustrates the complexity of its operation. The vaccine itself—the drug substance—is produced by contract manufacturers scattered around the globe, including Henogen, in Belgium; Catalent, in the United States; Halix, in the Netherlands; Oxford Biomedica, in the United Kingdom; and Serum Institute of India, the world's largest vaccine manufacturer.[32]

Once the vaccine has been produced, it is sent to a variety of places for the so-called fill-and-finish process: vials are filled with the vaccine and finished by being packaged for distribution. In the United Kingdom, the AstraZeneca vaccine is sent to Welsh-based CP Pharmaceuticals, a subsidiary of Wockhardt, a global biotechnology company headquartered in India. In the European Union, the vaccine is sent to IDT Biologika, in Germany; Catalent, in Italy; and Insud Pharma, in Spain; among other places.[33]

• • •

By partnering with innovative suppliers, Pfizer and AstraZeneca leapt ahead of their bigger rivals. Pfizer was predicted to achieve Covid-19 vaccine revenues of $15 billion in 2021, catapulting it to the top of the vaccine rankings.[34] Meanwhile, GSK, Merck, and Sanofi have been forced to play catch-up and, in some cases, serve as suppliers of basic manufacturing services to Pfizer, AstraZeneca, and other vaccine makers. GSK belatedly announced a deal with CureVac, a German biopharmaceutical company, to codevelop a Covid-19 vaccine using mRNA technology.[35] At the same time, it agreed to produce a fill-and-finish function for one of its smaller rivals, Novavax, and committed to helping Johnson & Johnson manufacture its vaccine.[36] Meanwhile, Sanofi unveiled plans to accelerate the development of an mRNA vaccine with its supplier, Translate Bio, a US-based therapeutics company, and struck agreements to support the manufacture of the vaccines developed by Pfizer-BioNTech and another pharmaceutical giant, Johnson & Johnson.[37]

Pfizer's and AstraZeneca's approach is likely to become a classic business-school case study in how companies can seize the competitive advantage if they collaborate with their suppliers to develop game-changing innovations.

Conclusion

A company's ability to innovate in a world of technological change and disruption is critical for survival. But innovating on your own is tough. For a start, it's expensive and there are no guarantees that the investment will pay off. It's also challenging—especially for companies that aren't technology companies and don't have the people with relevant high-tech expertise. But there is a solution: CEOs can tap the financial, intellectual, and other resources of their top suppliers by giving the CPO and procurement team a central role in the product-development process. By doing so, they can defray the costs of R&D and codevelop a pipeline of innovative solutions that meet the needs of consumers.

After cost savings, innovating new products and processes is probably the single most important way that the procurement team can help their company achieve competitive advantage. In a sense, it serves as a kind of catalyst, enabling companies to extract value from all the other sources of competitive advantage. It not only helps them save costs (as we showed with the stories of Apple, Siemens Gamesa, and 50Hertz), it also helps them deliver sustainability (the Apple story), increase speed (the 50Hertz and Covid-19 vaccine stories), reduce risk (the Apple and Siemens Gamesa stories), and create high-quality products and processes (all the stories)—which is the subject of the next chapter.

➡️ **Notes for the CEO**

Key Takeaway

If you want to deliver a pipeline of innovative products and services, you need to bring your suppliers into your product-development system.

Key Strategy

Instruct your CPO to tap the R&D resources of your suppliers. Focus on demand-driven, rather than producer-driven, innovation for product and process development. Concentrate on satisfying the needs and solving the real-world problems of consumers and society.

Key Tactics

- Get your CPO to listen to the voice of the consumer, the voice of society, and the voice of the product.

- Hand your CPO the responsibility for managing a coordinated intelligence-gathering effort and converting it into a program of innovation.

- Establish the procurement function as a source of ideas and insight. Ensure that the CPO has or hires go-to experts.

- Create nimble cross-functional teams so that different perspectives and corporate interests are reflected in the product-development process.

7

Settle for Perfection

Deliver *Unbeatable Quality* by Joining Forces with Your Suppliers to Wage a War on Errors

A t about 9:50 p.m. on Tuesday, April 20, 2010, a massive explosion ripped through a gargantuan oil rig drilling deep into the ocean floor forty miles off the coast of Louisiana in the Gulf of Mexico. Eleven workers were killed, and over the next three months, more than four million barrels of oil leaked into the Gulf, leaving a slick that stretched over 57,500 square miles and destroyed wildlife, ruined the pristine natural environment, and wrecked the local economy.[1]

The catastrophic blast at the Deepwater Horizon well is generally remembered as the "BP oil rig disaster." In its quest for new reserves of oil and gas, the British energy company had leased the rights to develop the so-called Macondo Prospect—an offshore zone estimated to hold about fifty million barrels of oil. But BP did not work alone. The oil rig was owned and operated by Transocean, the world's biggest oil-rig company, while Halliburton, a US oil-services company, had been hired to plug an exploratory "well from hell" with cement. These companies, contracted by BP's procurement team, played a key part in the unfolding disaster. It was Halliburton's failed efforts to properly cement the exploratory well that directly led to the explosion of high-pressure methane gas.

BP, as the buyer of the suppliers' services, was ultimately held responsible for what was, and remains, the worst marine oil spill in history. A drilling endeavor that was budgeted to cost $96.2 million ended up costing BP a record $18 billion for fines and the associated cleanup operation, as well as inflicting enormous damage on the company's reputation.[2] The tragic failure is a constant reminder that companies can never absolve themselves of the responsibility for the actions of their suppliers. If their suppliers fail, then they fail too. There is an old adage that says you should strive for perfection and settle for excellence. In these current times, however, we think companies need to set their bar much higher. This is why we recommend that CEOs follow our seventh principle: *Settle for perfection. Deliver unbeatable quality by joining forces with your suppliers to wage a war on errors.*

As often as not, quality breaches originate with one of the suppliers rather than with the company itself. But in our experience, quality issues are less likely to occur when companies build mutually beneficial alliances with their key suppliers. That's because these companies are closely entwined with their suppliers, and they can use their ultimate bargaining chip—giving more of their business to those suppliers that meet their most stringent quality targets.

This is a lesson that has been learned by several companies—including Toyota, Dell, and the top pharmaceutical corporations.

Targeting Zero Defects: How Toyota, Dell, and the Top Pharmaceutical Companies Double Down on High Quality

It is hard to believe it now, but Japanese cars used to have a reputation as cheap, shoddy vehicles. Toyota changed this, with the Toyota Production System, as we noted in the introduction. It practices a form of tough love with suppliers, something articulated in the company's uncompromising slogan: "It's the Toyota way or no way." In particular, it makes what might seem like excessive demands on suppliers by setting a goal of "zero defects," and that applies to every stage of the product life cycle—from design to production and distribution. To achieve this, it promotes *kaizen*—the principle of continuous improvement. Also, it manages a preferred supplier pyramid that operates like a game of snakes and ladders. If a supplier does well, it can hope to win more business. If it slips up, then it may slip down the pyramid. It mirrors our own approach, where suppliers can move up or down depending on their performance and their perceived strategic potential.

Despite Toyota's challenging reputation, suppliers do, on the whole, relish the opportunity to work with the company. This is because the corporation's rewards for top-performing suppliers are significant: wide-ranging business support, decent profit margins, mutual respect that manifests itself in top-level one-on-one exchanges and jointly managed development projects, and real opportunities to grow market share. Indeed, the best suppliers not only get more business, they also sometimes get financial support through the *keiretsu* system, by which Toyota takes an equity stake of between 20 percent and 50 percent to develop a "shared destiny."

But there is no fast track to the top of the pyramid. Those at the top—numbering about seventy-five—are long-standing suppliers that have typically taken fifteen to twenty years to get there. And what marks out these suppliers is the fact that they strive for zero defects by practicing not only *kaizen* but also a series of other less well-known principles. One of these is *jikotei kanketsu*, which requires every individual to take responsibility for their part in the process of creating an automobile: specifically, they must not pass on problems or poor quality to the next person in the process. Another of Toyota's key principles is *genchi genbutsu*, which means "going to the source," and requires every supplier to check, and double-check, the facts for itself. If there is a problem, it must determine the root of it. That sometimes means putting into practice one of the management strategies of Sakichi Toyoda, the founder of Toyota Industries Corporation (which gave rise to the car company). Long ago, he said it was important to "ask 'why' five times about every matter." That way, the cause of the problem can be discerned, and prevented from happening again.[3]

• • •

Toyota has built a formidable reputation for quality and reliability—and it is able to charge a premium as a result. But as we've said before, if there is a weakness to its approach, it is the overreliance on a stable set of suppliers. This limits the company's freedom to experiment with other suppliers and, ultimately, negatively affects its ability to innovate. So, what is the alternative?

One company that has tried a different approach is Dell Technologies. Like Toyota, it has made quality one of its defining characteristics. As Michael Dell said: from launch day in 1984, he made quality Dell's "big differentiator" as he tried to distinguish his startup "from the armies of companies jumping into the PC business."[4] To deliver high-quality products, he instructed his company to work closely with its suppliers. As he put it: "Sometimes we'd find incompatibilities in the components from our suppliers and would have to go back to them to ensure they met our standards. But the problems often continued. So . . . we formed close relationships with our suppliers, teaching them our requirements, sharing testing and validation data, and driving them for continuous improvement."[5]

Also, Dell built a coveted reputation for managing its supply chain in a way that prioritized quality assurance. When journalist Thomas Friedman, of the *New York Times*, chose a company through which to tell the story of a globalized supply chain in his Pulitzer Prize–winning book *The World Is Flat*, he chose Dell. Writing, as it happened, on a Dell Inspiron 600m notebook, Friedman related the story of how it took just thirteen days for the computer to reach his home after he picked up the phone to call Dell, spoke to a salesperson, and placed his order. That was astoundingly fast at the time, but it would actually have taken just four days if Dell's quality-assurance specialists had not noticed a problem with the machine's wireless card when it was being assembled in Penang, in Malaysia. Impressed by the slick operation, Friedman described Dell's "supply chain symphony" as "one of the wonders of the flat world."[6]

That was back in 2005. Since then, the proliferation of counterfeiters as well as cybercriminals has further complicated manufacturing and the management of suppliers. Companies must battle hard not only to minimize errors in their quest to develop, manufacture, and deliver high-quality products to their customers but also to minimize the impact of cybercriminals and others with malign intentions. Today, there is every possibility that such people have planted a counterfeit part or placed some malware onto a motherboard. In 2020, according to the World Economic Forum, data threats, and fraud and cyberattacks, were regarded as the sixth and seventh most likely global risks—after extreme weather, climate-action failure, natural disasters, biodiversity loss, and human-made environmental disasters.[7]

Tackling the threat from cybercriminals is no easy task for Dell, because the company produces roughly sixty million PCs every year and delivers them to customers in 180 countries. Dell's solution to the problem is a highly interventionist quality-assurance process that leaves little opportunity for any malign tampering with its products as they make their way from the design phase to the final distribution phase. "We know how to keep the bad guys out," Michael Dell once said. "We integrate security deeply at every step—from our supply chain to the security that's embedded deep inside our products to the network and application layer into the heart of our customers' operations."[8]

Dell's engineers design the products, from the outset, with "built-in" security.[9] The real challenge of providing quality assurance comes when the company has to turn to external suppliers for the raw materials, for the manufacturing capabilities needed to create the products at scale, and for the logistics services to convey the finished products to the doors of consumers. To make sure that the raw materials and other constituent parts used in the manufacturing process are genuine, authentic, and new, Dell procures them from a select list of approved original component manufacturers.

To track these components as they make their journey to the factories where the products are assembled, Dell uses a variety of electronic tags. Some high-risk components on servers destined for governmental and corporate clients carry a unique piece part identification (PPID) number. Other components are labeled with serial numbers or electronic identifiers. These tagged materials are sent to one of more than twenty-five factories that manufacture the products. Of these, Dell owns about one half, with the remainder owned by suppliers who offer contract manufacturing services as original design manufacturers.[10] Finally, once the finished products are ready, Dell distributes them with the help of a variety of logistics suppliers.

The CPO and procurement team have a critical role in selecting all of these different types of suppliers and monitoring their performance. Dell's modus operandi is "trust and verify": trust the suppliers it has selected as partners, and verify everything they do. The selection process is tough. Take the case of the contract manufacturers. First, Dell's commodity managers draw up a short list of potential suppliers. Second, these companies are sent a set of product specifications—for a motherboard, say, or a hard drive—and they are expected to provide what Dell calls "a clause-by-clause response, showing how they could meet the specifications." Third, if this response is satisfactory, Dell conducts a quality process audit, which takes place at the supplier's factory. Fourth, Dell's procurement team oversees a "bench" level test on the supplier's device: in some cases, the device is submitted to a comprehensive destructive physical analysis where it is broken into its constituent parts. Fifth, the device is placed in the finished Dell product—whether that is a PC, desktop, or server—to see how well it works. If the supplier comes through this rigorous examination, it is enrolled into Dell's preferred supplier list and obliged to undergo regular and routine performance reviews.

The finished Dell products can be either shipped directly to the consumer from the factory or, alternatively, sent to one of the company's fulfillment hubs. Either way, Dell relies on several trusted logistics suppliers who ship two units per second every day—carrying enough product to fill two 747 jumbo jets every day and 34,000 shipping containers every year. As a matter of routine, these suppliers are expected to use tamper-evident seals and door-locking mechanisms. Also, they have to offer a variety of tracking devices as well as the option for an armored security escort.

Nothing, in other words, is left to chance.

• • •

Toyota and Dell put quality at the very heart of their businesses. By pursuing zero defects, they are driven by a commercial imperative to differentiate themselves from their rivals. It's part of their unique selling point. But for pharmaceutical companies, quality is an expectation set by regulators. It's not a unique selling point. If they fail to deliver anything less than the very highest quality products, they do not simply risk losing out to their competitors—they risk losing their license to do business. As a result, they don't talk aspirationally about "zero defects"; they talk very practically about the altogether higher bar of "first time right," because they know that if they get things wrong, there are no second chances.

Given the pressure on pharmaceutical companies to get things right the first time, and every time, you would have thought their least risky option would be to do everything themselves—innovating new products, manufacturing them, and distributing them to hospitals and pharmacies. But over the years, they have learned that they need suppliers to help them grow their business. These companies can help them access new technology, add manufacturing capacity in a flexible way, enter new markets, and reduce the risks associated with creating pharmaceutical products at scale.[11]

If anything illustrates the way that pharmaceutical companies have benefited from their alliance with suppliers, it is their rapid development of the vaccines to tackle Covid-19. As described earlier, Pfizer worked with BioNTech and AstraZeneca worked with Oxford University's Jenner Institute to develop innovative new vaccines. And then, when it came to mass producing these vaccines, they turned to a variety of contract manufacturers in different markets around the world.

The fact that they were able to do this so quickly can be attributed to their sophisticated approach to buying services from suppliers. In the pharmaceutical industry, companies separate what we regard as core procurement activities—the buying of direct and indirect goods and services from suppliers. The procurement function handles the purchasing of indirect goods and services (for example, office supplies, IT systems, facilities management, marketing, and travel) while a separate, external supply function handles the purchasing of all the key elements of a company's medicinal products and the selection and management of the contract manufacturers.

The external supply function can strike up different kinds of relationships with contract manufacturers. The basic arms-length contract is a fee-for-service arrangement whereby the pharmaceutical company buys manufacturing capacity on an as-needed basis. Beyond this, a variety of strategic partnerships are possible. The simplest is a "take or pay" contract, whereby the company buys an agreed-upon volume of products for an agreed-upon number of days, weeks, or months (and reserves the option to switch products and shift timelines). The most sophisticated is a mutually beneficial coinvestment contract, whereby a company can expand capacity for several products, gain access to cutting-edge technologies and lucrative new emerging markets, and accelerate its go-to-market strategy.

The commercial benefits of striking a sophisticated, strategic relationship with contract manufacturers are significant. It is through innovation, speed to market, and cost efficiency that pharmaceutical companies can distinguish themselves in the market—not through quality. But of course, the challenges of delivering high-quality products increase with every additional supplier. So how can pharmaceutical companies tackle them? Some firms are experimenting with what are called "virtual plant" teams. These are cross-functional teams, comprising representatives from the company's quality-assurance, logistics, planning, manufacturing, and other departments. The team leader could be based in the external supply function, or in one of the other functions. The idea is that each member of the virtual-plant team builds a direct relationship with their equivalent expert at the contract manufacturer. For example, the company's quality specialist can talk with the quality specialist at the contract manufacturer, and this allows for a deeper conversation between two people who talk the same technical language and understand the main challenges and opportunities.[12]

To some extent, this approach goes a long way to meeting the first-time-right commitment. But pharmaceutical companies cannot afford to take any chances. As a result, they invest heavily in a separate quality-assurance function. Indeed, on average, one in every three people working in the big pharmaceutical companies is focused on quality assurance. This is the kind of investment that is just not affordable in other industries, where the pressures to deliver high-quality goods and services are commercial, not regulatory.

There is, however, another way that companies can pursue their quality agenda—and extract, or recoup, lost value—after their products have been purchased by consumers. It's called claim management, and it is a capability that the procurement functions of several companies have been busily developing in recent years.

After Production: How Companies Can Recoup Their Losses If Suppliers Deliver Poor-Quality Goods and Services

In the automotive industry, companies have been forced to undertake an increasing number of product recalls as a result of quality defects, safety concerns, and other faults. In the twenty years from 1996 to 2016, the number of recalls tripled, from 19.4 million to 53.1 million. Why is this happening? There are two main reasons: one, vehicles have become very complex, and are now routinely fitted with advanced technology and complicated software; and two, automakers' quality-assurance departments, which were scaled back in the wake of the global financial crisis, have not been built back because of the companies' need to invest in electric vehicles, self-driving capabilities, and other technology.[13]

All of these recalls are very costly for the companies. That's because they often require the company to repair or replace the faulty parts of a vehicle under warranty. On average, automakers spend about two percent of annual revenues on warranty payments. But smart companies have learned to recoup some of these warranty costs by claiming back money from their suppliers. Global Car Corporation (GCC), whose approach to digital procurement we discussed in chapter 4, spends, on average, $1.5 billion on warranty costs every year. These derive from several sources—for example, the expenses of the repair shop, which include replacement parts and work hours; salvage costs, such as providing stranded customers with towing services; and goodwill and other payments designed to restore customer satisfaction. But thanks to its procurement function, which runs a sophisticated claim-management operation, GCC reclaims about 10 percent of these costs—and $150 million is a significant sum.

How does the company do it?

The small team—with experts in supplier relations, contract law, and quality engineering—monitors the performance data for the vehicles, using advanced pattern-recognition technology. If the team detects a pattern of failure—rather than just a one-off anomaly—it undertakes a deep-dive analysis. From this, it determines whether the supplier's component is responsible for the failure. If the supplier is found to be at fault, the procurement team can implement a two-pronged strategy to recoup the costs and help the supplier implement the necessary quality improvements.

In one case, GCC started receiving complaints about faulty sensors designed to measure the amount of fuel in the tank. Drivers were being left stranded on the roadside when their vehicles unexpectedly ran out of fuel during a journey. At first, customers were invited to take their vehicle to the local dealer, where they could have it refitted with a new sensor—but this did not solve the problem, because over time, the new sensors failed too.

To get to the root of the problem, the procurement team's quality engineers, as the owners of the relationship with the supplier of the fuel-tank sensors, worked with the supplier. Together, they discovered that the type of glue used by the supplier disintegrated when it came into contact with gasoline, corroding the sensor's internal electronics. This meant that, under the terms of the agreement, the supplier had to pay the warranty costs. But in the spirit of collaboration, GCC helped find a new and more effective glue that ensured that the supplier would not be liable for future failures of the fuel-tank sensor.

The procurement team's expertise in claim management helped GCC recoup some warranty costs from other suppliers who, in turn, were given help to solve their quality issues. But what claim management cannot do is recover the intangible costs associated with a damaged reputation. More than a decade after the Deepwater Horizon disaster, it is BP that bears the biggest scars—not the suppliers. This is why it is always better to strive for zero defects or first time right.

The Search for Quality—It's Not Just about the Avoidance of Errors

When it comes to quality as a competitive advantage, there is much that the CPO and the procurement function can do to protect their company on the downside. As we have shown, they can work with suppliers to limit the frequency of faults in the finished products and, if faulty products are launched into the market, recoup some of the losses from suppliers. Also, there is much that they can do to help the company profit on the upside. When CPOs are made equal partners in the strategic development of a company's business—when the procurement function is freed from thinking narrowly about low-cost solutions—then they can help deliver solutions that combine quality *and* cost effectiveness.

Earlier, we noted how Apple strives to see the bigger picture in its approach to innovation, resisting the pressure to weigh the benefits of its design and engineering solutions against short-term cost and profit considerations. Now we will show how one of Thailand's biggest power-generating companies transformed the economics of its business by seeing the bigger picture when procuring fuel for its power plants.

Global Power Synergy, or GPSC, is the flagship power subsidiary of the Petroleum Authority of Thailand, which is the country's largest corporation and the only one ranked among the *Fortune* Global 500 list of companies.[14] It mostly uses natural gas, which accounts for two-thirds of the fuel used by its power plants. But it has several coal-fired power plants, which generate electricity in the conventional manner: the coal is burned, the heat this produces converts water into high-pressure steam, and this, in turn, drives a turbine that generates electricity. The relative efficiency of these power plants—and specifically how much electricity they can generate—depends on the quality of the coal, and this is where the procurement function is critical.

There are four main types of coal: anthracite, bituminous, subbituminous, and lignite. What distinguishes them is their carbon content. The highest quality of the four is anthracite, which contains anything between 86 percent and 97 percent carbon, and is mainly used to make steel. All the other types of coal are used in the power-generation industry, and their carbon content ranges from 86 percent down to 25 percent. The higher the carbon content, the greater the heat that is generated. But of course, higher-quality coal attracts a higher price. For this reason, GPSC's procurement function traditionally focused on buying the cheapest coal per MMBtu, the traditional unit for measuring heat content or energy value. But this approach had pros and cons: the pro was lower up-front costs; the con was the fact that it did not take into account the hidden costs of using different types of coal.[15]

Reflecting on this approach, GPSC decided to switch to a different method: the total cost of ownership (TCO). Essentially, senior executives asked the question: what is the most cost-effective coal to buy? To get an answer, the CPO and the procurement team started to assess a supplier's coal based on the consequential impact of each parameter of coal—for example, how ash, sulfur, or moisture content in coal affect the operating efficiency and, as a result, the total operating cost of different boilers. They then worked out the total cost of ownership in order to determine the competitiveness of a supplier's offer.

To implement this method, GPSC's procurement managers did two things. They changed *what* they asked for and they changed *how* they asked for it. Prior to the switch to the TCO method, they fixed the quality of the coal they wanted to buy and then conducted a simple bidding process, selecting companies that could supply the specified type of coal and picking the lowest bidder—usually after several rounds of bidding. After the switch, they invited suppliers to offer a wider variety of coal with different levels of quality, and they conducted an online bidding process—an e-auction—that took account of TCO factors. As a result, they received bids from a wider range of suppliers, including those who had previously ruled themselves out because they were not able to offer the specified type of coal. In effect, GPSC opened the bidding to all.

Once GPSC had received bids from coal suppliers, the procurement managers reviewed them against the total cost of ownership. To their amazement, they found that some of the lower-quality coal was overpriced and some of the higher-quality coal represented good value: every dollar spent on the higher-quality coal was calculated to generate more kilowatts of energy than every dollar spent on the lower-quality coal. After several further rounds of bidding—when a ceiling price was imposed—GPSC finally made an offer to one of the suppliers. Over the course of one year, GPSC saw the amount it spent on raw materials fall by eight percent. Given that the company was previously happy if it could squeeze raw-material costs by one percent, this result was transformative.

It is, on the face of it, something of a paradox that costs fell so dramatically after the focus of attention was extended beyond up-front cost. But by taking account of several parameters and using the e-auction bidding process, GPSC was able to make the whole process much more competitive, get the best out of the market, and ultimately purchase better-value coal.

Conclusion

In some business sectors, quality is a competitive advantage. In other sectors, such as the pharmaceutical industry, where products are a matter of life and death, quality is a regulatory requirement. But either way, companies cannot expect to deliver quality without the active participation of their suppliers. The CPO and the procurement team, as orchestrators of the network of suppliers, are well placed to help their companies deliver the highest-quality products and services. In the same way, as we will show in the next chapter, they can help their companies meet the rising expectations of consumers—and society at large—for sustainable products.

 Notes for the CEO

Key Takeaway

If you want to deliver products and services of unbeatable quality, you need to join forces with your suppliers.

Key Strategy

Demand that your CPO set a high bar for performance. Promote a first-time-right approach. Aim for zero defects. If a supplier does well, offer more business; if it doesn't, offer support but scale back your business with that supplier.

Key Tactics

- Expect your suppliers to invest in continuous improvement.

- Consider installing a highly interventionist quality-assurance process that takes a "trust and verify" approach to everything your suppliers do.

- Take account of the quality dimension and demand the de-livery of the lowest-*cost* (as opposed to the lowest-*priced*) goods and services.

- Establish a specialist claim-management team as an insur-ance policy in the event your suppliers do provide you with substandard products.

- Review the way your company manages contract manufac-turers. Consider creating a specialist "external supply" capa-bility with oversight of your company's relationships with contract manufacturers. Consider matching each contract manufacturer with a dedicated, cross-functional "virtual plant" team.

8

Share Your Tomorrows

Become *Truly Sustainable* by Allying with Your Suppliers to Meet Environmental, Social, and Governance Standards

n July 2020, in the midst of the global pandemic, the *Sunday Times*, the United Kingdom's biggest-selling upmarket newspaper, published an article by undercover reporters alleging that suppliers making clothes for Boohoo Group, one of the rising stars of the European fashion retail industry, were tolerating unacceptable working conditions and underpaying their workers.[1]

At one level, this kind of story is not unusual. Barely a week goes by without news of a human-rights abuse affecting the supply chain of one major company or another somewhere in the world: child labor in the sweatshops of Bangladesh, sexual exploitation in the garment factories of India, dangerous working conditions in the deep mines of Africa, "wage theft" (where companies have used the Covid-19 pandemic as an excuse to underpay workers) in the fabric manufacturers of Cambodia and Indonesia—the list could go on and on.

What made the Boohoo story different was the fact that the suppliers in question were not based in some far-distant country but much, much closer to home. Boohoo is headquartered in Manchester, the historic manufacturing city in the north of England once known as "Cottonopolis" because of its status in the Victorian era as the producer of one third of the world's cotton fabrics. The suppliers at the center of the human-rights allegations are based in Leicester, a city not thousands of miles away from Boohoo's offices but a mere hundred-mile drive down one of the United Kingdom's main highways.

The revelations, carried under the headline "Boohoo: Fashion Giant Faces 'Slavery' Investigation," caused a storm of anger and poor publicity for the company, whose leaders vowed to leave "no stone unturned" in their effort to resolve the problem. A senior lawyer, Alison Levitt QC, was hired by the company to conduct a rigorous investigation, and she concluded that the allegations were "not merely well-founded but substantially true."[2] In the wake of the report, Boohoo hired another lawyer, Sir Brian Leveson, a senior retired British judge, to oversee its self-described "agenda for change."[3]

The Boohoo story highlights the challenges facing companies as they endeavor to meet growing demands by consumers, investors, and citizens for products and services that do not violate environmental, social, and governance standards. It also highlights an increasingly robust regulatory regime that puts the onus on companies to take responsibility for their entire supply chain. In recent years, several companies have created a new role of chief sustainability officer in an attempt to demonstrate to their shareholders and stakeholders that they are taking action on the issue. Ultimately, though, the success with which a company meets these standards depends on its relationships with suppliers—and the responsibility for this success falls squarely within the domain of the CPO. Buyers and suppliers have different visions of their futures, but in this connected world, they are increasingly bound together, so they should follow our eighth essential principle: *Share your tomorrows. Become truly sustainable by allying with your suppliers to meet environmental, social, and governance (ESG) standards.*

When companies do this, they can expect to unlock tremendous value.

Doing Good, Doing Well

Ten years ago, companies routinely reported the ways that they fulfilled what was then called corporate social responsibility. It was regarded as little more than a box-ticking exercise. Nowadays, sustainability matters, and it encompasses everything from human rights and labor conditions to climate-change-related issues and ethical business governance. As Kevin Brown, Dell Technologies' CPO, puts it: "Sustainability is not only about doing the right thing—it's a better way of doing business."[4] In this regard, it's noteworthy that Ford published its first integrated sustainability and financial report in 2021 so that it could, as Bill Ford, the executive chairman and great-grandson of Henry Ford, put it: "share a more holistic view of our performance."[5] Increasingly, CEOs see sustainability as integral to the financial success of their companies.

In our work with companies, we have amassed evidence that companies that "do good" also "do well." Part of the challenge, of course, is "not doing bad." In its early incarnation, Google set the bar very high for itself, and for other companies, by pledging to do no evil. Since then, big institutional investors, reflecting the wishes of *their* investors, have signaled the importance of sustainability. In 2020, Larry Fink, CEO of BlackRock, announced that the world's biggest asset manager would "place sustainability at the center of our investment approach."[6] The following year, he pledged new commitments to addressing climate change, noting that "companies with better

ESG profiles are performing better than their peers, enjoying a 'sustainability premium.'"[7]

Meanwhile, governments, reflecting the wishes of their citizens, have started to raise the regulatory hurdle, leaving companies with little alternative but to prioritize sustainability. Governments are banning nonelectric vehicles as they steer their economies toward a future with net-zero emissions. Also, the European Union is actively considering the introduction of a carbon-border adjustment mechanism that would tilt the economic scales in favor of companies that have lower carbon emissions, by imposing a levy on high-carbon companies that try to sell their products in countries with strict carbon-pricing rules (and thereby undercut their rivals who have invested in carbon-reduction initiatives). Similarly, governments have been strengthening legislation regarding the use of forced labor and other human-rights abuses. In the United Kingdom, for example, the government has toughened its rules around modern slavery, and issues hefty fines to companies found to have done business with suppliers who rely on forced labor.[8] Likewise, in Germany, a law introduced in 2021 allows the government to issue substantial fines to companies whose suppliers breach environmental rules or human rights.

But sustainability is not just about doing the right thing and reducing risk. By our calculation, if companies get it right, they can expect to enjoy increased sales, increased profitability (we have recorded premiums in the 2 percent to 5 percentage range), decreased capital costs (rate reductions of 0.2 percent to 0.4 percent), and greater investor interest (one-third of all assets under management are now invested sustainably). Also, they can expect to spark greater interest from the next generation of employees—40 percent of millennials, those people born between 1981 and 1996, take ESG factors into account when choosing a job.

But getting it right isn't easy. Many companies are searching for a sustainable silver bullet, which simply doesn't exist. "Is there a single key performance indicator that I can show my shareholders to prove that we're a sustainable company?" one senior executive asked us. The answer, we said, was no. For companies to be truly sustainable, they must become masters of three distinct issues—the environment, society, and governance. Indeed, more than this, they must dig into the details and decide which specific environmental, social, and governance issues to prioritize—which ones will make a *material* impact on both business success and sustainable development. HP, one of the world's largest electronics companies, conducts a regular materiality assessment to, as it puts it, "review relevant environmental, social, and governance issues, reconfirm our long-standing areas of focus, and clarify and shape our sustainable impact strategy, investments, and disclosure." From this assessment, it draws up a materiality matrix, in which specific issues relating to the "planet," "people," "community," and "governance" are measured against two dimensions: their relative importance to HP's business success and their relative importance to sustainable development.[9]

Once CEOs have mapped out their way forward, they can start on their journey. But they should not travel alone—and indeed, there are many companies that are building effective alliances with their suppliers so that they can meet the growing expectations of consumers, citizens, and investors.

The Environment—the Race to Net Zero

In 2015, the world's nations met in Paris and committed to an ambitious goal: to limit the average rise in global temperatures to 2 degrees Celsius, or 3.6 degrees Fahrenheit, above preindustrial levels while trying more ambitiously to keep the increase below 1.5 degrees Celsius, or 2.7 degrees Fahrenheit. But it was another three years before the race to "net zero" really got underway. In 2018, the Intergovernmental

Panel on Climate Change finally declared that countries must bring carbon dioxide emissions to net zero by 2050 to keep global warming to below 2.7 degrees Fahrenheit.[10] Since then, companies, as well as countries, have made significant and well-publicized commitments.

Now CEOs must deliver on their promises. Among climate-change activists, there is significant skepticism that companies are serious about those pledges: even though many CEOs have set interim goals for 2025 and 2030, the net-zero goal is not, in most cases, expected to be achieved until long after they have retired. As one activist group observed when HSBC, the London-based global bank, unveiled its net-zero plans: "This is zero ambition, not 'Net Zero Ambition.'"[11] Under pressure to set out their route, or "pathway," to net zero, several CEOs are taking significant steps to transform their companies, in partnership with others. In Germany, for example, the Federation of German Industries (BDI) commissioned BCG to work with around eighty companies and affiliated associations to develop a way for them to comply with the German government's new target of greenhouse gas neutrality—where companies offset their emissions with measures to remove carbon from the atmosphere—by 2045. The resulting report shows that this can be achieved without compromising the country's competitiveness and industrial strength.[12]

What is clear is that CEOs won't be able to achieve their goals (and those set by national governments) without the active participation of their suppliers and the empowerment of the CPO and the procurement team. Why is this? It is a question of numbers. Half of all global carbon emissions are produced by just eight sectors. The largest contributor to global warming is the food sector, accounting for 25 percent of all carbon emissions. The other seven are construction (10 percent); fashion, fast-moving consumer goods (FMCG), and freight (5 percent each); and electronics, automotive, and professional services (2 percent each). But most of the carbon emissions are produced not by the end-product companies themselves but by their suppliers in the so-called hard-to-abate sectors, such as steel, cement, mining, textiles, agriculture, and chemicals.[13]

According to the Greenhouse Gas Protocol, the most widely used accounting standard, there are three types or scopes of carbon emission: Scope 1 relates to the direct emissions from a company's operations; Scope 2 relates to the indirect emissions from a company's consumption of electricity and other sources of power and heat; and Scope 3 relates to the indirect emissions from a company's suppliers (upstream) and customers (downstream).[14] In an analysis by BCG, produced in association with the World Economic Forum, some 90 percent of the carbon emissions generated by all the companies in the FMCG-products supply chain up to the point of sale are created by suppliers—specifically, chemicals and plastics, freight, and manufacturing companies. For other sectors, the percentage is similarly high: fashion (85 percent), food (83 percent), automotive (82 percent), construction (81 percent), and electronics (77 percent).[15]

In other words, if CEOs address the carbon emissions of their suppliers, they can go a long way toward achieving their goal of net zero. Equally, suppliers have every reason to collaborate with the buyer companies. Take the steel industry, for instance. It is one of the biggest polluters in the world as a result of the power and heat needed to create the fusion of iron and carbon. According to BCG's calculations, if a steel company resolved to become net zero, it would need to increase prices by around 50 percent to cover the costs of upgrading or rebuilding its factories. In a commodity business, where price is everything, this would soon make the company uncompetitive. But there is a solution. If the steel company worked closely with the automotive company buying the steel, it would still be able to increase prices by 50 percent, but the price tag for a typical €30,000 car would rise by only €500. That's because steel—as indeed all raw materials—accounts for a fraction of the price paid by the consumer, even though it accounts for the bulk of the car's overall carbon footprint.[16]

In its work with the World Economic Forum, BCG has identified several best practices that are being adopted by companies to tackle their supply-chain emissions.

Let's look at some of these practices in turn.

Work out the size of your carbon footprint

The first step for CEOs is to get clarity on the quantity of greenhouse gases—measured in metric tons of carbon dioxide equivalent—their company actually emits every year. This is difficult to do—and working out the scale of a company's Scope 3, or supply-chain, emissions is especially difficult, because many large global companies don't always know exactly which suppliers contributed to which products. As Dell acknowledges: "We have one of the world's largest supply chains [and] its size and complexity can make it hard to give a simple answer to the question 'Who makes your products?'"[17] One company addressing this problem is Mercedes-Benz, a subsidiary of Daimler with some two thousand suppliers. It is developing a digital solution, using blockchain technology to monitor emissions through its supply chain. Collaborating with Circulor, a UK-based startup that specializes in tracking raw materials with blockchain technology and AI, Mercedes-Benz has started mapping the production flow of cobalt used in rechargeable lithium-ion batteries as well as the associated CO_2 emissions.[18]

Another company trying to establish the size of its carbon footprint is HP. In 2019, HP's carbon footprint amounted to 46,785,800 metric tons of CO_2 equivalent—50 percent of which came from its supply chain. It knew this owing to its work with the Massachusetts Institute of Technology, which helped the company develop a series of life-cycle assessments (which estimate the total greenhouse-gas emissions associated with a product over its lifetime and which include emissions from materials extraction, manufacturing, distribution, usage by customers, and end-of-life management). These estimates allowed the company to come up with product carbon footprints (focusing on specific desktops, notebooks, tablets, and printers). With the information from these assessments, HP has been able not only to quantify the environmental impact of its products but also to assess possible alternatives and identify product-performance improvements.[19]

Set ambitious supply-chain targets
and report on progress

The second step, related to the first and part of a broader effort to become fully transparent, is to set ambitious, science-based, carbon-reduction targets for suppliers. Tesco, the United Kingdom's largest retailer, set its first businesswide carbon-reduction target in 2006, but in the wake of the 2015 Paris Agreement, it realized that it needed to commit to steeper absolute targets over the short and medium terms. It conducted a full supply-chain carbon-footprint survey of its product portfolio in order to identify what it called "the hot spots that should be targeted for greenhouse gas emission reductions." In 2017, Tesco set itself tough targets approved by the Science Based Targets initiative, a partnership of leading climate-change groups, including the United Nations Global Compact and the World Wide Fund for Nature. It was the first company in the world to do so. Science-based targets are goals deemed to be consistent with what the latest climate science indicates is necessary to meet the Paris Agreement objectives. Back then, Tesco committed to reducing Scope 3, or supply-chain, emissions by 17 percent by 2030, with 2015 as the baseline year. It has since committed to reducing them to net zero by 2050. To achieve this, it has set different targets for different supplier types, with more stretching targets for agriculture suppliers, who contribute 70 percent of Tesco's supply-chain emissions.[20]

While there are different ways for companies to track their carbon emissions, science-based targets are the most popular. Since Tesco's pioneering move, hundreds of major companies have set science-based targets, including Apple, BAE Systems, BMW, General Motors, Pfizer, and Twitter.[21] Microsoft, which has also set science-based targets, has vowed to become not just net zero (companies remove as much carbon as they emit) but carbon negative (companies remove more carbon that they emit). To achieve this requires active engagement with suppliers—three-quarters of Microsoft's carbon emissions (12 million metric tons) fall within the Scope 3 category.[22] In a variation on this theme, GlaxoSmithKline has pledged to have not only a net-zero impact on climate but also a "net-positive impact on nature": in other words, "to put back into nature more than the company takes out."[23]

Redesign your products, packaging, and product portfolio for low-carbon sustainability

Once a company has established the size of its carbon footprint and committed to a science-based target, it needs to start on its carbon-reduction journey. This should begin with a plan to redesign its products, packaging, and product portfolio. As we saw in chapter 3, Tesla reduced the length of the wire harness in its electric vehicles from three kilometers to just one hundred meters. It did this principally to improve the manufacturability of its new Model Y automobile. But in addition to making the vehicle less heavy, this innovation has reduced the speed with which power drains from the electric battery—making it more efficient and lowering its impact on the environment.

Another way that companies are redesigning their product is by incorporating more recycled materials. In the fashion and apparel industry, sportswear giant Adidas has collaborated with Parley for the Oceans, an environmental group dedicated to removing plastic waste from the sea. Every year, some eight million tons of plastic wind up in the world's oceans. In the Pacific Ocean, the Great Pacific

Garbage Patch is a vortex of plastic and other marine trash spread out across 1.6 million square miles: if it were a country, it would be bigger than Japan or Germany. To help tackle this, and to lower its carbon emissions, Adidas has created a sportswear range that uses high-performance polyester yarn produced from repurposed marine plastics. In 2015, when Adidas created the first prototype ocean-plastic sports shoe, it did so by working on what its material experts described as "a pallet of old, stinky, dead, crab-entangled fishing net." The fishing net was cleaned and sent to textile suppliers that the procurement team had found would be able to transform the plastic into yarn for a shoe's upper. By the end of 2020, Adidas had produced more than thirty million shoes using the upcycled plastic.[24]

In the automotive industry, Ford is looking for ways to make its vehicles even more sustainable. A typical vehicle comprises 40,000 parts from 1,200 first-tier suppliers who use approximately 1,000 materials and 10,000 chemicals. About 75 percent of the vehicle is made from metal, which is typically a mix of recycled metal and recyclable metal. Of the rest, about 17 percent comes from plastics, textiles, and elastomers or rubbers, and this is where the company is focusing its attention. Working with suppliers, Ford has repurposed a variety of composite materials for its vehicles. It uses soy-based foam in seats and armrests, wheat-straw-reinforced plastic in the Ford Flex SUV's storage bins, kenaf in the door bolster of the Ford Escape, and rice hulls in the F-150 wire harness. In a partnership with McDonald's, it has used coffee chaff—the dried skin of the coffee bean—to make a durable material for reinforcing headlight housings on the Lincoln Continental; and in a partnership with chemical giant BASF, it has developed polyurethane foam for seats that is reinforced with nanocellulose, which makes them lighter and stronger, and further reduces the company's carbon footprint.[25]

As well as focusing on their products, companies need to focus on their packaging. Many companies have set explicit near-term targets for their packaging to be 100 percent recyclable. But some companies are going further by committing to making packaging *from* recycled materials. In the electronics industry, Dell Technologies, like Adidas, is on a mission to recover ocean-bound plastics, recycle them into packaging, and thereby reduce its carbon emissions. To do this, Dell is working with suppliers to collect, process, and mix plastics with other recycled materials to create trays for packaging specific products. Ocean-bound plastic now accounts for half of these trays, with the other half being composed of recycled high-density polyethylene plastic.[26]

Companies should consider not only redesigning their products and associated packaging but also their product portfolio, by increasing the mix of products that have a lower environmental impact. In the food industry, Rügenwalder Mühle, one of Germany's biggest meat producers, which can trace its roots as a sausage-maker back to 1834, has shifted its portfolio toward vegetarian alternatives.[27] Indeed, it now produces more meat-free than meat-filled products.[28] The company has principally made this strategic move to take advantage of the growing popularity of vegan food in Germany (the US Department of Agriculture has noted that the country is leading "a vegan revolution in Europe").[29] Also, it helps Rügenwalder Mühle lower its carbon footprint. Vegetarian and vegan foods are unquestionably less damaging to the environment than meat products: an Oxford University report found that if everyone shifted to a vegetarian diet, it would cut global carbon emissions by 63 percent.[30]

Redesign your sourcing strategy for a low-carbon world

As a company redesigns its products, packaging, and product portfolio, it will simultaneously need to redesign its sourcing strategy. One way to do so is for the CPO and procurement team to find suppliers located closer to the company and its markets—which has become known as "near-shoring" (as opposed to off-shoring, which was the big movement in the early 2000s, when US and European companies established factories in Asia to take advantage of low labor costs). By shortening the length of their supply chain, companies can reduce not only the carbon emissions associated with transporting goods from one region to another but also the time it takes to get their products into the hands of consumers.

Another way is to find suppliers of low-carbon components, parts, and raw materials. Rügenwalder Mühle, for instance, has had to completely reengineer its sourcing strategy, switching from pig farmers to suppliers of the ingredients for its vegetarian and vegan products, which include soy, peas, potatoes, and wheat. To do so, it has collaborated with several groups, including Greenpeace, animal-rights organization PETA, and ProVeg, an international food-awareness organization.

In a similar manner, Lufthansa, Germany's flag carrier and Europe's biggest airline, and Dutch airline KLM have started to switch from jet kerosene to sustainable air fuel (SAF). Back in 2011, Lufthansa became the world's first airline to test alternative fuel in regular commercial flights; since then, the company has worked with Finland-based Neste, one of the world's largest suppliers of sustainable fuel for aircraft. Initially, Neste faced a challenge: sustainable fuel was derived from farmland crops, which led to growing alarm that fuel production would negatively affect the production of food needed to feed an expanding global population. Lufthansa was anxious to avoid being caught on the wrong side of the fuel-versus-food debate. So, much as NASA supported SpaceX to develop new solutions, Lufthansa worked with Neste to find a way to produce sustainable fuel from materials such as used cooking oil, municipal waste, and wood waste.[31]

Help your suppliers reduce their carbon emissions

As we have shown, the shift to a new low-carbon sourcing strategy may require replacing existing suppliers. But that isn't a possibility when it comes to suppliers who play an integral part in the company's product-development process. Instead, companies will need to help these suppliers rise to the sustainability challenge and reduce their own carbon emissions.

One company that understands it must assist, not abandon, suppliers struggling to adapt to the new consumer demand for sustainable products is Unilever, which spends €35 billion every year on around 56,000 suppliers in 190 countries. David Ingram, Unilever's CPO, says: "We have a fundamental responsibility to know our supply chain and address the issues that exist. If . . . waterways are being poisoned or forests are being chopped down illegally, we can't turn a blind eye because we are a few levels removed from where it is occurring." He adds: "If we fail to act in the right way, we will betray the trust we have built up with our consumers over decades and ultimately destroy the value of our brands."[32]

Accordingly, Unilever has taken several steps to work more closely with suppliers. First, it has translated its sourcing policy brochure into thirteen different languages, including Arabic, Chinese, Hindi, Indonesian, Thai, and Vietnamese. Second, it has instructed suppliers identified as high risk to undergo a desktop auditing assessment. Third, it has demanded that suppliers of raw materials and finished goods submit to an on-site face-to-face audit. Also, the company has been taking an active developmental role in some of its strategically important markets. For instance, in Indonesia and Malaysia, where it sources palm oil, Unilever has worked with regional governments to create what Ingram calls "a sustainable development zone where we know that standards will be high and our sourcing risks will be low."

• • •

With these best practices, CEOs stand a good chance of putting their companies in the best possible position to honor the commitments they have made but which do not have to be met for several decades. What is clear is that if the CEOs procrastinate, then the challenge facing their successors will be even greater. As it is, greenhouse-gas emissions must fall by half by 2030, with the other half dropping to net zero by 2050. It means the race is on to cut emissions dramatically during the 2020s. The sooner CEOs focus not only on Scope 1 and Scope 2 emissions but also on Scope 3 emissions—and the sooner they involve their CPO and procurement function—the better.

Social and Governance Sustainability

The race to save the planet has given an urgency to corporate efforts to make and deliver net-zero carbon commitments. But for their companies to be truly sustainable, CEOs must focus not only on the *E* in *ESG* but also on the *S* and the *G*. Human rights, workplace safety, fair pay for a fair day's work, ethical business practices—these are just a few of the social and governance issues that CEOs must address in their company and in the companies they do business with—their suppliers. This is not just about complying with regulations. It is about fulfilling the terms of an unwritten social license to operate. But doing the right thing is hard. To help CEOs, we have identified a series of actions that they should instruct their CPO and the procurement team to take in order to address social and governance issues.

To start with, companies should set out their social and governance expectations in their supplier code of conduct, alongside their environmental expectations. They should then incorporate these expectations in their supplier contracts, establish a clear reporting process, require their own local managers to monitor the suppliers, and commission formal—and ideally third-party—audits on a regular basis.

If evidence of human-rights abuses, poor working conditions, or bribery and corruption is found, the CPO should send personalized letters to the CEOs of the suppliers, demanding immediate improvement and offering business support and training. Dell Technologies takes great care to risk assess the factories where Dell products are manufactured and assembled. It helps the suppliers take corrective action if necessary, and supports them in developing new capabilities. In 2020, for example, Dell commissioned third-party audits for 346 high-risk suppliers in its supply chain. The auditors spent several days on-site, reviewing documents, observing daily work practices, and conducting interviews with thousands of supplier employees. To improve the suppliers' compliance with the code of conduct established by the Responsible Business Alliance—a nonprofit organization whose members have combined annual revenues of more than $7.7 trillion, directly employ more than 21.5 million people, and manufacture products in more than 120 countries—Dell required several factories to complete bespoke programs of "corrective actions" and to put 1,439 supplier employees through "capability building" programs.[33]

Sometimes suppliers fail to improve even after receiving substantial support. In these cases, CPOs should put the relationship on hold and review the situation. Sometimes suppliers refuse to engage in any way. In these cases, CPOs should not hesitate to terminate the relationship. Apple has done this on several occasions. The tech giant is striving to improve working conditions for mining communities around the world where it sources vital metals and minerals. As a result, miners, smelters, and refiners are expected to assess and identify risks under the terms of Apple's supplier code of conduct and its standard for the responsible sourcing of raw materials. In conflict zones, such as the

Democratic Republic of Congo and adjoining countries, where Apple sources tin, tantalum, tungsten, and gold, suppliers have to provide reassurance that they have not directly or indirectly financed or benefited armed groups. As part of this reassurance process, they are required to participate in traceability and third-party audit programs designed to address and mitigate identified risks. In 2020, Apple ejected seven smelters and refiners from its supply chain because they either did not meet its requirements for the responsible sourcing of minerals or were unwilling to participate in, or complete, a third-party audit.

Traceability is critical, and it can also be hard to do. Apple is committing to "one day" using only "recycled and renewable minerals and materials in its products and packaging." Until then, it is working with ITSCI (the international tin association) and RCS Global Group, a specialist responsible-sourcing auditor. The company acknowledges that "the challenges of tracking specific mineral quantities through the supply chain continue to impede the traceability of any specific mineral shipment through the entire product manufacturing process."[34]

Similarly, in the jewelry industry, which also has to deal with suppliers in conflict zones, some companies are working to improve the reliability of their track-and-trace processes. The issue of conflict or blood diamonds—those that have been mined in a war zone and sold to finance a warlord's activities—has become acute. To address this, Tiffany, the US-based jeweler, gives each diamond a unique serial number that is etched by laser onto the diamond's surface and provides a record of its provenance.[35] In a competitive industry, though, these actions may not be sufficiently radical. In 2021, Pandora, the world's biggest jeweler, not only unveiled its first laboratory-grown, or man-made, diamond collection but also announced that it would no longer use mined diamonds.[36] To do this, it is starting to redesign its supply chain.[37]

Conclusion

Sustainability is no longer just about doing the right thing. Increasingly, it is about doing business, full stop. If companies ignore the eighth principle and fail to take appropriate actions, they had better hope that their customers—and the citizens of the countries where they do business—aren't looking. It could spell the end, or the beginning of the end, of their business. After all, a company that is not sustainable is by definition unsustainable. This is why companies and their suppliers have a vested interest in helping each other meet all the environmental, social, and governance standards.

 # Notes for the CEO

Key Takeaway

If you want your company to be known as a high performer that meets its environmental, social, and governance (ESG) obligations, you need the active support of your suppliers.

Key Strategy

Require your CPO to work with suppliers to deliver ESG standards.

Key Tactics

- If you haven't already, join the race for net-zero carbon emissions. Ascertain the Scope 3 (upstream) emissions produced by your suppliers. Set ambitious targets and require progress reports.

- Redesign your products, your packaging, and your product portfolio for a low-carbon world. Incorporate more recycled and recyclable materials. Change your mix of products.

- Adjust your sourcing strategy for low-carbon business. Support near-shoring initiatives.

- Help your suppliers reduce their carbon emissions. Set out your expectations in a supplier code of conduct. Incorporate key points in your supplier contracts. Support suppliers in developing new capabilities. Sever ties with those that don't comply.

- Don't just focus on the *E* (environmental) in *ESG*. Ask your CPO to tackle the *S* (social) and the *G* (governance) as well.

9

Get Quicker,
Faster—as One

Go *Twice as Fast* by Collaborating with—
Not Competing Against—Your Suppliers

n February 2021, when the news broke that he would succeed Jeff Bezos as CEO of Amazon, Andy Jassy was quick to acknowledge his debt to the founder of the world's biggest retailer in an internal memo to staff. "It's hard," he wrote, "to overstate how much I've learned from Jeff over the past 24 years."[1] He then proceeded to list the lessons: how to obsess over customers, the importance of inventing, the criticality of hiring and developing great people, and the value of high standards and consistently speedy, outstanding delivery. Of these, it is speed—and specifically what Bezos himself calls the company's "insanely-fast shipping"—that has come to define the company's success.[2] Customer obsession may be Bezos's most sacrosanct principle, but speed is a close second, since it is a critical part of pleasing the customer. This was clear from Amazon's earliest days. In late August 1994, before he had settled on a name for what he claimed was his well-capitalized Seattle startup, Bezos posted his first job advertisement for computer programmers: "You must have experience designing and building large and complex (and yet maintainable) systems," he wrote, "but you should be able to do so in about one-third the time that most competent people think possible."[3]

Of course, by fixating on speed, Bezos was fixating on something that has long underpinned the success of the world's top-performing companies. As we have seen, Henry Ford invented the assembly line in the early 1900s, enabling him to churn out one Model T every ninety-three minutes and force competitors to play catch-up. Likewise, Toyota invented just-in-time manufacturing in the 1970s, allowing it to streamline production and race ahead of rivals in the United States and Europe. By the 1980s, Boston Consulting Group's George Stalk singled out time as "the next source of competitive advantage" in an article for *Harvard Business Review*.[4] Since then, speed has been a source of value, alongside cost, innovation, quality, sustainability, and risk management. Now the big question is not whether you can go fast but whether you can go faster—faster than your increasingly fast competitors.

This is not easy. We are living in a quickening world. In 2000, there were eighteen million Google searches every day. Now that number has risen to more than five billion. And in today's high-octane, always-on, 24-7 environment, consumers have come to expect Amazon-style same-day delivery. The situation is engendering a new creed for speed among top executives. "People ask, 'Is there a silver bullet?'" Ginni Rometty, then CEO of IBM, told the *New York Times* as she was working to turn around the 100-year-old technology behemoth. Her answer was clear: "The silver bullet, you might say, is speed, this idea of speed."[5]

But how do you speed up your business? There is, of course, an onus on every employee in the company to play their part. As Bill Gates put it in his book *Business @ the Speed of Thought*, "Everybody must realize that if you don't meet customer demand quickly enough, without sacrificing quality, a competitor will."[6] But in our view, there is a particular role for the CPO and the procurement team, hence our ninth principle: *Get quicker, faster—as one. Go twice as fast by collaborating with—not competing against—your suppliers.*

There are three main ways the CPO and the procurement team can help the CEO increase the speed with which their company anticipates, responds to, and meets the needs of customers. One way is to reconfigure the procurement process. Another way is to redesign the supply chain. A third is to reengineer the product-development process.

Reconfigure the Procurement Process

There are various ways that the CPO can reconfigure the procurement process. As we described earlier, one way is to use robots (which can do the job of four people) to automate all the routine administrative functions: this can reduce the time it takes to set in train complex capital projects by as much as 40 percent. Another way is to simplify the "red tape" that sometimes puts off up-and-coming, entrepreneurial suppliers that have significant strategic potential. These suppliers—often under-capitalized startups—may have some innovative product that will give the company first-mover advantage in the market, or they may even have some new way of speeding up the manufacturing process.

We advised one of the world's biggest white-goods manufacturers, which wanted to take on some of these innovative, energetic suppliers in a fast, frictionless way. We knew that most of them would find it difficult to jump through all the usual hoops that the company puts in the way of prospective suppliers. As a result, we recommended that the company completely reconfigure its procurement process for this special category of supplier. To start with, it ranked the suppliers among the important group—those that offered strategic potential and that may one day grow to become established key partners.

Then, to procure the services of these startups, it simplified the contracting process: it drew up a short, two-page contract with only the most essential commercial and technical terms (rather than a weighty document running into hundreds of pages designed to formalize a three-to-five-year relationship); it stripped out the warranty and indemnity clauses that would threaten to bankrupt startups; and it committed to paying bills in thirty days (rather than the standard ninety days) to alleviate cash-flow concerns.

By expediting the procurement process, the white-goods manufacturer became more attractive as a potential client to the up-and-coming suppliers—and it was able to bring new innovations more speedily to its customers.

Redesign the Supply Chain

As well as reconfiguring the procurement process, the CPO can redesign the supply chain in order to make the business more responsive to consumers. This is precisely what one fashion house has done, and it has come to define the entire industry.

It was in 1989 that Anne-Marie Schiro, a reporter for the *New York Times*, noticed that a new store, "an American outpost" of a little-known Spanish retailer, had just opened in Manhattan. She went to investigate, spoke with the store's manager, and was shocked to discover that, as she was told, "it takes 15 *days* between a new idea and getting it into the stores." Normally, fashion houses take between three and six *months* to launch a new collection. Back in the office, Schiro wrote up what she had found, and coined the term that has been used ever since to describe the business of delivering the latest on-trend apparel to customers in the quickest time possible: "fast fashion."[7]

The company Schiro had gone to see was Zara, and one of the big secrets of its success was—and remains—the way it works with suppliers. Now the flagship brand of Inditex, the world's biggest fashion retailer, Zara was founded in 1975 by Amancio Ortega in northern Spain (coincidentally, not far from where Ignacio López learned his trade).[8] Right from the start, his goal was to please his customers, and to do this, he decided he needed to overturn the traditional business model. Today, Ortega's approach is continued by Pablo Isla, Inditex's CEO. "Instead of designing a collection long before the season, and then working out whether clients like it or not," Isla once told the *Financial Times*, "we try to understand what our customers like, and then we design it and produce it."[9]

To design and produce garments in double-quick time, Inditex deploys several procurement strategies intended to take the complexity out of the process. First, it operates a dual-response supplier-manufacturer strategy that involves locating half of its factories close to its customers in Europe and the United States and the other half in the low-cost labor markets of Asia.[10] This approach contrasts with that practiced by traditional, or "slow," fashion houses, which are headquartered in Paris, New York, Milan, and London and which rely on manufacturers operating thousands of miles away in China and other countries in Asia.

Second, Inditex keeps a significant percentage of its factory capacity idle at certain points in the year, so that the company can be responsive to consumer sentiment. In other words, it pays manufacturers for keeping some flexibility in the system—just in case it needs to ramp up production at a moment's notice. This, of course, can be costly, but Inditex puts consumer responsiveness above cost effectiveness, because it believes that this ultimately leads to superior financial performance.

Third, it commits half of its inventory to fast fashion, in stark contrast to the standard practice of most fashion houses, which typically acquire as much as four-fifths of their inventory some six months in advance of a new season. By doing so, Inditex leaves room to tweak or completely overhaul its collection in response to new trends during the season.

Fourth, Inditex's world-beating fabric specialists on the procurement team (the kind of go-to experts we described in chapter 4 and chapter 6) focus on buying the *fabric* for the following year from suppliers—not the *finished goods*. They make a calculated bet on how much fabric they will need, knowing that it can be repurposed for different collections throughout the year.

Fifth, Inditex fosters a collaborative environment—inside and outside the company. Outside, procurement managers work closely with suppliers, looping them into the product-development process and coinvesting in new machinery and other technology. Inside the company, everything is centered at The Cube, Inditex's futuristic headquarters. At most fashion houses, the designers and other creative types call the shots. Not at Inditex. Here, where there is no single chief designer, hundreds of designers share offices with procurement executives and production managers. So when suppliers visit the company, they invariably end up meeting the design, procurement, and production managers. This collaboration, fostered by a close physical proximity, has created strong bonds among Inditex's executives in the different functions, encouraging them to feel that they co-own the product, ensuring that decisions flow through the company quickly, and allowing the company to be ultraresponsive to consumer demands.[11]

As a result of Inditex's unconventional approach to working with suppliers, the founder, Amancio Ortega, is now ranked among the world's richest billionaires. Not surprisingly, he has attracted many fast followers.

• • •

Many companies are now choosing local suppliers—not only for speed but also to reduce their carbon footprint or avoid geopolitical tangles. Responding to this trend, some major suppliers have started shifting or setting up operations close to *their* traditional buyers. For example, TSMC, which serves Apple and Tesla, has begun construction of a $12 billion facility in Arizona.[12]

But it is not always possible or desirable for companies to use local suppliers. In some cases, the necessary expertise may just not be available. So, what then? One option is to simplify the supply chain by taking out any strictly unnecessary links. This is what one US computer company did after its CPO and procurement team investigated the supply of microchips they used and found a very convoluted supply chain. The microchips' journey started in Singapore, at a New York–headquartered firm's factory. Once made, the microchips were flown nearly 2,800 miles to Beijing, where they were packaged or incorporated into an integrated circuit board by a European-headquartered company. Next, they were sent another 6,500 miles east to Phoenix, Arizona, where the microchips were programmed with the latest software by a local electronics business. After that, they were flown back 6,700 miles to China, this time to Shanghai, where the microchips were installed into computer hardware by another US-based corporation. Finally, they were sent on a relatively short hop west—500 miles—to the computer company's sprawling factory in Wuhan to be incorporated into the finished product. Reviewing this extraordinary, 16,500-mile odyssey for just one part (albeit an important part) of the company's computers, the CPO decided to shorten the supply chain and withdrew the software-programming contract from the Arizona-based company. In so doing, the company cut the journey the microchips were taking by 80 percent and reduced the production time by five weeks.

Reengineer the Product-Development Process

As well as reconfiguring the procurement process and redesigning the supply chain, CEOs should consider reengineering the product-development process to increase speed to market. Here, once again, the CPO and procurement function can play an important role in getting suppliers to work in a collaborative way. As we saw earlier with Ocean Victory Corporation and the big pharmaceutical companies, CPOs can be instrumental in a company's efforts to get early, privileged access to products and advanced technology being developed by startups and other suppliers. It goes without saying that by being first to the market with new innovations, companies can gain a significant competitive advantage. But there are other ways to achieve this market-leading edge.

Use a diversity of suppliers to accelerate product development—how the US Army built the Humvee's successor

In late 2006, five years after the 9/11 terrorist attacks, the US military decided it needed a new vehicle to help prosecute the Global War on Terror in Afghanistan and Iraq. Soldiers riding in the High-Mobility Multipurpose Wheeled Vehicle—the HMMWV, or Humvee—were falling victim to the growing number of improvised explosive devices (IEDs), which were cheap, easy to make, and deadly. The mighty vehicle may have become an icon of America's assault on Osama bin Laden, Al-Qaeda, and their fanatical supporters, but its flat-bottomed design was leaving soldiers vulnerable to murderous roadside bombs.

It did not take long for US generals to select the MRAP—a mine-resistant ambush-protected vehicle—as the Humvee's successor. This

vehicle was not actually state-of-the-art. It was developed by South African Defense Force engineers in the 1960s. But its defining features—a raised chassis and a V-shaped hull—were highly effective in nullifying the impact of a mine blast. In other words, it could do the job of protecting American soldiers fighting on the front line.[13]

The big problem was time: the US commanders needed the MRAPs *now*. How could they get them fast? The procurement, or acquisition, chiefs decided to accelerate the normal product-development cycle, overturning decades of conventional military procurement practice by ordering vehicles not from one carefully selected supplier but from a small group of specialist suppliers. In a way, it was mirroring what NASA did when it commissioned Boeing and SpaceX to develop rocket-powered transport vehicles to succeed the iconic Shuttle spacecraft.

In November 2006, the US military issued a request for proposal for designing and manufacturing 1,185 MRAPs. It received ten bids, and by January 2007, it had awarded nine companies so-called indefinite delivery, indefinite quantity (IDIQ) contracts with production orders for a minimum number of prototype vehicles that could be submitted for testing. Three months later, after the prototypes had been tested at Aberdeen Proving Ground, in Maryland, the list of suppliers was whittled down to five: BAE Systems, Armor Holdings (now owned by BAE Systems), General Dynamics Land Systems, Force Protection Industries (now owned by General Dynamics Land Systems), and Navistar's International Military and Government subsidiary (now called Navistar Defense). The decision to select five suppliers proved critical, because over the next five months, field commanders increased their demand for MRAPs—first to 7,774 vehicles, in May, and then to 15,374, in September.

What made the MRAP product-development process a success was the way the US military, as buyer, collaborated with the five different vehicle supplier-manufacturers. First, the IDIQ contract was important: the US military agreed to buy all of the minimum amounts ordered from each manufacturer, reducing the usual risk suppliers bear when pitching for business. Second, a generous cash incentive—$100,000 per vehicle for delivery of test MRAPs ahead of agreed schedules—encouraged willing participation. Third, the product specifications were broad: in essence, the suppliers could work to their own designs, and as long as their vehicles passed the "survivability" test, they were given the green light. Fourth, the different phases of contracting, testing, and launching that would historically have been conducted consecutively were managed concurrently to fast-track development. Fifth, the US high command did not guarantee that all manufacturers would be given a production contract, leaving them with the thought that there was a winner-take-all opportunity for the fastest to design, test, and deliver their MRAPs. Sixth, the US military helped orchestrate the network of suppliers who supplied the MRAP manufacturers—for example, steelmakers and tire manufacturers—to make sure there was no delay in the delivery of all the necessary raw materials and components for making the vehicles.

The first MRAPs started entering battle zones in October 2007—less than a year after companies were invited to bid for contracts. This represented a dramatic reduction in the speed-to-market of military vehicles, which normally takes ten years.

Build country-specific or region-specific supplier ecosystems—how big tech companies can learn from Chinese smartphone manufacturers

Another way CEOs can increase their companies' speed-to-market is to build ecosystems of suppliers in the countries or regions where they are targeting specific consumers. Depending on the country and the industry, this approach offers real value to companies looking to fast-track their product-development process. Take China's smartphone industry, for example. Now the biggest smartphone market in the world—in 2020, some 325 million units were shipped in the country, 25 percent of the total shipped around the world—China has provided a tremendous proving ground for several domestic smartphone companies that have expanded internationally, including Huawei (until the United States restricted sales of vital American-made components to the company, slowing the smartphone maker's growth), Xiaomi, Oppo, and Vivo.[14] One of the keys to Chinese smartphone makers' astonishing success is the speed with which the companies can develop a new smartphone and launch it into the market. On average, it takes less than six months for Chinese smartphones to go from the drawing board to consumers' hands. By contrast, US and European companies can take three years to develop a new smartphone from scratch.

What is the secret? China's extraordinary network of technology suppliers.

This network, or ecosystem, emerged initially to create so-called *shanzhai* products—cheap, imitation, and even counterfeit smartphones (and other consumer goods). But two factors have helped transform the ecosystem into a sophisticated network of design and manufacturing suppliers. First, Chinese consumers have developed the taste for high-end, but affordable, products. Second, the US decision to put some Chinese companies on its so-called Entity List (which effectively prevents US corporations from selling critical components to listed companies) forced these companies to rely more heavily on Chinese-sourced components. According to a report published in the *Financial Times*, a teardown of Huawei's Mate 30 smartphone found that parts made in China constituted 42 percent of the total value of the components—up from 25 percent when the company could still buy US-made components.[15]

As a result, China's suppliers now have the technical expertise to deliver globally branded products for the local market. (This means that global companies have the option to develop products that respond to the needs and reflect the tastes of Chinese consumers in an affordable and fast way.) Also, China's smartphone makers have developed some fast-track product-development techniques that global companies should consider applying in their own domestic as well as other international markets. One strategy is to relax product specifications (as the US military did in the case of MRAPs): China's smartphone makers are happy with slightly older (rather than next-generation) technology and slightly lower-grade components as long as these meet certain minimum performance standards. Another strategy is to buy from one local supplier (rather than multiple global suppliers), pay cash immediately (rather than after a ninety-day period), and make monthly (rather than one-time) purchase orders. A third strategy is to use a modular approach with common off-the-shelf parts—battery cells, LCD panels, and circuit boards—across several products.

Test out "gigafactories," microfactories, and smart factories—how Tesla and Unilever are accelerating their products' journey to consumers

As well as building local and regional ecosystems, CEOs should instruct the CPO and the rest of the executive team to optimize their company's manufacturing process for speed-to-market. Obviously, the manufacturing function must be the key driver, but the procurement procurement has a critical but often overlooked role to play as the orchestrator of not only the contract manufacturers (if the company itself does not do the manufacturing) but also the suppliers of raw materials to the factories.

Tesla is betting on so-called gigafactories to accelerate the production of battery cells and other key components to meet consumer demand for its electric vehicles. In a sense, Elon Musk is harking back to the glory days of Henry Ford, whose River Rouge factory complex in Dearborn, Michigan, sprawled over nine hundred acres. Tesla's massive gigafactories present significant procurement challenges. Building the facilities is the least of those challenges. (Tesla's Shanghai factory took just eleven months to construct.) Feeding those factories with enormous supplies of raw materials to make the lithium-ion batteries that power the electric vehicles is a far greater challenge. So too is managing the relationship with the various battery makers that partner with Tesla in these gigafactories—notably Japan's Panasonic, South Korea's LG Chem, and China's CATL.[16]

By contrast, several other companies are experimenting with microfactories that are equipped with 3D printing technology, that make parts as well as finished products in small batches, and that can be erected quickly in different markets to be ultraresponsive to local consumers. Again, the CEO should instruct the CPO to play a critical role, sourcing not only the latest digital manufacturing equipment but also, if the factories are actually portable, the suppliers in the different local markets. Unilever, for example, has built what it calls nanofactories in forty-foot shipping containers. They are, as the company says, a completely movable asset that can be picked up and dropped anywhere. Not only that, but these mobile minimanufacturing hubs house "everything we need to produce a batch, from the point where raw materials go in at one end to where finished products come out at the other—bottled, capped, and labeled."[17]

Conclusion

In a quickening world, speed is paramount. Working on their own, companies may be able to go fast, but working with suppliers, they can go faster—twice as fast. It's a proven fact. This is why our ninth principle is so essential for all companies. It pays due recognition to the fact that suppliers can act like booster rockets for a company's business (and vice versa).

 # Notes for the CEO

Key Takeaway

If you want to increase the speed with which your company anticipates, responds to, and meets the needs of customers, you need to find faster ways to work with your suppliers.

Key Strategy

Tell your CPO to reconfigure the procurement process, redesign the supply chain, and reengineer the product-development process.

Key Tactics

- Reconfigure your procurement process by automating all of the routine administrative tasks and simplifying the contracts for up-and-coming suppliers that offer game-changing innovations.

- Redesign your supply chain by using local suppliers, keeping some spare manufacturing capacity, encouraging suppliers to relocate nearer to you, and reducing the number of suppliers.

- Reengineer the product-development process by using a diversity of suppliers, building country- or region-specific supplier networks, and testing out a variety of very large and very small manufacturing plants.

10

Anticipate the Inevitable

Halve Your Risks by Working with Your Suppliers to Predict the Unexpected

On the last day of 2019, the China office of the World Health Organization received unconfirmed accounts of a new virus, and within weeks, as the contagion circulated more widely, reports of the first deaths from Covid-19 hit the headlines. Over the next eighteen months, the virus spread around the world, causing countries to impose strict lockdown measures and sending the global economy into a tailspin. With global supply chains broken, companies were forced to shutter factories, abandon offices, and lay off workers. Thousands of companies closed for business—and some closed down altogether.

Business leaders were mostly unprepared for this kind of natural disaster. As a result, they soon started calling the global pandemic a "black swan" event. This phrase, coined by the mathematician and philosopher Nassim Nicholas Taleb, describes random, highly improbable events that have enormous impact.[1] It echoes an earlier and equally memorable phrase coined by Donald Rumsfeld, former US Secretary of Defense, to describe such unusual events: "unknown unknowns."[2] As the Covid-19 pandemic swept around the world, business leaders started applying the black-swan label to several other disruptive events for which they were similarly unprepared. In mid-February 2021, a fierce ice storm swept through Texas, home to some of the world's biggest manufacturers of semiconductors, plastics, and other petrochemical products. It was one of the worst winter weather events on record in Texas, and triggered a worldwide shortage of plastics and compounded the troubles already affecting the semiconductor supply chain.[3]

Then, in late March 2021, one of the world's largest container ships, *Ever Given*, was passing through the narrow Suez Canal when a sandstorm caused the ship's captain to lose control of the vessel. It veered off course, ran aground, and blocked the canal for every other ship. For the next six days, workers struggled to free the stranded giant, which was laden with 18,300 containers filled with a variety of goods. Some three hundred other ships were forced to queue up outside the canal, through which 12 percent of global trade must pass to get to market.[4]

And in May 2021, Colonial Pipeline, the operator of a 5,500-mile pipeline that carries gasoline and other fuel from Texas up the East Coast to New York, was hit by a ransomware cyberattack undertaken by a Russia-based group of hackers.[5] The most disruptive cyberattack in US history, it affected some fifty million Americans and thousands of companies, creating fuel shortages, stalling business transactions, leaving airplanes grounded, and interrupting shipments.

In their different ways, these disparate and unconnected events were hugely disruptive for companies. But if they were unusual, they should not be categorized as black-swan events. Every one of them was perfectly predictable. No one can truly say they weren't warned.

A global pandemic, a breach of cybersecurity, a blockage in one of the main trade arteries—these should all be recognized not as distant possibilities but as distinct *probabilities.*

So, how should CEOs prepare for these kinds of events? They should follow our tenth principle and instruct the CPO and procurement team to: *Anticipate the inevitable. Halve your risks by working with your suppliers to predict the unexpected.* CPOs should codevelop long-term strategies designed to make their companies more resilient in the face of disruptive, if predictable, events. Also, they should put in place short-term contingency plans designed to help their companies cope when the unexpected really does happen. But first, before doing any of this, they should commit to a new kind of leadership, one forged by US commanders during the Global War on Terror.

Leadership in a Crisis: "Extreme Ownership" and the Lessons of the US Navy SEALs

"Whose fault is it?" That was the question Jocko Willink, a top US Navy SEAL commander, asked his platoon. He was looking for someone to blame. His SEALs—members of the elite special forces that tracked down and killed Osama bin Laden—had just participated in a brutal firefight on the streets of Ramadi, in Iraq. They thought they had been shooting terrorists. But they weren't. It was only when the fog of war lifted that they discovered they had engaged in friendly fire, killing one Iraqi soldier, wounding others, and suffering their own casualties. As Willink put it, the battle was "a firefight between us and . . . us."[6]

After a brief silence, the SEAL who had fatally shot the Iraqi soldier raised his hand. "It was my fault," he said. "I should have positively identified my target." Willink praised the SEAL for his honesty but said, "No, it wasn't your fault." Again he looked around the room, this time with a menacing stare. Another SEAL put up his hand. Once more, Willink said, "No, it wasn't your fault." For the next few minutes, more SEALs raised their hands to admit their guilt in the tragedy. But every time, Willink said, "No, it wasn't your fault, either."

"So whose fault is it?" Willink asked one more time. There was silence, and then he spoke again. "There is only one person to blame for this: me. I am the commander. There is no one to blame but me. And I will tell you this right now: I will make sure that nothing like this ever happens to us again." As leader, he understood that he had to take full responsibility for *everything*. In other words, he had to take *extreme ownership*. "On any team, in any organization, all responsibility for success and failure rests with the leader," he writes in his book *Extreme Ownership: How US Navy SEALs Lead and Win*. "The leader must acknowledge mistakes and admit failures, take ownership of them, and develop a plan to win."

It is this kind of extreme ownership, the kind that military leaders show on the battlefield, that business leaders should show in the boardroom. In the context of putting suppliers at the core of their business and empowering the CPO and procurement team, this means CEOs taking (rather than shirking) responsibility for anticipating inevitable, if unusual, events. But it raises a question: Why should CEOs have to spend so much time, so many resources, and such reputational capital on anticipating events that, according to the definition, are highly improbable and few and far between? There are several answers.

First, most of the admittedly challenging events affecting companies are not true black-swan events. Far from being highly improbable, they are what have been called "gray rhinos"—highly probable, highly predictable, high-impact, but neglected threats that are charging toward the company like a crash of rhinos.[7] The big freeze that forced the Texas petrochemical and semiconductor complex to shut down in

2021 was caused by a polar vortex—a band of strong westerly winter winds that forms in the stratosphere up to thirty miles above the North Pole—that is becoming increasingly common as a result of climate change.[8] But if it hadn't been a polar vortex that closed factories, it could have been any number of other common natural phenomena, such as hurricanes or floods. In 2017, Hurricane Harvey swept through the Lone Star state, killing more than a hundred people, destroying homes, forcing factories to stop production, and causing more than $125 billion worth of damage.[9] As certain as night follows day, such disasters will happen again.

Similarly, the Suez Canal blockage and the closure of the East Coast pipeline could have been foreseen. As recently as 2017, there was a temporary blockage in the Suez Canal, when the captain of *OOCL Japan* lost control of the container ship after its steering gear malfunctioned. Before that, there were blockages in 2006 and 2004.[10] Meanwhile, Colonial Pipeline has regularly had to halt the operation of parts (if not all) of its East Coast pipeline as a result of hurricanes, leaks, explosions, and "integrity issues."[11]

Even the Covid-19 pandemic, which on the face of it has the biggest claim to being a black-swan event, was predictable—and, indeed, predicted. Back in 2015, Bill Gates, speaking after the outbreak of Ebola, had said that the world needed to prepare to fight microbes, not "missiles, because if anything kills over 10 million people in the next few decades, it's most likely to be a highly infectious virus rather than a war."[12] Then, in September 2019, just three months before the Covid-19 outbreak, the Global Preparedness Monitoring Board, a panel of experts convened by the World Health Organization and the World Bank, reported that "there is a very real threat of a rapidly moving, highly lethal pandemic of a respiratory pathogen killing 50 to 80 million people."[13] Its warning, which garnered little attention, followed the devastating impact of the SARS epidemic in 2003, the H1N1 influenza pandemic in 2009, and the West African Ebola outbreak in

2014—all of which were, like Covid-19, caused by zoonotic viruses that spread from animals to humans.

So these are "when," not "if," events. Thus, CEOs really have no excuse not to prepare for them. But preparing for them is not just about protecting on the downside but also about profiting on the upside. There are some real, tangible benefits for CEOs who get their company ready for the next crisis. For a start, companies that are well prepared and as a result prosper in a crisis can expect to recover more quickly than their competitors. In a review of corporate performance during the past four US downturns (since 1985), Boston Consulting Group (BCG) found that 14 percent of companies *increased* their sales and their profit margin.[14] Also, it is clear that investors are starting to reward companies that build for the future by becoming more innovative and more resilient. In June 2020, during the depths of the Covid-19 pandemic, BCG surveyed major institutional investors and found that nine out of ten believed it was "important for healthy companies to prioritize the building of business capabilities—even if it means lowering earnings-per-share guidance or delivering below consensus."[15]

CEOs have every reason to prepare for the next crisis—and no reason not to. But how, exactly, should they prepare? If they buy the idea that they must take extreme ownership, what do they need to do to, as Jocko Willink said, "develop a plan to win"? They need to build long-term resilience and short-term responsiveness.

From Just-in-Time to Just-in-Case: How to Prepare for "When," Not "If"

Over several decades, companies have, in their quest for ever greater lean efficiency and improved customer service, perfected their global supply chains according to the principles of just-in-time: keeping costly inventories to a minimum and coordinating deliveries of raw materials and components from suppliers so that they arrive just in time to be incorporated into the finished product. This system is unlikely to be scrapped anytime soon. Anders Williamsson, the head of purchasing at the VW-owned Swedish truckmaker Scania, which has production facilities in Europe, Latin America, China, and India, has described the situation well: "It would be a romantic dream to think we would be able to get all the competencies and capabilities we need into European or Swedish soil. That will never happen."[16]

On the other hand, the shock of the Covid-19 pandemic to global supply chains has forced companies to accept that they must build in some overcapacity—or redundancy, to use the jargon—as well as some flexibility and forward-thinking. In short, they must switch from just-in-time to just-in-case. To do that, they must establish an effective sensing and risk-monitoring operation, simplify their product portfolio, de-risk their supply chain, and take back control of the supply of critical raw materials and components.

Create a world-class risk-monitoring operation

When Jeff Bezos launched Amazon, he liked to quote the American computer scientist Alan Kay, who said: "It's easier to invent the future than predict it."[17] Some twenty-seven years later, Bezos returned to this theme when he stood down as Amazon's chief executive. Signing off with an email to employees, he wrote: "Keep inventing, and don't despair when at first the idea looks crazy. Remember to wander. Let curiosity be your compass. It remains day one."[18]

But although invention and innovation are key to a company's future, and prediction is hard to do, CEOs must nevertheless prepare for what comes next by getting a clear view of the likely risks in their supply chain—as well as the unlikely risks, to the extent that's possible. To do this, they need to invest in risk intelligence and strategic foresight, creating a team of procurement superforecasters equipped with the latest AI-powered sensing technology. If the Covid-19 pandemic has taught them anything, it is that they should never again be blindsided by a perfectly predictable, if only occasional, natural occurrence.

Too often, a company's monitoring efforts rarely extend beyond its direct, or Tier 1, suppliers and tend to be decentralized, typically relying on manual and gut-feel analysis, and the resulting insights are often poorly disseminated through the organization. All this needs to change: risk monitoring should extend to Tier N suppliers, encompass multiple risk factors in a single supplier-risk score, and draw on the latest AI and other digital technologies. Also, the insights should be distributed across the organization through compelling dashboard presentations customized for different audiences. For global companies, there is no single provider that offers a one-stop solution with the sophistication that is really required in these uncertain times. Companies must therefore develop their own bespoke risk-sensing and risk-mitigation solution. What are the critical elements of such a system?

First, companies need to understand the different types of risk. We see eight essential risk categories—four associated with individual suppliers (operational, financial, reputational, and structural risks), three associated with a supplier's country or region (disaster, and geopolitical and fiscal risks), and one associated with a supplier's industry (industry risks). Within each of these categories, there are three or four specific risks, and a total of around thirty. For example, a supplier's structural risk might be its dependence on one or two Tier N suppliers, or its involvement in a hostile-takeover bid. A supplier's geopolitical risk might be its operations in a war zone or a territory that imposes tariffs and other trade barriers. And a supplier's industry risk might be its dependence on one or two monopolistic suppliers who then suffer a production delay.

Having established the framework of the risk-sensing and risk-mitigation system, companies need to feed it with internal and supplier data drawn from the company and the supplier's enterprise-resource-planning system, as well as data drawn from external news, public information, and other such sources. The data should be linked to specific key-risk indicators (KRIs). For example, operational-risk KRIs might be the age of a supplier's machinery or the percentage of employees in workers' unions; industry-risk KRIs might be the concentration of suppliers that could lead to bottlenecks, or a supplier's R&D into innovative technology and the risk of obsolescence. Disaster-risk KRIs might be the number of people vaccinated in the country and at the supplier, or the number of power outages suffered by the company.

This data-feeding process is not a one-time effort—it must be automated so that the company gets an ongoing, real-time view of the changing risks to the business. With this data, and with the help of an AI-powered algorithm, the specific risk can be plotted on a two-by-two matrix, with the y-axis reflecting the detectability of the risk and the x-axis reflecting the impact of the risk. The four quadrants of the matrix correspond to: limited risk, or hard-to-detect events that have a noncritical impact; manageable risk, or easy-to-detect events that have a noncritical impact; disruptive risk, or hard-to-detect events that have a critical impact; and high-risk, or easy-to-detect events that have a critical impact.

After doing this, companies can then determine what they need to do next. If a risk is deemed to be limited, then it can be deprioritized and occasionally reviewed for any increased detectability. If a risk is found to be manageable, then it can be subject to automated tracking and daily review. If a risk is disruptive, then a company must establish its likely probability, hedge proactively, simulate any possible negative impact, and prepare a reaction plan. Finally, if a risk is deemed high, then a company must actively monitor the situation and take urgent steps to reduce the risk.

Simplify your product portfolio

In the past few years, it has been the goal of companies to give consumers what they, as individuals, really want. Niche, highly personalized, "segment of one" products and services, made cost-effective by a lean supply chain and supported by targeted advertising that uses data mined from consumers' online activity, have become the norm. The trouble is that the number of stock-keeping units (SKUs) has risen dramatically.[19] Often low-margin, and lacking a strategic purpose, they can be so specialized that they do not share common raw materials and components with other SKUs, require a broader range of suppliers, and lead to higher manufacturing, freight, and out-of-stock costs and an increased risk of waste.

For these reasons, the product portfolio should be scrutinized and probably scaled back. But how do you decide which products to keep and which to cut? More than fifty years ago, Bruce Henderson, Boston Consulting Group's founder, wrote a short essay, simply called "The Product Portfolio," in which he introduced the simple two-by-two growth-share matrix to help CEOs make their decisions. He encouraged companies to divide their products into four groups: stars (whose "high share and high growth assure the future"), cash cows (whose high market share but low growth prospects "supply funds for . . . future growth"), question marks (whose low market share but high growth prospects could be "converted into stars with the added funds" from the cash cows), and finally pets (whose "failure . . . to obtain a leadership position during the growth phase" means they are simply "not necessary").[20]

After all these years, there is still no easier way to simplify your product portfolio than to use the BCG growth-share matrix. A variation on this theme is to take a cost–value approach. With this, the four quadrants in the matrix are: advance (which includes high-margin, high-advantage products that should be supported for their differentiating value); streamline (which includes low-margin, high-advantage products that are highly differentiated but need a margin boost through increased prices, reduced service levels or lower complexity); maintain (which includes high-margin, low-advantage products that are profitable but lack a competitive edge and need some differentiating customer value); and phase out (which includes low-margin, low-advantage products that should be eliminated immediately or over time if their cash contribution becomes negative).[21]

As well as eliminating entire product lines and minimizing SKUs, companies should modify their remaining products by simplifying their design, harmonizing their specifications, and standardizing their constituent raw materials, components, and other ingredients, as well as their packaging materials.[22]

De-risk your supply chain

In the face of all these risks, the lean mantra that procurement leaders have been reciting for several decades now needs to be accompanied by another: on resilience. But there is no single, straightforward way to create a resilient supply chain. That's because different crises create different challenges for companies. For example, it is clear from the Covid-19 outbreak that pandemics badly affect *labor-intensive* supply chains: the world's workforce was prevented from working for extended periods of time. By contrast, hurricanes, floods, and earthquakes badly affect *asset-intensive* supply chains. When the Great Tohoku earthquake and resulting tsunami struck the northeast of Japan, in March 2011, the sole factory manufacturing the world's supply of Xirallic pigment, which gives cars their glittering shine, was damaged in the disaster. As a consequence, stocks of the glossy paint were quickly depleted, forcing carmakers to switch to duller colors or postpone production. Meanwhile, the United States–China trade war showed how global supply chains are vulnerable to geopolitical risks.

So, how should companies de-risk their supply chains?

They need to consider a series of risk-mitigation actions that encompass the three elements of the supply chain: *sourcing* the raw materials, components, and other parts of products; *manufacturing* the products; and *delivering* the parts to the factories and the products to the customers.[23] In all cases, companies should take a just-in-case perspective by building in some overcapacity and greater flexibility. Clearly, these decisions need to be made jointly by the CEO and the executive board—but the CEO should make sure the CPO takes the central role.

For sourcing, companies should optimize (which today can mean increasing, not just reducing) the inventory of raw materials and other key components, persuade suppliers to shift some production to more-convenient locations (as TSMC has done), qualify new ready-to-go suppliers in various countries, and commit to a program of dual or multiple sourcing so that the supply of essential components is never interrupted by problems with one supplier.

For manufacturing, companies should review their make-or-buy strategy, consider investing in digital technologies such as 3D printing, qualify ready-to-go contract manufacturers who can step up production in cases of disruption, and above all, switch manufacturing to locations at home (reshoring), closer to home (near-shoring), or closer to consumer markets (regionalization).

As we have seen, the fast-fashion industry has long valued local manufacturing—primarily for speed. It is now enjoying the additional benefits of improved sustainability and lower supply-chain risk. Also, Unilever has invested in highly mobile "nanofactories" that can be sited pretty much anywhere. Likewise, Airbus, the world's largest aircraft manufacturer, has built assembly plants in several key locations around the world. Initially, its A320 aircraft, which was launched in 1987, was assembled exclusively in Toulouse and Hamburg, with components coming from four countries—France, Germany, Spain, and the United Kingdom. Since then, Airbus has opened an assembly plant in the Chinese city of Tianjin to supply A320s to Chinese airlines, and opened another assembly plant in Mobile, Alabama.

For delivering, companies should qualify new and additional distribution partners, rethink types of freight transport (land, air, or ocean), and shift warehousing and finished-goods distribution closer to consumer markets.

Take back control of mission-critical supplies

It is a bizarre fact that many global companies (and small companies too) do not necessarily know which supplier contributed which part to which of their products. Given this, it is not surprising that they rarely know the identity of the suppliers to their suppliers. It is perhaps not essential that a company knows who supplies the paper clips and other low-value office supplies, but it's a very different story when it comes to mission-critical supplies. This was brought into sharp relief during the Covid-19 global pandemic. All kinds of companies—high-tech companies, automotive companies, makers of electronic household goods—were left floundering as they tried to secure access to regular supplies of the usually ubiquitous semiconductor.

The semiconductor is the workhorse of the modern world. Otherwise known as a microchip or integrated circuit, it is found in everything from computers and smartphones to cars, airplanes, container ships, health-care devices, gaming consoles, fridges, vacuum cleaners, and power drills. When it is there, no one thinks about it. When it's not, the whole world stops—and that's what happened in 2020. In March, as Covid-19 cases rose exponentially and countries went into lockdown, many companies revised their sales forecasts and canceled their orders for semiconductors. But as soon as countries emerged from the first lockdowns in the summer and sales picked up faster than expected, the companies that had canceled orders called their suppliers to resume deliveries. But they were told that there was a semiconductor shortage.

What had happened?

There were three reasons for the shortage. First, there had been a big (but predicted) rise in the number of devices with increased semiconductor technology—from image-signal processors in cameras to display-touch controllers in smart watches and electric cars. Second, there had been a big (and also predicted) rollout of new devices, such as Apple's new 5G iPhones and Sony and Microsoft's new gaming consoles. Third (and this was the curveball), the migration to working from home, as governments imposed lockdowns during the Covid-19 pandemic, had led to a significant spike in the sales of personal computers (up 5 percent, after years of decline) and an even steeper rise in cloud-computing investment by the big technology companies.

The shortage affected all electronics companies. But it particularly hurt automotive companies. Why? When they canceled their orders in March, they went to the back of the queue for semiconductors. And in their case, it is a very long queue, because as an industry, the automakers account for approximately 10 percent of semiconductor sales and less than 5 percent of the revenues of the foundries that make the semiconductors. This exposed what is a very unequal balance of power: the auto industry is a relatively insignificant customer of the semiconductor industry, yet semiconductors are mission-critical to the auto industry. It is odd, therefore, that automakers typically have no meaningful relationship with the full range of semiconductor companies. Instead, they rely on the services of general automotive suppliers, such as Bosch and Continental, who procure the semiconductors for them.

Clearly, this needs to change. Companies need to take back control.

Not so long ago, during a previous semiconductor shortage (they happen on a frequent, if irregular, basis), we helped a US technology company take back control of its supply of semiconductors. Facing the prospect of temporarily shutting down production—at a cost of $100 million—the company solved the short-term problem by sourcing emergency supplies of semiconductors from new suppliers. It then addressed the long-term problem by developing contractual relationships with companies that are instrumental in every stage of the semiconductor supply chain. These include the semiconductor vendors (such as Infineon and NXP), the foundries (such as TSMC and GlobalFoundries), the integrated-circuit makers (such as JCET and Amkor), and the distributors (such as Avnet and Arrow Electronics).

Some automakers were less affected by the semiconductor shortage. Tesla, for example, goes one step beyond what most automakers are currently contemplating—not only do the company's procurement leaders build direct relationships with foundries, but the company even takes ownership of the vital components by designing its own microchips.

The Crisis Playbook: What to Do If the Unexpected *Really Does Happen*

Most of a CPO's time spent on risk-reduction activities should be focused on foreseeable events. But what if a real black-swan event does affect the company? What then? Actually, the experience of many companies during the Covid-19 global pandemic is instructive. Of course, as we have explained, it was not a black-swan event—it was perfectly predictable. But the fact that few, if any, companies had made adequate preparation for an epidemic made the Covid-19 disaster a de facto black-swan event.

What are the lessons?

We found that the companies that fared best—other than those companies that were in the right industry at the right time, such as Zoom (video communication) or Amazon (home delivery and cloud computing) or a variety of other digital firms, including CrowdStrike (cybersecurity), Sea Group (Southeast Asia's most valuable company, focusing on gaming, e-commerce, and digital payments), and Chewy (the online retailer of pet food and accessories)—were those that moved swiftly to do three things: stabilize their supply chain, harvest cost-reduction and cash opportunities, and prepare for the rebound.[24]

Stabilize your supply chain

If a crisis hits, the first thing CEOs need to do is stabilize their supply chain. They should start by approaching their most important suppliers, who will be the A suppliers in their company's 360° program, as well as all the vendors (whether they are A suppliers or not) of mission-critical raw materials, components, and other parts. Ideally, CEOs (or CPOs) should call, text, or email the CEOs of these suppliers and pose four questions:

1. What is the best way for both of our companies to ride out this storm, including measures to protect against financial difficulties?

2. What can we as a customer do to help stabilize your supply chain?

3. What can you as a supplier do to make our products more competitive in a shrinking market?

4. What can we do jointly to come out on top in the rebound?

As part of this outreach, CEOs need to instruct their CPOs to seek preferred access to the suppliers' production capacity for the duration of the crisis as well as for the post-crisis period.

Having done this, CPOs should be encouraged to focus on the company's top ten products, prepare a dashboard of missing parts, and develop a mitigation plan that might include agreeing to new delivery times and order volumes, changing freight routes, drawing on prequalified backup suppliers, and finding alternative parts.

And while this is going on, CEOs should establish a 24-7 command, or war, room to coordinate all of the activities and communication with suppliers. This should be staffed with a cross-functional team of experts from procurement as well as from operations, marketing, quality control, and finance. There should be a directly responsible individual (DRI) for each critical activity: safeguarding production output (and, if necessary, switching suppliers to ensure minimal disruption of goods and services), tracking shipments using the most-advanced monitoring technology, proactively supporting mission-critical suppliers, and spotting cost-reduction opportunities.

Harvest cost-reduction and cash opportunities

"Never let a good crisis go to waste." These words, spoken by Sir Winston Churchill when he was working with world powers to create the United Nations, are still as relevant today as they were then. However, the move to cut costs in the middle of a crisis is not about profiting from others' misfortune but rather about strengthening a company so that it can survive a black-swan event. Cost cutting is essential for a company to remain competitive in a shrinking market, to retain an active workforce so that production does not have to be interrupted, and to fund the continuing supply of mission-critical parts. During the Covid-19 pandemic, companies found a variety of ways to benefit from market-price fluctuations and suppliers' lower input costs.

For example, at the start of the crisis, there was a sharp drop in global demand for industrial plastics, as automotive and other companies canceled orders (of course, this would later change, after the Arctic blast hit the Texas petrochemical complex). In the space of three months, the price of phenolic resins fell by 45 percent, reducing the costs of plastics manufacturers, who are suppliers to a wide variety of companies. Some of these companies hurriedly renegotiated their contracts with the plastics manufacturers and shared some of the savings. In another case, companies carried out should-cost analyses after a big decrease in diesel prices caused by a drop in global demand for the fuel, and they promptly renegotiated their contracts with suppliers of logistics services who were not passing on the savings.

Prepare for the rebound

In the midst of a crisis, it is hard to extract yourself from the here-and-now to contemplate what might happen next. But it is essential that you do—and one of the senior DRIs in the war room should be tasked with focusing on the future. To some extent, companies that have already taken steps to make their supply chain more resilient by simplifying their product portfolio, de-risking the supply chain, and taking back control of critical supplies will be well positioned for the post-crisis phase.

Nevertheless, the crisis is a key moment to revisit these activities. Which products will be critical as the world emerges from the downturn? Which suppliers will be vital partners during the recovery? These and other questions will need to be asked and answered. It's also important that CEOs create a series of ramp-up scenarios, so that the company can cope with all eventualities.

Conclusion

Companies can double their savings, their innovation, their quality, their sustainability, and their speed. But as we have shown, if they are to claim the full range of supplier-related benefits, they must also double their risk-reduction capability—and thereby halve the number of risks they run every day. As always, suppliers hold the key to success. Help them, and they will help you. Do so in a crisis, and their loyalty will be all the greater.

 ## Notes for the CEO

Key Takeaway

If you want to halve your risks from possible existential crises, you need to call on the help of your suppliers.

Key Strategy

Order your CPO to anticipate the inevitable by codeveloping with your suppliers both long-term strategies designed to make your company more resilient and short-term contingency plans designed to help your company cope when the unexpected really does happen.

Key Tactics

- Commit to a new kind of leadership: "extreme ownership." Don't make excuses for poor preparation by labeling predictable crises as highly improbable black-swan events.

- Switch from just-in-time thinking to just-in-case thinking. Set aside resources for building some overcapacity, flexibility, and forward thinking.

- Prepare for events triggered by gray rhinos—highly probable, highly predictable, high-impact, but neglected threats.

Create a team of procurement superforecasters. Simplify your product portfolio. Reduce the number and variety of your products. De-risk your supply chain. Take back control of mission-critical supplies.

- Cope with an unexpected crisis by stabilizing your supply chain, harvesting cost-reduction and cash opportunities, and preparing for the rebound.

AFTERWORD

No company has yet found a way to maximize all the potential value from the relationships with its suppliers. Even companies with a deserved reputation for procurement—the function that owns the corporate relationship with suppliers—have not yet found a way to implement the kind of transformation program that would enable them not only to contain costs but also to tap five mission-critical sources of competitive advantage: innovation, quality, sustainability, speed, and risk reduction.

In *Profit from the Source*, we have shown how this can be done.

No one's pretending that it's easy to accomplish. After all, what we're advocating is nothing less than a fundamental overhaul of the whole company. Of course, over the past ten years or so, since the global financial crisis, many CEOs have embarked on what they grandly called "transformation" programs. But looking back, many of these were transformations in name only. If the catastrophic Covid-19 pandemic and the massive disruption to global supply chains exposed anything, it was the fact that companies (as well as governments) were shockingly unprepared for what was a perfectly predictable crisis.

Now CEOs must undertake a real transformation—one that, as the word suggests, truly changes the form, the *shape*, of the company. Clearly, the starting point will be different for different companies—depending on their stage of development, their industry, their geography, their competitors, and their history of tackling the big sustainability issues, among other things. But wherever they start, they should put suppliers at their core and empower their procurement function to extract the maximum possible value from them. That's because if they change a part of the business that is effectively responsible for spending 60 percent of the revenue, then it stands to reason that they are going to make a profound impact on the rest of the business.

The approach we present in *Profit from the Source* should form the foundation of any major business transformation. But this is not painting by numbers. This is why we recommend some strategic prioritization. All CEOs will want their CPO and procurement function to do what they have always done—take responsibility for containing costs. Also, they should want the CPO and procurement function to help the company become truly sustainable—that should be a mandatory task for all senior executives. But whether CEOs want to tap all or some of the other sources of competitive advantage will depend on the very particular needs of their company.

Whatever CEOs choose to do, they must, if they are to succeed in maximizing the full value from their suppliers, change the way their company works, by forging new dynamic relationships with the most important suppliers, putting the CPO and procurement function at the center of the company's product life cycle, and creating a "bionic" procurement function that combines the virtues of digital technology and human creativity. Above all, they must change the way they, themselves, work.

So much rests on the shoulders of the CEO—the individual leader. There is no question that the challenge is a mighty one. But mighty, too, is the prize. If they succeed, they can expect not only to double their savings but also to double the rate of innovation, double the quality of their products and services, double the sustainability of their business, double their speed to market—and do so while taking half the risks.

Ultimately, the degree to which they seize this prize is up to them. The choice is theirs. Quite legitimately, they could continue to follow the example of their predecessors and treat suppliers as marginal to the business and procurement as a cost-focused, administrative capability. This may work tolerably well, at least for a short while. It has, after all, worked in the past. But as the old investment adage has it, past performance is no guarantee of future success. And it is our view that if CEOs want to turn the dreams they have for their company into reality, they should follow the blueprint for success we have presented in *Profit from the Source*.

ACKNOWLEDGMENTS

As management consultants who spend our working lives with companies and their suppliers, we know only too well how many people play a critical role in the creation of a smartphone, an automobile, or an athletic shoe—indeed, all kinds of products. And a book is no different. In the course of writing *Profit from the Source*, we have drawn on the support of a long chain of people who have supplied us with their expertise, feedback, and encouragement. We now take great satisfaction in acknowledging them.

Dr. Simon Targett, a former associate editor of the *Financial Times* and former editor-in-chief of the Boston Consulting Group, kept us going, organized our thinking, helped us write the manuscript, and was an inspiration with his books—first and foremost, *New World, Inc.* Thank you, Simon.

Also, we relied on a fantastic inner circle of colleagues who provided research, detailed reviews, and tremendous case studies. Big thanks go to Florian Burgdorf, Michael Jonas, Harald Jordan, Christian Niebuhr, Nino Mori, Yulia Oleynikova, Boris Sidopoulos, and Dominik Steffani.

Jeff Kehoe, our editor at Harvard Business Review Press, gave us valuable and constructive feedback throughout the writing of the book. Thank you, Jeff. We are also grateful for the support of Melinda Merino, HBRP's executive editor, and the entire HBRP team.

Our literary agent, Todd Shuster, from Aevitas Creative Management, provided wise counsel as we sought a publisher and spoke to journalists in the US media. Thank you, Todd.

We would like to thank BCG's leaders for their warm encouragement: BGC's CEO, Christoph Schweizer, who encouraged us to share our vision with the broadest possible audience; BCG's global chair, Rich Lesser, who took special interest in the chapter on sustainability; and BCG's global chair emeritus, Hans-Paul Bürkner, who has long championed BCG's book-publishing program.

Many of our wonderful BCG colleagues have been remarkably generous with their time, providing invaluable comments, suggesting ideas, offering insights and considerable expertise, reading parts of the draft manuscript, providing feedback, and putting us in touch with business leaders. We would like to thank Inigo Aranzabal, Johanna Benesty, Jens Burchardt, Frank Cordes, Alex Dolya, Stephen Easton, Miranda Hadfield, Patrick Herhold, Daniel Kaegi, Aman Modi, Elton Parker, Aaron Snyder, Elia Tziambazis, Elliot Vaughn, and Eduard Viladesau.

The book would not have been possible without the sponsorship of BCG's Operations Practice and the backing of BCG's Book Committee. We would like to thank Ravi Srivastava, the current leader of the Operations Practice; Christian Greiser, the Operations Practice leader when we started the book; and the whole Operations Practice global leadership team. We would also like to thank the members of the Book Committee: Brian Bannister, David Fine, Sharon Marcil, Paul Michelman, Martin Reeves, and Amanda Wikman.

We are grateful to Payal Sheth for masterminding the marketing of the book, and Eric Gregoire and BCG's global marketing team. Also, we are grateful to Christine Hall, Heather Lockwood Hughes, and John Kerr for their copy-editing support as the manuscript neared completion.

Above all, we would like to thank our families, who have patiently supported us, even when we had to steal away in the evenings and on weekends to work on the book. Christian would like to thank his son, Nico, a budding economist, who took a keen interest in the book and

helped develop key themes. Wolfgang would like to thank his wonderful wife, Nur, and his children, Leyla and Levent. Alenka would like to thank her partner, Blaz, and son, Lars, for giving her the time to work on the book while nursing baby Frida. Daniel would like to thank his beloved wife, Sonja, and two sons, Karl and Otto, who made the home office a fun and inspirational place to be.

We couldn't have done it without you.

NOTES

Introduction

1. Nicholas Thompson, "Tim Cook's iPhone," *New Yorker*, October 5, 2011, https://www.newyorker.com/news/news-desk/tim-cooks-iphone.

2. Magdalena Petrova, "We Traced What It Takes to Make an iPhone, from Its Initial Design to the Components and Raw Materials Needed to Make It a Reality," *CNBC*, December 14, 2018, https://www.cnbc.com/2018/12/13/inside-apple-iphone-where-parts-and-materials-come-from.html.

3. Lionel Sujay Vailshery, "Apple iPhone Sales Worldwide 2007–2018," Statista, January 22, 2021, https://www.statista.com/statistics/276306/global-apple-iphone-sales-since-fiscal-year-2007/.

4. Patrick McGee, "Apple Becomes First $3tn Company After Boost from Pandemic Demand," *Financial Times*, January 3, 2022, https://www.ft.com/content/57f57303-82b9-49db-89ee-54888e1c714d.

5. Michael E. Porter and Nitin Nohria, "How CEOs Manage Time," *Harvard Business Review*, July–August 2018, https://hbr.org/2018/07/how-ceos-manage-time.

6. For more on the slow-moving challenges facing CEOs, see Martin Reeves et al., "The Challenge of Slow," Boston Consulting Group, July 7, 2020, https://www.bcg.com/publications/2020/challenge-of-slow.

7. "The New Coronavirus Could Have a Lasting Impact on Global Supply Chains," the *Economist*, February 15, 2020, https://www.economist.com/international/2020/02/15/the-new-coronavirus-could-have-a-lasting-impact-on-global-supply-chains.

8. Daniel Yergin and Matteo Fini, "For Auto Makers, the Chip Famine Will Persist," *Wall Street Journal*, September 22, 2021, https://www.wsj.com/articles/auto-car-makers-industry-semiconductor-chip-shortage-covid-19-taiwan-vietnam-11632329226.

9. Sameera Fazili and Peter Harrell, "When the Chips Are Down: Preventing and Addressing Supply Chain Disruptions," White House Briefing Room, September 23, 2021, https://www.whitehouse.gov/briefing-room/blog/2021/09/23/when-the-chips-are-down-preventing-and-addressing-supply-chain-disruptions/.

10. "Building Resilient Supply Chains, Revitalizing American Manufacturing, and Fostering Broad-Based Growth: 100-Day Reviews under Executive Order 14017," White House report, June 2021, https://www.whitehouse.gov/wp-content/uploads/2021/06/100-day-supply-chain-review-report.pdf.

11. "Remarks by President Biden at Signing of an Executive Order on Supply Chains," White House Briefing Room, February 24, 2021, https://www.whitehouse

.gov/briefing-room/speeches-remarks/2021/02/24/remarks-by-president-biden-at
-signing-of-an-executive-order-on-supply-chains/.

12. Amy Davidson Sorkin, "The Supply-Chain Mystery," *New Yorker*, September 26, 2021, https://www.newyorker.com/magazine/2021/10/04/ the-supply-chain-mystery.

13. Henry Ford, *My Life and Work* (New York: Garden City Publishing Co., Inc., 1922; Enhanced Media Publishing, 2017), 45. Kindle edition.

14. Franklin D. Roosevelt, "December 29, 1940: Fireside Chat 16: On the 'Arsenal of Democracy,'" Miller Center, University of Virginia, https://millercenter .org/the-presidency/presidential-speeches/december-29-1940-fireside-chat-16 -arsenal-democracy.

15. Robert Lacey, *Ford: The Men and the Machine* (Boston: Little Brown & Co., 1986), 390n.

16. Peter F. Drucker, *Concept of the Corporation* (New York: John Day Company, 1946).

17. Lacey, *Ford*, 434.

18. Michael A. Cusumano, "Manufacturing Innovation: Lessons from the Japanese Auto Industry," *MIT Sloan Management Review*, October 15, 1988, https:// sloanreview.mit.edu/article/manufacturing-innovation-lessons-from-the-japanese -auto-industry/.

19. John F. Krafcik, "Triumph of the Lean Production System," *MIT Sloan Management Review*, Fall 1988, Reprint 3014, https://www.lean.org/downloads/ MITSloan.pdf.

20. Michael Dell, *Direct from Dell: Strategies That Revolutionized an Industry* (New York: Harper Business, 1999), 172.

21. Thomas Friedman, *The World Is Flat: A Brief History of the Twenty-First Century* (New York: Farrar, Straus & Giroux, 2005).

22. Martin Reeves and Simon Levin, "The Biology of Corporate Survival," Boston Consulting Group, February 29, 2016, https://www.bcg.com/publications/2016/ strategy-business-unit-strategy-biology-of-corporate-survival.

23. Martin Reeves et al., "Advantage in Adversity: Winning the Next Downturn," Boston Consulting Group, February 4, 2019, https://www.bcg.com/publications/2019/ advantage-in-adversity-winning-next-downturn.

Chapter 1

1. A.G. Lafley, "The Game-Changer: How Every Leader Can Drive Everyday Innovation," *Chief Executive Officer*, October 15, 2008, https://www.the-chief executive.com/features/feature43911/index.html.

2. This section is based on a variety of sources, including Micheline Maynard, *Collision Course: Inside the Battle for General Motors* (New York: Carol Publishing Group, 1995); Alex Taylor III and Joyce E. Davis, "GM's $11,000,000,000 Turnaround CEO," *CNN*, October 17, 1994, https://money.cnn.com/magazines/fortune/ fortune_archive/1994/10/17/79852/index.htm; Judith H. Dobrzynski, "Jack and John: Two for the Road at GM," *New York Times*, July 9, 1995, https://www.nytimes .com/1995/07/09/business/jack-and-john-2-for-the-road-at-gm.html; "The Quiet Man," the *Economist*, May 8, 1999, https://www.economist.com/business/1999/05/06/ the-quiet-man; Donald W. Nauss, "Executive's Fall as Dramatic as His Rise," *Los*

Angeles Times, November 30, 1996, https://www.latimes.com/archives/la-xpm-1996 -11-30-fi-4213-story.html; Michael Hirsh, "GM vs. VW," *Newsweek*, August 12, 1996, https://www.newsweek.com/gm-vs-vw-175298; and John Eisenhammer, "Crusader at the Wheel," the *Independent*, July 3, 1993, https://www.independent.co.uk/news/ business/crusader-at-the-wheel-ignacio-lopez-sees-himself-as-a-saviour-of-the -western-car-industry-writes-john-eisenhammer-but-his-move-from-gm-to-vw-led -to-its-biggest-upheaval-for-years-1482815.html.

3. Maynard, *Collision Course*, 91.

4. Maynard, *Collision Course*, 93. This page has the other performance figures referenced in this section.

5. Larry Black, "The Man Who Left GM Standing at the Altar," the *Independent*, March 18, 1993, https://www.independent.co.uk/news/business/the-man-who-left -gm-standing-at-the-altar-larry-black-profiles-the-volkswagen-chief-whose-defection -1498432.html.

6. Robin Meredith, "VW Agrees to Pay G.M. $100 Million in Espionage Suit," *New York Times*, January 10, 1997, https://www.nytimes.com/1997/01/10/business/ vw-agrees-to-pay-gm-100-million-in-espionage-suit.html.

Chapter 2

1. Andrew Edgecliffe-Johnson and Patrick McGee, "Companies' Supply Chains Vulnerable to Coronavirus Shocks," *Financial Times*, March 9, 2020, https://www.ft .com/content/be05b46a-5fa9-11ea-b0ab-339c2307bcd4.

2. Adam Smith, *The Wealth of Nations. Books I-III. With an introduction by Andrew Skinner* (First published 1776. This edition: London: Penguin Books, 1986), 117.

3. For a useful analysis of NASA's commercial program, see Scott Manley, "The Story of How NASA Went from Space Shuttles to SpaceX & Commercial Rockets," YouTube, June 3, 2020, https://www.youtube.com/watch?v=HGICHa1IZKo&t=172s.

4. Ensign John Minnehan, "Non-Nuclear Submarines? Choose Fuel Cells," *Proceedings of the US Naval Institute*, June 2019, https://www.usni.org/magazines/ proceedings/2019/june/non-nuclear-submarines-choose-fuel-cells.

5. For Boeing's involvement, see "Space Shuttle Orbiter: Historical Snapshot," Boeing, https://www.boeing.com/history/products/space-shuttle-orbiter.page.

6. "Space Act Agreement between National Aeronautics and Space Administration and Space Exploration Technologies Corp. for Commercial Orbital Transportation Services Demonstration (COTS)," NASA, May 30, 2006, https://www .nasa.gov/centers/johnson/pdf/189228main_setc_nnj06ta26a.pdf.

7. Richard Waters, "SpaceX on the Verge of Sending Astronauts into Orbit," *Financial Times*, May 26, 2020, https://www.ft.com/content/17a13157-9ab7-4d5e-820e -34e48b4c2c40.

8. Jessica E. Lessin, Lorraine Luk, and Juro Osawa, "Apple Finds It Difficult to Divorce Samsung," *Wall Street Journal*, July 1, 2013, https://www.wsj.com/articles/SB1 0001424127887324682204578513882349940500.

9. Kif Leswing, "Apple Is Spending More Than Ever on R&D to Fulfill the 'Tim Cook Doctrine,'" *CNBC*, August 3, 2019, https://www.cnbc.com/2019/08/03/apple-rd -spend-increases-fulfilling-tim-cook-doctrine.html.

10. Dave Lee, "Nokia: The Rise and Fall of a Mobile Giant," BBC, September 3, 2013, https://www.bbc.co.uk/news/technology-23947212.

11. Lorraine Luk, "TSMC Starts Shipping Microprocessors to Apple," the *Wall Street Journal*, July 10, 2014, https://www.wsj.com/articles/tsmc-starts -shipping-microprocessors-to-apple-1404991514.

12. Linley Gwennap, "Apple's 5 Nanometer Chip Is Another Signpost That Moore's Law Is Running Out," *Forbes*, October 12, 2020, https://www.forbes.com/ sites/linleygwennap/2020/10/12/apple-moores-law-is-running-out/?sh=847134f529ab.

13. Filipe Espósito, "Former Intel Engineer Says Skylake Problems Were Turning Point for Apple's ARM Mac Transition," 9to5Mac, June 24, 2020, https://9to5mac .com/2020/06/24/former-intel-engineer-says-skylake-problems-were-turning-point -for-apples-arm-mac-transition/.

14. Tim Bradshaw, "Apple's In-House Chip Design Unit Gives It Smartphone Edge," *Financial Times*, December 18, 2015, https://www.ft.com/content/ 06815bee-a560-11e5-97e1-a754d5d9538c.

15. "TSMC 5 nm Node Supply Fully Booked, Apple the Biggest Customer," *Techpowerup*, September 18, 2020, https://www.techpowerup.com/272303/tsmc-5-nm -node-supply-fully-booked-apple-the-biggest-customer.

16. Richard Waters, "Apple Chips Away at a New Strategy for Computing," *Financial Times*, November 12, 2020, https://www.ft.com/content/2efc9861-3d07-4e33 -8ca7-db1654373fcd.

Chapter 3

1. "Our History," Alexander Dennis, https://www.alexander-dennis.com/about -us/our-history/.

2. "Who We Are," Alexander Dennis, https://www.alexander-dennis.com/about -us/who-we-are/.

3. "Opportunities in Engineering and Operations," Alexander Dennis, https:// www.alexander-dennis.com/media/84253/opportunities-in-engineering-and -operations.pdf.

4. For more on this story, see *Hearings Before the Subcommittee on Economy in Government of the Joint Economic Committee, Congress of the United States, Ninety-First Congress, First Session, Part 1, December 29, 30, and 31, 1969* (Washington: US Government Printing Office, 1970), https://www.jec.senate.gov/reports/91st%20 Congress/The%20Acquisition%20of%20Weapons%20Systems%20Part%20I%20 (485).pdf; Eric M. Lofgren, "Cost and Competition in U.S. Defense Acquisition," International Cost Estimating and Analysis Association, June 2018, http://www .iceaaonline.com/ready/wp-content/uploads/2018/07/AO05-Paper-Cost-and-Com petition-in-U.S.-Defense-Acquisition-Lofgren-1.pdf.

5. For information on the growth of data, see Martin Reeves et al., "The Integrated Strategy Machine: Using AI to Create Advantage," Boston Consulting Group, May 14, 2020, https://www.bcg.com/publications/2016/strategy -technology-digital-integrated-strategy-machine-using-ai-create-advantage.

6. This can be viewed as a three-part series on YouTube: "Killing a Toyota, Part 1," https://www.youtube.com/watch?v=xnWKz7Cthkk, "Killing a Toyota, Part 2," https://www.youtube.com/watch?v=xTPnIpjodA8, and "Killing a Toyota, Part 3," https://www.youtube.com/watch?v=kFnVZXQD5_k.

7. "Tesla Overtakes Toyota to Become World's Most Valuable Carmaker," BBC, July 1, 2020, https://www.bbc.co.uk/news/business-53257933.

8. For a summary of the decisions by different countries, see Isabella Burch and Jock Gilchrist, "Survey of Global Activity to Phase Out Internal Combustion Engine Vehicles," The Climate Center, March 2020, https://theclimatecenter.org/wp-content/uploads/2020/03/Survey-on-Global-Activities-to-Phase-Out-ICE-Vehicles-update-3.18.20-1.pdf.

9. Jamie Powell, "Tesla Is Asked to Recall 158,000 Cars in the US over Touchscreen Issues," *Financial Times*, January 14, 2021, https://www.ft.com/content/4a489993-f8b5-4bb8-87be-a7684eb8dccd.

10. "Cost Reduction Engineer," LinkedIn, https://www.linkedin.com/jobs/view/cost-reduction-engineer-supercharger-service-at-tesla-2795374438/.

11. "Supply Chain Manager—Singapore," LinkedIn, https://www.linkedin.com/jobs/view/supply-chain-manager-singapore-at-tesla-2720491853/?trackingId=OZ1eczBCmfAKnGll5%2BK96Q%3D%3D&refId=AjUPMhZMuQdcr1LHN88Nhg%3D%3D&pageNum=0&position=7&trk=public_jobs_jserp-result_search-card&originalSubdomain=sg.

12. Joe Miller, "Daimler to Cut Out Suppliers to Fund Software Hiring Spree," *Financial Times*, December 3, 2020, https://www.ft.com/content/6173af2c-2ea8-4e90-876a-5cc189e3342b.

13. "Everything to Know about Apple's Big iPhone Profits and a Big Potential Acquisition," Counterpoint, December 21, 2019, https://www.counterpointresearch.com/everything-know-apples-big-iphone-profits-big-potential-acquisition/; and Karn Chauhan, "Apple Continues to Lead Global Handset Industry Profit Share," Counterpoint, December 19, 2019, https://www.counterpointresearch.com/apple-continues-lead-global-handset-industry-profit-share/.

14. "Prospering in the Pandemic: 2020's Top 100 Companies," *Financial Times*, January 1, 2021, https://www.ft.com/content/f8251e5f-10a7-4f7a-9047-b438e4d7f83a.

Chapter 4

1. "The Bionic Company," Boston Consulting Group, https://www.bcg.com/capabilities/digital-technology-data/bionic-company.

2. Gil Golan, "Automotive: GM," Invest in Israel, https://investinisrael.gov.il/InvestInIsrael/Pages/GM.aspx.

3. "Procurement & Supply Chain Roles," Odgers Berndtson, https://www.odgersberndtson.com/en-gb/roles/procurement-supply-chain-roles.

4. For more on voestalpine's "greentec steel" program, see "voestalpine Holds Patent for Carbon-Neutral Pre-material Used in Green Steel Production," voestalpine, June 15, 2021, https://www.voestalpine.com/group/en/media/press-releases/2021-06-14-voestalpine-holds-patent-for-carbon-neutral-pre-material-used-in-green-steel-production/.

5. "The World's Most Valuable Resource Is No Longer Oil, But Data," *Economist*, May 6, 2017, https://www.economist.com/leaders/2017/05/06/the-worlds-most-valuable-resource-is-no-longer-oil-but-data.

6. Jeff Desjardins, "How Much Data Is Generated Each Day?" World Economic Forum, April 17, 2019, https://www.weforum.org/agenda/2019/04/how-much-data-is-generated-each-day-cf4bddf29f/.

7. "The State of Dark Data," Splunk, 2019, https://www.splunk.com/pdfs/dark-data/the-state-of-dark-data-report.pdf.

8. Christian Schuh et al., *The Purchasing Chessboard: 64 Methods to Reduce Costs and Increase Value with Suppliers* (New York: Springer-Verlag, 2011).

Chapter 5

1. James P. Womack, Daniel T. Jones, and Daniel Roos, *The Machine That Changed the World: The Story of Lean Production* (New York: Simon & Schuster, 1990), 149–153.

2. Tripp Mickle, "Jobs, Cook, Ive—Blevins? The Rise of Apple's Cost Cutter," *Wall Street Journal*, January 23, 2020, https://www.wsj.com/articles/jobs-cook -iveblevins-the-rise-of-apples-cost-cutter-11579803981.

Chapter 6

1. Martin Neil Baily and Nicholas Montalbano, "Why Is U.S. Productivity Growth So Slow?" working paper 22, Hutchins Center on Fiscal & Monetary Policy at Brookings, Washington, DC, September 2016, https://www.brookings.edu/wp -content/uploads/2016/09/wp22_baily-montalbano_updated1.pdf.

2. Lawrence H. Summers, "The Age of Secular Stagnation: What It Is and What to Do about It," *Foreign Affairs*, March/April 2016, https://www.foreignaffairs.com/ articles/united-states/2016-02-15/age-secular-stagnation.

3. Robert J. Gordon, "Is U.S. Economic Growth Over? Faltering Innovation Confronts the Six Headwinds," working paper 18315, National Bureau of Economic Research, Cambridge, MA,, August 2012, https://www.nber.org/papers/w18315.

4. Christopher Mims, "Why There Are More Consumer Goods Than Ever," *Wall Street Journal*, April 25, 2016, https://www.wsj.com/articles/ why-there-are-more-consumer-goods-than-ever-1461556860.

5. Jeff Desjardins, "In the Race to 50 Million Users There's One Clear Winner— and It Might Surprise You," World Economic Forum, June 26, 2018, https://www .weforum.org/agenda/2018/06/how-long-does-it-take-to-hit-50-million-users.

6. Richard Waters, "Microsoft Growth Accelerates as Pandemic Boosts Cloud Business," *Financial Times*, April 30, 2020, https://www.ft.com/content/ ac054397-eb9a-4198-a050-18961f39feb9.

7. For more on Bell Labs, see Jon Gertner, *The Idea Factory: Bell Labs and the Great Age of American Innovation* (New York: Penguin Books, 2012).

8. "Partnering for Mutual Value," Procter & Gamble, https://www.pgconnect develop.com/.

9. "Innovation," Procter & Gamble, https://www.pg.co.uk/innovation/.

10. "Open Innovation in Action," Procter & Gamble, https://www.pgconnect develop.com/needs/.

11. For the history of Xerox Palo Alto Research Center, see "PARC History," PARC, https://www.parc.com/about-parc/parc-history/.

12. *Triumph of the Nerds*, PBS, 1996, https://www.pbs.org/nerds/.

13. "What's Wrong with This Picture: Kodak's 30-Year Slide into Bankruptcy," Knowledge@Wharton, University of Pennsylvania, February 1, 2012, https:// knowledge.wharton.upenn.edu/article/whats-wrong-with-this-picture-kodaks -30-year-slide-into-bankruptcy/.

14. Patrick Vlaskovits, "Henry Ford, Innovation, and That 'Faster Horse' Quote," hbr.org, August 29, 2011, https://hbr.org/2011/08/henry-ford-never-said -the-fast.

15. "Genrikh Altshuller," Altshuller Institute for TRIZ Studies, https://www.aitriz .org/altshuller.

16. Kif Leswing, "Apple Is Spending More Than Ever on R&D to Fulfill the 'Tim Cook doctrine,'" *CNBC*, August 3, 2019, https://www.cnbc.com/2019/08/03/apple-rd -spend-increases-fulfilling-tim-cook-doctrine.html.

17. Joel M. Podolny and Morten T. Hansen, "How Apple Is Organized for Innovation," *Harvard Business Review*, November–December 2020, https://hbr .org/2020/11/how-apple-is-organized-for-innovation.

18. "Method to Create an Enclosure for an Electronic Device," United States Patent 8,341,832, United States Patent and Trademark Office, January 1, 2013, https://patft.uspto.gov/netacgi/nph-Parser?Sect1=PTO1&Sect2=HITOFF&d= PALL&p=1&u=%2Fnetahtml%2FPTO%2Fsrchnum.htm&r=1&f=G&l=50&s1 =8,341,832.PN.&OS=PN/8,341,832&RS=PN/8,341,832.

19. "Apple MacBook Pro Aluminum Unibody Design Video," YouTube, June 22, 2009, https://www.youtube.com/watch?v=sxbiIpXZfG8.

20. "Blade Services," Siemens Gamesa, https://www.siemensgamesa.com/en-int/ products-and-services/service-wind/blade-services.

21. "Artificial Intelligence Solution from Fujitsu Helps Siemens Gamesa Significantly Accelerate Quality Assurance Procedures," Fujitsu press release, November 7, 2017, https://www.fujitsu.com/uk/news/pr/2017/fs-20171107-4.html. See also "Your Vision, and Fujitsu. Together We Can Change the World," Fujitsu, 2017, https://www.fujitsu.com/global/Images/Fujitsu%20EBook%20EMEIA%20 2018.pdf. For a Siemens Gamesa video on how it works, see "Hermes AI: The Future of Blade Health Management," YouTube, March 29, 2019, https://www.youtube.com/ watch?v=3VGAdgs5seQ.

22. "SuedOstLink," 50Hertz, https://www.50hertz.com/en/Grid/ Griddevelopement/Onshoreprojects/SuedOstLink.

23. "Naming the Coronavirus Disease (COVID-19) and the Virus That Causes It," World Health Organization, https://www.who.int/emergencies/diseases/novel -coronavirus-2019/technical-guidance/naming-the-coronavirus-disease-(covid-2019) -and-the-virus-that-causes-it.

24. For the World Health Organization announcement, see https://www.youtube .com/watch?v=sbT6AANFOm4.

25. David Crow, "Merck Chief Casts Doubt on Coronavirus Vaccine Timeframe," *Financial Times*, May 26, 2020, https://www.ft.com/content/7b72a568 -9eed-460f-b100-7bf74e3f4cbf.

26. "Sanofi and GSK to Join Forces in Unprecedented Vaccine Collaboration to Fight COVID-19," GlaxoSmithKline press release, April 14, 2020, https://www.gsk .com/en-gb/media/press-releases/sanofi-and-gsk-to-join-forces-in-unprecedented -vaccine-collaboration-to-fight-covid-19/.

27. "Pfizer and BioNTech to Co-Develop Potential Covid-19 Vaccine," Pfizer press release, March 17, 2020, https://investors.pfizer.com/investor-news/press-release -details/2020/Pfizer-and-BioNTech-to-Co-Develop-Potential-COVID-19-Vaccine/ default.aspx.

28. "AstraZeneca and Oxford University Announce Landmark Agreement for COVID-19 Vaccine," AstraZeneca press release, April 30, 2021, https://www .astrazeneca.com/media-centre/press-releases/2020/astrazeneca-and-oxford-university -announce-landmark-agreement-for-covid-19-vaccine.html.

29. Louise Richardson, "An Oxford Vaccine for the World," University of Oxford, November 23, 2020, https://staff.admin.ox.ac.uk/article/an-oxford-vaccine-for-the -world#/.

30. "Sanofi and GSK Announce a Delay in Their Adjuvanted Recombinant Protein-Based COVID-19 Vaccine Programme to Improve Immune Response in the Elderly," GlaxoSmithKline press release, December 11, 2020, https://www.gsk.com/ en-gb/media/press-releases/sanofi-and-gsk-announce-a-delay-in-their-adjuvanted -recombinant-protein-based-covid-19-vaccine-programme-to-improve-immune -response-in-the-elderly/.

31. "Merck Discontinues Development of SARS-CoV-2/COVID-19 Vaccine Candidates; Continues Development of Two Investigational Therapeutic Candidates," Merck press release, January 25, 2021, https://www.merck.com/news/merck-discontin ues-development-of-sars-cov-2-covid-19-vaccine-candidates-continues-development -of-two-investigational-therapeutic-candidates/.

32. For information on Henogen, Catalent, and Oxford Biomedica, see "COVID-19 Vaccine AstraZeneca," January 29, 2021, https://www.ema.europa.eu/en/documents/ product-information/covid-19-vaccine-astrazeneca-product-information-approved -chmp-29-january-2021-pending-endorsement_en.pdf. For information on Serum Institute of India, see "Serum Institute of India Obtains Emergency Use Authorisation in India for AstraZeneca's COVID-19 Vaccine," AstraZeneca press release, January 6, 2021, https://www.astrazeneca.com/media-centre/press-releases/2021/serum-institute -of-india-obtains-emergency-use-authorisation-in-india-for-astrazenecas-covid-19 -vaccine.html.

33. For information on Wockhardt, see Victoria Rees, "UK Government Reserves Wockhardt Production Line to Fill Finish COVID-19 Vaccines," *European Pharmaceutical Review*, August 4, 2020, https://www.europeanpharmaceuticalreview .com/news/125137/uk-government-reserves-wockhardt-production-line-to-fill-finish -covid-19-vaccines/. For information on other European contract manufacturers, see Ashutosh Pandey, "AstraZeneca COVID Vaccine's Complex EU Supply Chain," Deutsche Welle, February 2, 2021, https://www.dw.com/en/astrazeneca -covid-vaccine-oxford/a-56427963.

34. Hannah Kuckler, "Pfizer Expects $15bn in COVID Vaccine Revenue This Year," *Financial Times*, February 2, 2021, https://www.ft.com/content/0f1ab138-401d -40ff-824f-f6879704f10e.

35. For the GSK CureVac announcement, see "GSK and CureVac to Develop Next Generation mRNA COVID-19 Vaccines," GlaxoSmithKline press release, February 3, 2021, https://www.gsk.com/en-gb/media/press-releases/gsk-and-curevac-to-develop -next-generation-mrna-covid-19-vaccines/.

36. For the GSK Novavax announcement, see "GSK to Support Manufacture of Novavax' COVID-19 Vaccine," GlaxoSmithKline press release, March 29, 2021, https://www.gsk.com/en-gb/media/press-releases/gsk-to-support-manufacture- of-novavax-covid-19-vaccine/; for the Merck announcement, see "Merck to Help Produce Johnson & Johnson's COVID-19 Vaccine; BARDA to Provide Merck with Funding to Expand Merck's Manufacturing Capacity for COVID-19 Vaccines and Medicines," Merck press release, March 2, 2021, https://www.merck.com/news/merck -to-help-produce-johnson-barda-to-provide-merck-with-funding-to-expand-mercks -manufacturing-capacity-for-covid-19-vaccines-and-medicines/.

37. For the Sanofi announcements, see "Sanofi and Translate Bio Initiate Phase 1/2 Clinical Trial of mRNA COVID-19 Vaccine Candidate," Sanofi press release,

March 12, 2021, https://www.sanofi.com/en/media-room/press-releases/2021/2021 -03-12-07-00-00-2191846; "Sanofi to Provide Support to BioNTech in Manufacturing Their COVID-19 Vaccine to Help Address Public Health Needs," Sanofi press release, January 27, 2021, https://www.sanofi.com/en/media-room/press-relea ses/2021/2021-01-27-07-30-00; and "Sanofi to Provide Manufacturing Support to Johnson & Johnson for Their COVID-19 Vaccine to Help Address Global Supply Demands," Sanofi press release, February 22, 2021, https://www.sanofi.com/en/media -room/press-releases/2021/2021-02-22-11-40-00-2179318.

Chapter 7

1. National Commission on the BP Deepwater Horizon Oil Spill and Offshore Drilling, *Deep Water: The Gulf Oil Disaster and the Future of Offshore Drilling: Report to the President*, January 2011, https://www.govinfo.gov/content/pkg/GPO -OILCOMMISSION/pdf/GPO-OILCOMMISSION.pdf.

2. National Commission, *Deep Water*, 2. It has been estimated that the total cost incurred by BP—calculated seven years after the disaster—was $144.89 billion. See Yong-Gyo Lee, Xavier Garza-Gomez, and Rose M. Lee, "Ultimate Costs of the Disaster: Seven Years after the Deepwater Horizon Oil Spill," *Journal of Corporate Accounting & Finance* 29, no. 1 (2018): 69, https://www.researchgate.net/publication/322574747_Ultimate_Costs _of_the_Disaster_Seven_Years_After_the_Deepwater_Horizon_Oil_Spill.

3. Olivier D. Serrat, "The Five Whys Technique," Asian Development Bank, February 2009, https://www.adb.org/publications/five-whys-technique. See also "Ask 'Why' Five Times about Every Matter," Toyota, https://www.toyota-europe.com/ world-of-toyota/feel/quality.

4. Michael Dell, *Direct from Dell: Strategies That Revolutionized an Industry* (New York: Harper Business, 1999), 24.

5. Dell, *Direct from Dell*, 24.

6. Thomas Friedman, *The World Is Flat: A Brief History of the Twenty-First Century* (New York: Farrar, Straus & Giroux, 2005), 214.

7. "The Global Risks Report 2020," World Economic Forum, January 15, 2020, https://www.weforum.org/reports/the-global-risks-report-2020.

8. Mark Haranas, "Michael Dell's 5 Biggest Statements at Dell Technologies World," *CRN*, April 29, 2019, https://www.crn.com/slide-shows/storage/ michael-dell-s-5-biggest-statements-at-dell-technologies-world/4.

9. "A Partnership of Trust: Dell Supply Chain Security," Dell Technologies, 2020, https://i.dell.com/sites/csdocuments/CorpComm_Docs/en/supply-chain-assurance .pdf?newtab=true.

10. "2019 Public Supplier List," Dell Technologies, https://i.dell.com/sites/ doccontent/corporate/corp-comm/en/Documents/dell-suppliers.pdf?newtab=true.

11. Ben Aylor et al., "Creating More Powerful Partnerships in Pharma Manufactur-ing," Boston Consulting Group, September 10, 2018, https://www.bcg.com/en-gb/ publications/2018/how-to-make-pharma-manufacturing-partnerships-more-strategic.

12. Louis Garguilo, "Biogen's 'Virtual' Plant Manager Goes to Switzerland," *Outsourced Pharma*, October 25, 2019, https://www.outsourcedpharma.com/doc/ biogen-s-virtual-plant-manager-goes-to-switzerland-0001.

13. Peter Campbell, "Car Recalls Rise as Industry Becomes More High-Tech," *Financial Times*, May 19, 2018, https://www.ft.com/content/15e283a0-59eb-11e8-b8b2 -d6ceb45fa9d0.

14. For more information on GPSC: "The Innovative Power Flagship of PTT Group. Corporate Presentation," GPSC, October 1, 2019, https://investor.gpscgroup .com/misc/presentation/20190927-gpsc-singapore-corporate-presentation-02.pdf.

15. For more on the varieties of coal and the coal production process, see "Coal Explained," US Energy Information Administration, https://www.eia.gov/ energyexplained/coal/, and "What Is Coal Used For?" US Geological Survey, https://www.usgs.gov/faqs/what-coal-used?qt-news_science_products=0#qt-news _science_products.

Chapter 8

1. Caroline Wheeler et al., "Boohoo: Fashion Giant Faces 'Slavery' Investigation," *Sunday Times*, July 5, 2020, https://www.thetimes.co.uk/article/ boohoo-fashion-giant-faces-slavery-investigation-57s3hxcth.

2. Alison Levitt, "Independent Review into the Boohoo Group PLC's Leicester Supply Chain," Boohoo Group, September 24, 2020, https://www.boohooplc.com/ sites/boohoo-corp/files/final-report-open-version-24.9.2020.pdf.

3. Patricia Nilsson, "Boohoo Hires Leveson to Monitor Its Supply Chain," *Financial Times*, November 26, 2020, https://www.ft.com/content/08e6a92f-1e5e -489e-bf5e-11877169bf5c.

4. "Supply Chain Sustainability Progress: 2018 Annual Report," Dell Technologies, https://corporate.delltechnologies.com/content/dam/delltechnologies/ assets/corporate/pdf/progress-made-real-reports/scs-report-2018.pdf.

5. "Helping Build a Better World: Making Life Electric: Integrated Sustainability and Financial Report 2021," Ford Motor Company, https://corporate.ford.com/ microsites/integrated-sustainability-and-financial-report-2021/files/ir21.pdf.

6. Larry Fink, "Larry Fink's 2020 Letter to CEOs: A Fundamental Reshaping of Finance," BlackRock, 2020, https://www.blackrock.com/corporate/ investor-relations/2020-larry-fink-ceo-letter.

7. Larry Fink, "Larry Fink's 2021 Letter to CEOs," BlackRock, 2021, https:// www.blackrock.com/corporate/investor-relations/larry-fink-ceo-letter.

8. Jasmine Cameron-Chileshe, "UK Companies Face Fines over 'Slave Labour' China Suppliers," *Financial Times*, January 12, 2021, https://www.ft.com/content/ 0249203b-ce34-406c-ae4d-1bd031ced55b.

9. "Sustainable Impact Report 2020," HP, https://h20195.www2.hp.com/v2/getpdf .aspx/c07539064.pdf.

10. Intergovernmental Panel on Climate Change, *Global Warming of 1.5°C* (IPCC, 2019), https://www.ipcc.ch/site/assets/uploads/sites/2/2019/06/SR15_Full_Report_ High_Res.pdf.

11. Matthew Vincent, "The Problem with Zero Carbon Pledges," *Financial Times*, November 30, 2020, https://www.ft.com/content/83edfedd-77e7-4877-a016 -b00b6b6d0307.

12. "Climate Paths 2.0: A Program for Climate and Germany's Future Development," Boston Consulting Group, October 2021, https://web-assets.bcg .com/02/a6/91958a6f4287a0490e24ef56d2b5/climate-paths2-summary-offindings -en.pdf.

13. "Net-Zero Challenge: The Supply Chain Opportunity," World Economic Forum, in collaboration with Boston Consulting Group, January 21, 2021, https:// www.weforum.org/reports/net-zero-challenge-the-supply-chain-opportunity.

14. "Briefing: What Are Scope 3 Emissions?" Carbon Trust, https://www .carbontrust.com/resources/briefing-what-are-scope-3-emissions; "Standards," Greenhouse Gas Protocol, https://ghgprotocol.org/standards.

15. "Net-Zero Challenge," World Economic Forum.

16. Jens Burchardt, "How We Can Curb Climate Change by Spending Two Percent More on Everything," TED, April 22, 2021, https://www.youtube.com/watch?v=lR _WNPGVENU.

17. "Our Suppliers," Dell Technologies, https://corporate.delltechnologies.com/ en-gb/social-impact/advancing-sustainability/sustainable-supply-chain/our-suppliers .htm.

18. "Blockchain Pilot Project Provides Transparency on CO_2 Emissions," Daimler, https://www.daimler.com/sustainability/resources/blockchain-pilot-project-supply -chain.html.

19. "Sustainable Impact Report 2019," HP, https://h20195.www2.hp.com/v2/getpdf .aspx/c06601778.pdf.

20. "Case Study—Tesco," Science Based Targets, https://sciencebasedtargets .org/companies-taking-action/case-studies/tesco; and "Britain's Tesco Extends Net Zero Pledge," Reuters, September 23, 2021, https://www.reuters.com/business/ sustainable-business/britains-tesco-extends-net-zero-pledge-2021-09-23/.

21. "Companies Taking Action," Science Based Targets, https://sciencebasedtargets .org/companies-taking-action.

22. Brad Smith, "Microsoft Will Be Carbon Negative by 2030," Official Microsoft Blog, January 16, 2020, https://blogs.microsoft.com/blog/2020/01/16/microsoft-will -be-carbon-negative-by-2030/.

23. "GSK Sets New Environmental Goals of Net Zero Impact on Climate and Net Positive Impact on Nature by 2030," GlaxoSmithKline press release, November 3, 2020, https://www.gsk.com/en-gb/media/press-releases/gsk-sets -new-environmental-goals-of-net-zero-impact-on-climate-and-net-positive-impact -on-nature-by-2030/; and "Protecting and Restoring the Planet's Health to Protect and Improve People's Health," GlaxoSmithKline, https://www.gsk.com/en-gb/ responsibility/environment/.

24. "How We Turn Plastic Bottles into Shoes: Our Partnership with Parley for the Oceans," Adidas, March 2021, https://www.adidas.co.uk/blog/639412-how-we-turn -plastic-bottles-into-shoes-our-partnership-with-parley-for-the-oceans.

25. "Helping Build a Better World," Ford, https://corporate.ford.com/microsites/ integrated-sustainability-and-financial-report-2021/files/ir21.pdf; and "A Better World for Generations to Come," Ford, https://corporate.ford.com/microsites/integrated -sustainability-and-financial-report-2021/environment/index.html.

26. "Waste as a Resource: Finding Raw Materials in the Most Unlikely Places," Dell Technologies, https://corporate.delltechnologies.com/en-gb/social-impact/advancing -sustainability/sustainable-products-and-services/materials-use/waste-as-a-resource .htm.

27. "We Are a Seventh-Generation Family Business," Rügenwalder Mühle, https:// www.ruegenwalder.de/en/our-familiy-history.

28. "Germany: Rügenwalder Mühle Sees 50% Increase in Meat-Free Sales," *Vegconomist*, August 28, 2020, https://vegconomist.com/companies-and-portraits/ germany-rugenwalder-muhle-sees-50-increase-in-meat-free-sales/.

29. US Department of Agriculture and Global Agricultural Information Network, "Germany: Germany Is Leading a Vegalution—Vegan Revolution—in Europe,"

January 16, 2020, https://www.fas.usda.gov/data/germany-germany-leading-vegalution-vegan-revolution-europe.

30. "Veggie-Based Diets Could Save 8 Million Lives by 2050 and Cut Global Warming," University of Oxford, March 22, 2016, https://www.ox.ac.uk/news/2016-03-22-veggie-based-diets-could-save-8-million-lives-2050-and-cut-global-warming.

31. Satu Dahl, "Welcoming an Age of Sustainable Flight," Neste, December 16, 2019, https://www.neste.com/corporate-info/news-inspiration/articles/welcoming-an-age-of-sustainable-flight#f189b2ff.

32. "Unilever's Chief Procurement Officer Talks 400 Brands, Trust and Palm Oil," *Observe Magazine*, Odgers Berndtson, October 8, 2019, https://www.odgersberndtson.com/en-gb/insights/unilevers-chief-procurement-officer-talks-400-brands-trust-and-palm-oil.

33. Kevin Brown, "Supply Chain Responsibility Is a Core Part of Our Business," Dell Technologies, 2020, https://corporate.delltechnologies.com/en-gb/social-impact/reporting/2020-supply-chain-sustainability-progress-report.htm; "About the RBA," Responsible Business Alliance, http://www.responsiblebusiness.org/about/rba/.

34. "Conflict Minerals Report 2020," Apple, https://www.apple.com/supplier-responsibility/pdf/Apple-Conflict-Minerals-Report.pdf.

35. Tiffany Hsu, "You Know Your Diamond's Cut and Carat. But Does It Have Ethical Origins?" *New York Times*, January 8, 2019, https://www.nytimes.com/2019/01/08/business/diamonds-origin-tiffany-consumers.html?searchResultPosition=2.

36. "Pandora Launches Lab-Created Diamond Collection," Pandora press release, May 4, 2021, https://pandoragroup.com/investor/news-and-reports/newsdetail?id=24186.

37. Tim Barsoe, "Carbon Copy? Pandora Takes a Shine to Lab-Made Diamonds," Reuters, May 3, 2021, https://www.reuters.com/business/carbon-copy-pandora-takes-shine-lab-made-diamonds-2021-05-04/.

Chapter 9

1. Kara Swisher (@karaswisher) Twitter, February 2, 2021, https://twitter.com/karaswisher/status/1356848079132065793.

2. Jeff Bezos, "Email from Jeff Bezos to Employees," Amazon, February 2, 2021, https://www.aboutamazon.com/news/company-news/email-from-jeff-bezos-to-employees.

3. Isobel Asher Hamilton, "As Jeff Bezos Steps Down, a Single Line from His First Amazon Job Ad Posted 27 Years Ago Tells You Everything about His Obsession with Speed," *Business Insider*, February 3, 2021, updated July 5, 2021, https://www.businessinsider.com/jeff-bezos-first-amazon-job-ad-reveals-obsession-with-speed-2019-7?r=US&IR=T.

4. George Stalk Jr., "Time—the Next Source of Competitive Advantage," *Harvard Business Review*, July 1988, https://hbr.org/1988/07/time-the-next-source-of-competitive-advantage. For more on time-based competition, see: https://www.bcg.com/en-gb/about/overview/our-history/time-based-competition.

5. Steve Lohr, "IBM's Design-Centered Strategy to Set Free the Squares," *New York Times*, November 14, 2015, https://www.nytimes.com/2015/11/15/business/ibms-design-centered-strategy-to-set-free-the-squares.html. Also, see "The Creed

of Speed," *Economist*, December 5, 2015, https://www.economist.com/briefing/2015/12/05/the-creed-of-speed.

6. Bill Gates, *Business @ the Speed of Thought: Using a Digital Nervous System* (New York: Penguin, Kindle Edition, 2000), 155.

7. Anne-Marie Schiro, "Fashion: Two New Stores That Cruise Fashion's Fast Lane," *New York Times*, December 31, 1989, https://www.nytimes.com/1989/12/31/style/fashion-two-new-stores-that-cruise-fashion-s-fast-lane.html.

8. For more on Zara and Inditex, see Suzy Hansen, "How Zara Grew into the World's Largest Fashion Retailer," *New York Times*, November 9, 2012, https://www.nytimes.com/2012/11/11/magazine/how-zara-grew-into-the-worlds-largest-fashion-retailer.html.

9. Tobias Buck, "Fashion: A Better Business Model," *Financial Times*, June 18, 2014, https://www.ft.com/content/a7008958-f2f3-11e3-a3f8-00144feabdc0.

10. "Our Suppliers," Inditex, https://www.inditex.com/our-commitment-to-people/our-suppliers.

11. Hau L. Lee, "How Extreme Agility Put Zara Ahead in Fast Fashion," *Financial Times*, December 10, 2019, https://www.ft.com/content/3f581046-cd7c-11e9-b018-ca4456540ea6.

12. "TSMC Says Has Begun Construction at Its Arizona Chip Factory Site," Reuters, June 1, 2021, https://www.reuters.com/technology/tsmc-says-construction-has-started-arizona-chip-factory-2021-06-01/.

13. Seth T. Blakeman, Anthony R. Gibbs, and Jeyanthan Jeyasingam, "Study of the Mine Resistant Ambush Protected (MRAP) Vehicle Program as a Model for Rapid Defense Acquisitions" (MBA professional report, Naval Postgraduate School, 2008), https://calhoun.nps.edu/handle/10945/10285.

14. Daniel Slotta, "Smartphone Market in China—Statistics & Facts," Statista, May 6, 2021, https://www.statista.com/topics/1416/smartphone-market-in-china/.

15. Fumie Yaku, "Huawei Shown to Have Switched to Chinese Parts after US Blacklisting," *Financial Times*, May 26, 2020, https://www.ft.com/content/449f6962-a705-437e-8679-f6a7057594c4. The US Department of Commerce, Bureau of Industry and Security put Huawei on its Entity List in May 2019, https://www.bis.doc.gov/index.php/all-articles/17-regulations/1555-addition-of-certain-entities-to-the-entity-list-final-rule-effective-may-16-2019. See also Bureau of Industry and Security, "Huawei Entity List Frequently Asked Questions (FAQs)," December 3, 2020, https://www.bis.doc.gov/index.php/documents/pdfs/2447-huawei-entity-listing-faqs/file.

16. "Tesla Gigafactory," Tesla, https://www.tesla.com/en_GB/gigafactory.

17. "How Our Engineers Fitted a Factory into a 40-Foot Container," Unilever, January 17, 2021, https://www.unilever.com/news/news-and-features/Feature-article/2021/how-our-engineers-fitted-a-factory-into-a-40-foot-container.html.

Chapter 10

1. Nassim Nicholas Taleb, *The Black Swan: The Impact of the Highly Improbable* (New York: Random House, 2007).

2. "Rumsfeld/Knowns," CNN, December 2, 2002, https://www.youtube.com/watch?v=REWeBzGuzCc.

3. Asa Fitch, "Texas Winter Storm Strikes Chip Makers, Compounding Supply Woes," *Wall Street Journal*, February 17, 2021, https://www.wsj.com/

articles/texas-winter-storm-strikes-chip-makers-compounding-supply-woes
-11613588617; Christopher M. Matthews, Austen Hufford, and Collin Eaton,
"Texas Freeze Triggers Global Plastics Shortage," *Wall Street Journal*, March 17,
2021, https://www.wsj.com/articles/one-week-texas-freeze-seen-triggering
-monthslong-plastics-shortage-11615973401.

    4. Mary-Ann Russon, "The Cost of the Suez Canal Blockage," BBC, March 29,
2021, https://www.bbc.co.uk/news/business-56559073.

    5. David E. Sanger, Clifford Kraus, and Nicole Perlroth, "Cyberattack Forces
a Shutdown of a Top U.S. Pipeline," *New York Times*, May 13, 2013, https://www
.nytimes.com/2021/05/08/us/politics/cyberattack-colonial-pipeline.html.

    6. Jocko Willink and Leif Babin, *Extreme Ownership; How U.S. Navy
SEALs Lead and Win* (New York: St. Martin's Press, 2015), 27. Jocko Willink,
"Extreme Ownership," TEDx Talks, February 2, 2017, https://www.youtube.com/
watch?v=ljqra3BcqWM.

    7. Michele Wucker, *The Gray Rhino: How to Recognize and Act on the Obvious
Dangers We Ignore* (New York: St. Martin's Press, 2016): and Michele Wucker, "Was
the Pandemic a Grey Rhino or a Black Swan?" the *Economist*, November 17, 2020,
https://www.economist.com/the-world-ahead/2020/11/17/was-the-pandemic-a-grey
-rhino-or-a-black-swan.

    8. Rebecca Lindsey, "Understanding the Arctic Polar Vortex," Climate.gov,
March 5, 2021, https://www.climate.gov/news-features/understanding-climate/
understanding-arctic-polar-vortex.

    9. Tom Dart and Jessica Glenza, "Harvey Shines a Spotlight on a High-Risk
Area of Chemical Plants in Texas," the *Guardian*, September 1, 2017, https://www
.theguardian.com/us-news/2017/sep/01/harvey-shines-a-spotlight-on-a-high
-risk-area-of-chemical-plants-in-texas.

    10. Yelena Dzhanova, "The Suez Canal Has a Contentious History and Has
Been Blocked and Closed Several Times Since Opening," *Business Insider*, March 28,
2021, https://www.businessinsider.com/the-suez-canal-blocked-and-closed-several
-times-since-opening-2021-3?r=US&IR=T.

    11. "Here Are the Other Times When All or Part of the Colonial Pipeline System
Was Shut," CNBC, May 9, 2021, https://www.cnbc.com/2021/05/09/colonial-pipeline
-cyberattack-heres-when-it-was-previously-shut-down.html.

    12. Bill Gates, "The Next Outbreak? We're Not Ready," TED, March 2015,
https://www.ted.com/talks/bill_gates_the_next_outbreak_we_re_not_ready/tran
script?language=en.

    13. Global Preparedness Monitoring Board, *A World at Risk: Annual Report on
Global Preparedness for Health Emergencies* (World Health Organization, 2019), 6,
https://www.gpmb.org/docs/librariesprovider17/default-document-library/annual
-reports/gpmb-2019-annualreport-en.pdf?sfvrsn=d1c9143c_30.

    14. Martin Reeves, David Rhodes, Christian Ketels, and Kevin Whitaker,
"Advantage in Adversity: Winning the Next Downturn," Boston Consulting Group,
February 4, 2019, https://www.bcg.com/publications/2019/advantage-in-adversity
-winning-next-downturn.

    15. Hady Farag, Gerry Hansell, Veronica Chau, and Douglas Beal, "ESG
Commitments Are Here to Stay," Boston Consulting Group, June 23, 2020, https://
www.bcg.com/en-gb/publications/2020/esg-commitments-are-here-to-stay.

16. Eoin McSweeney, "Europe's Carmakers Keep Faith in 'Just-in-Time' Supply," *Financial Times*, March 24, 2021, https://www.ft.com/content/a6cf50c5-b6bf-4c7c-8752-8d21025ea52f.

17. Isobel Asher Hamilton, "As Jeff Bezos Steps Down, a Single Line from His First Amazon Job Ad Posted 27 Years Ago Tells You Everything about His Obsession with Speed," *Business Insider*, February 3, 2021, updated July 5, 2021, https://www.businessinsider.com/jeff-bezos-first-amazon-job-ad-reveals-obsession-with-speed-2019-7?r=US&IR=T.

18. Jeff Bezos, "Email from Jeff Bezos to Employees," aboutamazon.com, February 2, 2021, https://www.aboutamazon.com/news/company-news/email-from-jeff-bezos-to-employees.

19. Christopher Mims, "Why There Are More Consumer Goods Than Ever," *Wall Street Journal*, April 25, 2016, https://www.wsj.com/articles/why-there-are-more-consumer-goods-than-ever-1461556860.

20. Bruce Henderson, "The Product Portfolio," Boston Consulting Group, January 1, 1970, https://www.bcg.com/publications/1970/strategy-the-product-portfolio; "What Is the Growth Share Matrix?" Boston Consulting Group, https://www.bcg.com/en-gb/about/overview/our-history/growth-share-matrix; Martin Reeves, Sandy Moose, and Thijs Venema, "BCG Classics Revisited: The Growth Share Matrix," Boston Consulting Group, June 4, 2014, https://www.bcg.com/en-gb/publications/2014/growth-share-matrix-bcg-classics-revisited; "Growth Share Matrix," the *Economist*, September 11, 2009, https://www.economist.com/news/2009/09/11/growth-share-matrix.

21. Bernd Elser et al., "Mastering Complexity: Capture the Hidden Opportunity," Boston Consulting Group, July 8, 2010, https://www.bcg.com/publications/2010/mastering-complexity#replaceMeMigration-tcm8-52282.

22. Love Edquist, "Less Can Be More for Product Portfolios: Attacking Complexity While Enhancing the Value of Diversity," Boston Consulting Group, August 25, 2014, https://www.bcg.com/publications/2014/lean-manufacturing-consumers-products-less-can-be-more-for-product-portfolio-attacking-complexity-while-enhancing-the-value-of-diversity.

23. Ben Aylor et al., "Designing Resilience into Global Supply Chains," Boston Consulting Group, August 3, 2020, https://www.bcg.com/publications/2020/resilience-in-global-supply-chains.

24. "Prospering in the Pandemic: 2020's Top 100 Companies," *Financial Times*, January 1, 2021, https://www.ft.com/content/f8251e5f-10a7-4f7a-9047-b438e4d7f83a.

INDEX

Adidas, 180–181

AI programs
emissions monitoring, 178
haircutter tool, 131, 133
negotiation tool, 101, 115, 129
wind-turbine safety checks, 145–146

Airbus, 216–217

Altshuller, Genrich, 140–141

Amazon, 191–192, 211

anticipating the inevitable (principle 10).
See unexpected crises

Apple, 1–3, 45
Cook's management of, 1–2
cost savings with suppliers and, 128
global supply chain and, 2, 15, 65, 91
innovation and use of experts at,
142–144, 152
integration of suppliers by, 55,
63–65
suppliers' working conditions and,
186–187

AstraZeneca, 149–152, 162

AT&T, 137, 138

audits, of suppliers, 184, 186, 187

augmented intelligence, 104, 110–118
game theory and, 111–112, 113, 116
supplier negotiations using, 111–116

automotive industry
challenges of suppliers with broad
range of commodities in, 44
Covid-19 disruption of supply chains
and, 4
Japanese manufacturing processes and,
12, 13
oil crisis (1970s) and, 11–12
product recalls and, 88, 164–165
See also specific companies

BCG Henderson Institute, 16

Bell Labs, 137, 138

Bezos, Jeff, 191–192, 211

Big Tech companies
collaborating with suppliers by, 14–15
cost savings in 360° program with
current suppliers and, 45–50
innovation by, 137
key role of CPOs and procurement
function at, 38
procurement function in, 95–96
supplier networks used by, 91

bionic, use of word, 97

bionic companies (principle 4), 19, 95–119
augmented intelligence (AI) in,
110–118
big data and advanced analytics in,
107–110
blockchain technology and, 104, 178
CPO selection in, 98–99
digital dimension of, 97, 103–118
Heidelberger Druckmaschinen
example of, 114–116
human dimension of, 97, 98–103
key strategy in, 118–119
key tactics in, 119
key takeaway in, 118
National Grid example of, 105–107
procurement team hiring in, 99–101
robotic process automation and,
104–107
supplier negotiations using, 111–116
technology companies' procurement
function as model for, 95–96
voestalpine's procurement specialists
in, 102–103

BioNTech, 149, 150, 152, 162

black swan events, 205–206, 208, 209, 219, 221
Blevins, Tony, 128
blockchain technology, 104, 119, 178
BMW, 26, 180
boards
   CEO's extreme ownership approach to suppliers and, 208
   CPO's role in decision-making by, 216
   López cost-cutting program at GM with support from, 32, 35
   making suppliers as top agenda item for, 34
Boeing, 58–59, 61–62, 199
Boohoo Group, 171–172
Bosch, 44, 90, 218
Boston Consulting Group (BCG), 17, 176, 177–178, 210
BP oil rig disaster, 155–156
Bracken, Vivienne, 105
Brandstätter, Ralf, 26
Brown, Kevin, 173
building blocks of a revitalized company, 17
   first, 18 (see also CEO change)
   second, 18–19 (see also company change)
   third, 20–21(see also ecosystem change)

captive suppliers, 10–11, 12, 28
carbon emissions, 175–185
   best practices in tackling, 178
   business and industry sectors contributing to, 176–177
   determining carbon footprint in, 178–179
   examples of CEO goals in, 175
   helping suppliers to reduce, 184
   net-zero goal in, 175–177, 179, 180, 185
   redesigning products and packaging for, 180–182
   redesigning sourcing strategy for reduction in, 182–183
   setting supply-chain targets in, 179–180
   three types or scopes of, 177

caretaker procurement managers, and cost savings, 128–132
CEO change (building block 1), 23–40
   as a building block of a revitalized company, 17, 18
   cultivating a new corporate mindset about suppliers and procurement in, 25, 34–35
   giving CPOs a leadership team role and strategic mandate in, 26, 35–38, 60
   Jack Smith's transformation of GM as example of, 27–33
   key strategy in, 39
   key tactics in, 39–40
   key takeaway in, 39
   starting at the top (principle 1) and, 25–40
   suppliers and procurement function leadership imperatives in, 25–27
CEOs
   bionic company's procurement function and, 97, 98
   brief history of suppliers and procurement and, 7–15
   carbon-emission goals and, 176, 177, 178, 185
   cost-savings pressures on, 123
   Covid-19 disruption of supply chains and challenges for, 4, 5, 6
   cross-functional product development teams and, 74–78
   extracting maximum value from supply chain relationships by, 7
   extreme ownership and, 208
   former CPOs as, 1, 2, 3, 26
   giving CPOs a role on leadership teams and, 26, 34–35
   risk monitoring by, 211–212
   social and governance issues and, 185
   supplier stabilization during crises and, 220–221
   sustainability and financial success and, 173
   ten principles for relationships between suppliers and, 17–21
   unexpected crises preparedness and, 207, 208, 210, 211–212, 214, 216, 220–221, 222

chief procurement officers. *See* CPOs
chief sustainability officers, 172
China
    Apple's product manufacturing in, 2
    cost savings in 360° program with
        suppliers from, 53
    growth of globalization and, 13
    network of technology suppliers in,
        201–202
    US trade war with, 51, 215
claim management, 164, 165–166, 170
collaborative relationship with suppliers
    CPO's fostering of, 36–38
    innovation and, 137, 143–144, 145,
        149–152
    NASA's use of, 58–59
    Procter & Gamble's approach to, 26
    procurement strategies and, 196
    Tesla's approach to, 89, 93
    Toyota and, 86
    US Army project and, 199–200
Commercial Orbital Transportation
    Services (COTS) program, 59–60, 61
commodity procurement managers, 44,
    47, 52, 161
communication with suppliers, 46–48, 52
company change (building block 2),
    41–119
    as a building block of a revitalized
        company, 17, 18–19
    going bionic and, 95–119
    treating your suppliers as friends and,
        43–67
Cook, Tim, 1–2, 26, 63
costs
    growth of globalization and, 13–14
    product reviews focused on, 84–85
    should-cost analyses of, 78, 79–80
    traditional product development cycle
        and, 70–74
cost savings (principle 5, cutting costs—
    fast), 20, 123–133
    A suppliers and, 126–128
    caretaker managers for C suppliers in,
        129–132
    CPO's responsibility for A suppliers
        in, 126, 133
    CPO's responsibility for product
        development and, 70, 124

    customizing strategies for supplier
        groups in, 125
    dividing suppliers into A, B, and C
        categories for, 125
    key strategy in, 132
    key tactics in, 133
    key takeaway in, 132
    negotiating supplier contract terms and
        prices for, 71–74
    Pareto principle and, 125, 126, 133
    pressure on CEOs for, 123
    procurement managers for B suppliers
        in, 128–129
    360° program with current suppliers
        and, 45–50
    Toyota's approach to, 124–125
    traditional approach to, 123–124
Covid-19 pandemic
    challenges for CEOs from, 6
    global economy and, 205–206
    supply chain disruptions and, 4–5, 6,
        211, 217, 219, 221–222, 225
    transformative innovations in vaccines
        during, 147–152
CPOs
    big data ownership by, 108
    bionic company's procurement
        function and, 97, 98–99
    carbon-emission goals and, 176, 183,
        184, 185
    as CEOs, 1, 2, 3, 26
    CEOs' relationship with, 25
    collaborative relationship between
        suppliers and, 36–38
    corporate relationship with suppliers
        owned by, 4
    cross-functional development teams
        with, 76–77
    cultivating a new corporate mindset
        about, 34–35
    digital manufacturing and, 203
    extracting maximum value from
        supply chain relationships by, 7
    extreme ownership and, 208
    giving a leadership team role and
        strategic mandate to, 26, 35–38,
        60
    innovation projects and, 142, 145,
        152, 153

CPOs (*continued*)
    involvement in entire product-development cycle by, 69–70, 87
    Jack Smith's transformation of GM and support for, 31–33, 34, 35
    López cost-cutting program at GM as CPO, 13, 31–33, 36
    mandate focused on profitable growth to, 36–38
    manufacturing process speed-to-market and, 198, 202, 203
    market performance related to leadership teams with, 17–18
    misunderstanding of procurement function and, 3–4
    negotiating supplier contract terms and prices by, 35, 70, 71–74, 80
    one-on-one communication with suppliers by, 47–48, 52
    performance/potential approach to suppliers and, 54
    personal relationship with suppliers, 34
    procurement process reconfiguring by, 193
    product-development process reengineering and, 198, 202, 203
    product development responsibility of, 69–70, 124, 152
    quality products and services and, 160–161, 166, 168, 169
    social and governance issues and, 185–186, 189
    speed and, 193
    supplier stabilization during crises and, 220–221
    supply chain redesign and, 194, 197
    sustainability programs with suppliers and, 172,173, 176, 183, 184, 185, 186, 188
    technology companies and, 38
    360° program with current suppliers and, 47–48
    unexpected crises preparedness and, 207, 208, 216, 219, 220, 223
    viewed as a company's "shoppers," 70
cross-functional product-development teams
    Alexander Dennis company example of, 76–77
    product development and, 74–78
    Tesla's use of, 89–90
cutting costs—fast (principle 5). *See* cost savings

Daimler, 91, 178
decision-making, and procurement departments, 35, 49
decision trees, 113–114
Deepwater Horizon well disaster, 155–156
Dell, Michael, 14, 158, 160
Dell Technologies, 91, 156, 173, 178
    computer tower redesign by, 82–84
    high-risk suppliers and, 186
    plastics recycling by, 182
    zero-defects goal of, 158–162
demand-driven innovation, 138–142
design engineers
    concept development and, 70, 73
    cost targets and, 75
    cross-functional teams with, 77–78
    product specifications for specific suppliers used by, 71, 72
development projects. *See* product development
Diess, Herbert, 26
Dolsten, Mikael, 149
dreaming big together (principle 6). *See* innovation
Drucker, Peter, 10

Economist, 4
ecosystem, definition of, 17
ecosystem change (building block 3), 121–224
    anticipating the inevitable and, 205–224
    as building block of a revitalized company, 17, 20–21
    cutting costs—fast and, 123–133
    dreaming big together and, 135–153
    getting quicker, faster—as one and, 191–204
    settling for perfection and, 155–170
    sharing your tomorrows and, 171–189

empowering your procurement team
(principle 3), 19, 69–94
Alexander Dennis company example
of, 76–77
cross-functional teams and, 74–78
Dell's computer tower redesign
example of, 82–84
involvement in entire product
development cycle by, 69–70, 87
key strategy in, 94
key tactics in, 94
key takeaway in, 94
product-development responsibility
in, 69–70
technical and tactical toolbox for,
78–84
Tesla's product-development approach
and, 87–93
Toyota's fixed relationship with
suppliers in, 85–87
traditional product development
approach and, 70–74
environmental, social, and governance
(ESG) standards, 174, 182, 188
demand-driven innovation and, 142
social and governance issues and,
185–187
suppliers and, 172–173
sustainability decisions and, 175
voice of society and, 139–140
See also carbon emissions
external supply function, 163, 170

Federation of German Industries (BDI),
176
50Hertz Transmission GmbH, 146–147,
152
Financial Times, 93, 195, 201
Fink, Larry, 173–174
Ford, Bill, 173
Ford, Henry, 7–9, 139, 192, 203
Ford, Henry II, 10–11
Ford Motor Company, 203
ownership of supply chain by, 8–9, 14
Quiz Kids' management changes at,
10–11
sustainability and, 173, 181
World War II bombers made by, 10

Foxconn, 2, 64, 144, 216
Frazier, Ken, 148
Friedman, Thomas, 14, 159
friends, suppliers as. *See* supplier
relationships
Fujitsu, 145, 146

game theory, 111–112, 113, 116
Gates, Bill, 192–193, 209
genchi genbutsu (Toyota principle), 158
General Motors (GM), 180
Alfred Sloan's use of captive suppliers
at, 10–11, 12
CEO Smith's support for CPO at, 34,
35, 36
CEO Smith's transformation of, 27–33
global sourcing program of, 13, 30
CPO López cost-cutting program
with suppliers at, 13, 31–33, 36

getting quicker, faster—as one (principle
9). *See* speed
gigafactories, 202–203
Gilbert, Sarah, 149
GlaxoSmithKline (GSK), 148–149, 150,
151
global economy
Covid-19 pandemic and, 205–206
data in, 82, 107
iPhones as global product in, 2
Suez Canal blockage and, 206
globalization
Apple's supply chain and, 2, 15, 65, 91
CEO challenges from, 4
Chinese suppliers and, 201–202
Dell's suppliers and, 14, 178
GM's sourcing program and, 13, 30
initial benefits of and later challenges
from, 13–14
transformative innovations and, 147
Global Power Synergy (GPSC), 167–169
Global Preparedness Monitoring Board,
209
global supply chains
cost impact of, 13–14
Covid-19 pandemic and, 4–5, 211, 217,
219, 221–222, 225
geopolitical risks affecting, 215–216

global supply chains (*continued*)
    growth in globalization and, 13
    just-in-time principles and, 210–211
    United States–China trade war and,
        51, 215
global warming, 175–176
going bionic (principle 4). *See* bionic
    companies
Google, 173
Gordon, Robert, 135
gray rhino events, 208–209, 223
Greenhouse Gas Protocol, 177
growth, CPO's mandate focused on,
    36–38

Halliburton, 155–156
Hasenkamp, Peter, 44
Heidelberg Druckmaschinen, 114–116
Henderson, Bruce, 214
HP, 91, 175, 178–179
HSBC, 176
Hudson, Paul, 148
Humvee replacement project, 198–200,
    202

IBM, 192
indefinite delivery, indefinite quantity
    (IDIQ) contracts, 199–200
Inditex, 195–196
Ingram, David, 184
innovation (principle 6, dreaming big
    together), 20, 135–153
    Apple's use of experts for, 142–144
    collaboration with suppliers and, 137,
        143–144, 145, 149–152
    companies' need for, 136
    Covid-19 vaccine development example
        of, 147–152
    demand-driven, 138–142
    environmental, social, and governance
        (ESG) factors and, 139–140
    50Hertz cable project example of,
        146–147
    funding as critical element for, 136–137
    key strategy in, 153
    key tactics in, 153
    key takeaway in, 153

process innovation, 144–147
product and process innovation,
    147–152
producer driven, 138–139
product innovation, 142–144
productivity growth related to, 135
R&D resources of suppliers and, 20,
    64, 87, 137, 142–143, 152, 153
Russian navy's Shkval torpedo
    example of, 141–142
Siemens Gamesa wind turbine example
    of, 145–146
speed of technological change and, 136
TRIZ approach to, 141–142
voice of society and, 139–140
voice of the consumer and, 139
voice of the product and, 140–142
Intel, 64, 65, 92
Intergovernmental Panel on Climate
    Change, 175–176
iPhones, 1–2, 38, 45, 63, 64, 91–92, 218

Japanese automakers, 12, 13, 157. *See also
    specific companies*
Jenner Institute for Vaccine Research,
    149–150, 162
jikotei kanketsu (Toyota principle), 158
Jobs, Steve, 1, 2, 16, 138
just-in-case thinking, 211, 216, 223
just-in-time manufacturing, 12, 192,
    210–211
just-in-time thinking, 211–12, 216, 223

kaizen, 12, 87, 157–158
Kaser, Kenneth Lee, 146
Kay, Alan, 211
keiretsu, 12, 15, 86, 157
Kennedy, John F., 11, 79
Kodak, 138
Krafcik, John, 12

Lafley, A. G., 26, 137
leadership teams, giving CPOs a role on,
    26, 34–35, 36
lean production, 12, 32, 86, 215
lean supply chain, 214, 214

Leveson, Sir Brian, 172
Levitt, Alison, 172
López de Arriortúa, José Ignacio, 13,
    28–33, 34, 35–36, 49, 71, 79, 124, 195
Lufthansa, 183

machine learning, 104, 111, 116, 119, 145
market performance, and CPOs on
    leadership teams, 17–18
McNamara, Robert, 11, 79
Mercedes-Benz, 178
Merck, 148, 149, 150, 151
microfactories, 203
Microsoft, 91, 136, 180
military
    extreme ownership in, 207–210
    game theory used by, 112
    procurement and, 7, 10–11, 26, 200
    technology conventions with suppliers
        used in, 56–58
    US Army Humvee replacement project
        and, 198–200, 202
    War Production Board and, 9–10
Musk, Elon, 55, 60, 62, 89, 202–203

Nadella, Satya, 136
NASA, 55, 58–63, 183, 199
National Grid, 105–107
near-shoring, 183, 216
negotiations with suppliers, augmented
    intelligence (AI) in, 111–116
Neste, 183
net-zero emissions goal, 175–177, 179,
    180, 185
new product development. *See* product
    development
Newtron, 110
New Yorker, 2, 5
Nohria, Nitin, 3
Nokia, 64

Ohno, Taiichi, 12
oil crisis (1970s), 11–12
Opel (GM subsidiary), 28–30, 36
Organization of Petroleum Exporters
    (OPEC), 11–12

Ortega, Amancio, 195–196
Oxford University, 149–150, 162, 182

packaging, and sustainability, 181–182
Palo Alto Research Center, 138
Pandora, 187
Pareto, Vilfredo, 125
Pareto principle, 125, 126, 133
Paris Agreement, 175, 179
Parley for the Oceans, 180–181
performance/potential approach to
        suppliers
    categories of supplies in, 54–55
    description of, 44–45
Pfizer, 149–150, 151–152, 162, 180
pharmaceutical companies, Covid-19
    vaccine innovation by, 147–152
Piëch, Ferdinand, 32
plastics, recycling of, 180–181, 182
Porter, Michael, 3
problem-solving, and innovation,
    140–142
Procter & Gamble (P&G), 26, 137
procurement function
    big data and advanced analytics used
        in, 108–110
    big data ownership by, 108
    brief history of, 7–15
    CEOs' lack of experience in, 26
    claim management and, 164, 165–166
    company's costs related to, 5, 6–7
    cost cutting and, 13
    cultivating a new corporate mindset
        about, 25, 34–35
    decision-making versus instruction-
        taking function of, 35
    economic forces of supply and demand
        and, 46
    extracting maximum value from
        relationships in, 7
    giving CPOs a strategic mandate on,
        26, 35–38, 60
    impact of organization of, 43–44, 52
    innovation projects and, 142, 153
    Jack Smith's transformation of GM
        and support for, 30–33, 34, 35, 36
    as a leadership imperative for CEOs,
        25–27

procurement function (*continued*)
  misunderstanding of CPOs and, 3–4
  product-development process
    reengineering and, 198
  quality products and services and,
    162–163, 166, 167
  roles of, 5–6
  specialist commodity managers in, 44,
    47, 52, 161
  strategic, decision-making role of, 35,
    49
  technology companies and, 38
procurement managers
  building blocks for empowering, 17
  CEO's current relationship with, 25
  collaborative environment and, 196
  cost savings with suppliers and,
    128–132
  cross-functional development teams
    with, 76–77
  as a leadership imperative for CEOs,
    25–27
  product-development process
    reengineering and, 199
  quality products and services and,
    168–169
  structured supplier questionnaires and,
    81–82
procurement process, reconfiguring for
    speed, 193–194
procurement teams
  bionic company's hiring of 97, 98–99,
    99–101
  carbon-emission goals and, 176, 183,
    185
  Dell's computer tower redesign
    example and, 82–84
  Dell's quality-assurance process and,
    171
  innovation projects and, 145, 152
  involvement in entire product-
    development cycle by, 69–70, 87
  manufacturing process speed-to-
    market and, 202
  negotiating supplier contract terms and
    prices by, 35, 70, 71–74, 80
  price factors in supplier selection by,
    73–74
  procurement strategies of, 196

product development responsibility of,
    69–70, 152
  quality engineers on, 165, 166
  quality products and services and,
    160–161, 166, 168, 169
  social and governance issues and, 185
  speed and, 193
  supply chain redesign and, 197
  sustainability programs with suppliers
    and, 176, 181, 183, 185
  viewed as a company's "shoppers," 70
  voestalpine's procurement specialists
    in, 102–103
  See also empowering your
    procurement team (principle 3)
producer driven innovation, 138–139
product and process innovation, 142–152
product development, 69–94
  Alexander Dennis company example
    of, 76–77
  cost creep in, 71–72
  country- or region-specific suppliers
    in, 200–202
  CPO and procurement team
    involvement in, 69–70, 87, 124
  cross-functional teams in, 74–78
  Dell's computer tower redesign
    example of, 82–84
  diversity of suppliers in, 198–200
  gigafactories in, 202–203
  microfactories with 3D printing
    technology in, 203
  need for a cross-functional team in,
    74–78
  product review for cost after contract
    award and, 84–85
  reengineering for speed, 193, 198–203
  technical and tactical toolbox in, 78–84
  Tesla's approach to, 87–93, 202–203
  Toyota's fixed relationship with
    suppliers in, 85–87
  traditional approach to, 70–74
  US Army Humvee replacement project
    example of, 198–200
  vigilance to the end of the product
    cycle in, 84–85
productivity growth related to, 135
profitable growth, CPO's mandate
    focused on, 36–38

quality (principle 7, settling for
  perfection), 20, 155–170
  claim management and, 164, 165–166,
    170
  as a competitive advantage, 166
  Dell example of, 158–162
  example of impact of breach of,
    155–156
  external supply function in, 163,
    170
  Global Power Synergy example of,
    167–169
  key strategy in, 170
  key tactics in, 170
  key takeaway in, 169
  pharmaceutical companies and,
    162–164
  product recalls and, 164–165
  total cost of ownership (TCO) method
    in, 168–169
  Toyota example of, 157–164, 161–162
  zero-defects goal in, 157–164
quality-assurance process
  Dell's use of, 159–161
  pharmaceutical companies and, 164
  "trust and verify" in, 161, 170
quality engineers, 165, 166

R&D resources of suppliers, 20, 64, 87,
    137, 142–143, 152, 153
Responsible Business Alliance, 186
risk-monitoring, 211–213
robotic process automation (RPA), 102,
    104–107, 193
Rometty, Ginni, 192
Roosevelt, Franklin D., 9–10
Rügenwalder Mühle, 182, 183
Rumsfeld, Donald, 206

Şahin, Uğur, 149
Samsung Electronics, 63, 64, 65, 90, 93
Sanofi, 148–149, 150, 151
Schiro, Anne-Marie, 194–195
semiconductors, supply chain shortage
    of, 4, 5, 206, 217–219
settling for perfection (principle 7). See
  quality

shared economy, collaborating with
  suppliers in, 15
sharing your tomorrows (principle 8). See
  sustainability
Shkval torpedo, 141–142
should-cost analyses, 78, 79–80
Siemens Gamesa, 145–146, 152
Sloan, Alfred, 10–11
Smith, Adam, 15, 46
Smith, John F. "Jack," 13, 27–33, 34,
    35–36, 39, 79
sourcing strategy, and carbon emissions,
    182–183
space shuttle program, 58–59
SpaceX, 55, 58, 60–63, 183, 199
speed (principle 9, getting quicker,
    faster—as one), 21, 191–204
  Bezos at Amazon and, 191–192
  as competitive advantage, 192, 198
  CPO and procurement team and, 193
  key strategy in, 204
  key tactics in, 204
  key takeaway in, 204
  procurement process reconfiguring for,
    193–194
  product-development process
    reengineering and, 198–203
  supply chain redesign and, 194–197
  three main ways of increasing a
    company's speed, 193
Stalk, George, 192
structured supplier questionnaires, 78,
    81–82
Summers, Larry, 135
supplier networks, 90–94
supplier relationships (principle 2,
    treating your suppliers as friends),
    18–19, 43–67
  Apple's approach to, 63–65
  description of 360° program with
    current suppliers in, 44, 45–50
  economic forces of supply and demand
    and, 46
  influencing suppliers in, 54, 55–58, 67
  integrating suppliers in, 63–65, 67
  investing in suppliers in, 58–63, 67
  key strategy in, 66–67
  key tactics in, 67
  key takeaway in, 66

supplier relationships (*continued*)
  NASA's approach to SpaceX
    development and, 58–63
  performance/potential approach in,
    44–45, 54–55
  procurement department organization
    and, 43–44
  technology conventions used in,
    56–58
  three categories of suppliers in, 54–55,
    67
  two possible approaches in, 44–45
suppliers
  audits of, 184, 186, 187
  augmented intelligence (AI) in
    negotiations with, 111–116
  Big Tech's collaboration with, 14–15
  brief history of procurement and, 7–15
  building blocks for putting suppliers at
    the core of your business, 17–21
  carbon-emissions reduction by, 184
  challenges from broad range of
    commodities offered by, 44
  claim management and, 164, 165–166,
    170
  company's network of (*see* ecosystem)
  CPO's ownership of corporate
    relationship with, 4
  cultivating a new corporate mindset
    about, 25, 34–35
  environmental, social, and governance
    (ESG) standards and, 172–173,
    185–187
  external supply function in, 163, 170
  GM's cost-cutting program with, 13,
    31–33, 36
  impact of procurement department
    organization on, 43–44
  Inditex fashion procurement strategies
    with, 195–196
  innovation through collaboration with,
    137, 143–144, 145, 149–152
  investing in, 58–63, 67
  near-shoring of, 183, 216
  negotiating contract terms and prices
    with, 35, 70, 71–74, 80
  pharmaceutical companies' quality
    products and, 162–164

price factors in selection of, 73–74
  R&D resources of, and innovation, 20,
    64, 87, 137, 142–143, 152, 153
  risk-management tool for, 117–118
  ten principles for CEO relationships
    with, 17–21
  Tesla's use of networks of, 90–94
  Toyota's fixed relationship with, 85–87,
    124–125
  traditional product development cycle
    and, 70–74
  US Army example of diversity of,
    198–200
  World War I's impact on, 8
  World War II War Production Board
    and, 9–10
  zero-defects quality goal and,
    158–162
  See also collaborative relationship with
    suppliers; supplier relationships
    (principle 2)
supply chains
  Dell's quality-assurance process in,
    159–160
  de-risking in unexpected crises,
    215–217
  emission targets in, 178, 179–180
  Ford's taking over ownership of, 8–9,
    14
  GM's use of captive suppliers in, 10–11,
    12
  global (*see* global supply chains)
  redesigning for speed, 193, 194–197
  social and governance issues and,
    185–187
  stabilizing during crises, 220–221
  Toyota Production System and, 12
  vertical integration of, 9, 10, 14
sustainability (principle 8, sharing your
    tomorrows), 21, 171–189
  carbon emissions and, 175–185
  financial performance and, 173–174
  government regulation and, 174
  key strategy in, 187
  key tactics in, 187–188
  key takeaway in, 187
  social and governance aspects of,
    185–187

Taiwan Semiconductor Manufacturing
    Company (TSMC), 55, 63–65, 93,
    197, 216, 219
Taleb, Nassim Nicholas, 205
Taylor, Frederick Winslow, 8, 12
teardowns, in product development, 78,
    79, 84–85
Tesco, 179–180
Tesla, 44, 180
    gigafactories used by, 202–203
    product-design approach of, 87–90
    supplier network used by, 90–94
3D printing technology, 203, 216
360° program with current suppliers, 44
    collaborative projects in, 48
    description of, 45–50
    one-on-one communication in, 46–48,
        52
total cost of ownership (TCO) method,
    168–169
Toyoda, Kiichiro, 12
Toyoda, Sakichi, 158
Toyota, 156
    fixed relationship between suppliers
        and, 85–87, 124–125
    lean production practices of, 32, 86
    zero-defects goal of, 157–158, 161–162
Toyota Production System, 12, 86–87, 157
treating your suppliers as friends
    (principle 2). *See* supplier
    relationships
TRIZ approach, 141–142
"trust and verify," in quality assurance,
    161, 170
TSMC, 55, 63–65, 93, 197, 216, 219

unexpected crises (principle 10,
    anticipating the inevitable), 21,
    205–224
    black swan events as, 205–206
    contingency plans for, 207, 223
    control of mission-critical supplies in,
        217–219
    CPO's role in, 207, 208, 216, 219, 220,
        223
    crisis playbook in, 219–222
    examples of 205–207
    extreme ownership in, 207–210
    gray rhino events as, 208–209, 223
    key strategy in, 223
    key tactics in, 223
    key takeaway in, 223–224
    product portfolio simplification and,
        214–215
    risk-monitoring in, 211–213
    supply chain de-risking for, 215–217
    US Navy SEALs example of response
        in, 207–208
    See also Covid-19 pandemic
Unilever, 184, 203, 216
US Army, 198–200
US Navy SEALs, 207–208

vaccine innovation, 147–152
vegetarian and vegan products, 182, 183
vertical integration, 9, 10, 14
voestalpine, 102–103
Volkswagen, 26, 32–33, 91
von Neumann, John, 111

Wagoner, Rick, 33, 35
Walmsley, Emma, 148–149
War Production Board, 9–10
Whiz Kids, at Ford, 10–11
Willink, Jocko, 207–208, 210
Womack, James, 32
working conditions, of suppliers,
    186–187
World Economic Forum, 108, 159, 177,
    178
World Health Organization, 148, 205,
    209

Xerox, 138

Zara, 195

ABOUT THE AUTHORS

Christian Schuh is a managing director and senior partner in BCG's office in Vienna, Austria. He has led procurement-transformation projects for companies in the automotive, construction-equipment, defense, high-tech, packaging, and steel industries in China, Europe, Russia, and the United States. He is a coauthor of five books on procurement, including *The Purchasing Chessboard*. He has a YouTube channel on supply-chain and procurement issues, called *Procurement in the Park*. He studied aeronautical engineering and holds a doctorate in business administration from Graz University of Technology.

Wolfgang Schnellbächer is a managing director and partner in BCG's office in Stuttgart, Germany. He is BCG's leader for the procurement topic in Central Europe and the Middle East, and he has advised global leaders in industrial goods, oil and gas, and the consumer industry. He is an author and a coauthor of several publications on procurement, including *Jumpstart to Digital Procurement*. He studied at Johannes Guttenberg University in Mainz before completing a doctorate at Stuttgart University in procurement and game-theory-based negotiations.

Alenka Triplat is a managing director and partner in BCG's office in Vienna, Austria. She spends most of her time with clients in Europe, North America, and Asia, in the high-tech, defense, heavy-equipment, and process industries. She is a coauthor of several books on procurement, including *The Purchasing Chessboard*. She studied economics at the University of Ljubljana in Slovenia and business administration at the Vienna University of Economics and Business Administration.

Daniel Weise is a managing director and partner in BCG's office in Düsseldorf, Germany. He is BCG's global leader for the procurement topic, and he has advised leaders in the industrial-goods, energy, consumer-goods, and public sectors. He is also chief executive of Inverto, a BCG subsidiary and specialist consultancy in procurement and supply-chain management. He is an author and a coauthor of several publications on procurement, including *Jumpstart to Digital Procurement*, and some reports with the World Economic Forum on sustainability in supply chains. He studied at the WHU-Otto Beisheim School of Management before completing an MSc in Finance at London Business School.